P9-EES-948

The Making of the 20th Century

This series of specially commissioned titles focuses attention on significant and often controversial events and themes of world history in the present century. Each book provides sufficient narrative and explanation for the newcomer to the subject while offering, for more advanced study, detailed source-references and bibliographies, together with interpretation and reassessment in the light of recent scholarship.

In the choice of subjects there is a balance between breadth in some spheres and detail in others; between the essentially political and matters economic or social. The series cannot be a comprehensive account of everything that has happened in the twentieth century, but it provides a guide to recent research and explains something of the times of extraordinary change and complexity in which we live. It is directed in the main to students of contemporary history and international relations, but includes titles which are of direct relevance to courses in economics, sociology, politics and geography.

The Making of the 20th Century

Series Editor: GEOFFREY WARNER

Titles in the Series include

4593662

Japan and the Decline of the West in Asia 1894–1943

Richard Storry

St. Martin's Press   New York

ST. PHILIPS COLLEGE LIBRARY

© Richard Storry 1979

All rights reserved. For information, write:
St. Martin's Press, Inc. 175 Fifth Avenue, New York, N.Y. 10010
Printed in Great Britain
First published in the United States of America in 1979

ISBN 0-312-44050-2

Library of Congress Cataloging in Publication Data

Storry, George Richard, 1913–
    Japan and the decline of the West in Asia 1894–1943.

    (The Making of the 20th century)
    Bibliography: p.
    1. Japan—Foreign relations—1912–1945. 2. World
politics—1900–1945. I. Title.
DS885.S84 1979   327.52   78-31872
ISBN 0-312-44050-2

322.52
S 887

Contents

The cover illustration shows the surrender of the Americans to the Japanese at Corregidor in 1942. The photograph is reproduced by kind permission of the Mainichi Newspaper Company of Japan.

62075

For
my brother
Jack

Preface

This book attempts to describe and interpret certain features of one of the most significant developments of modern times; namely, the rise to world power between 1894 and 1943 of the Japanese Empire, and the consequences thereof for the nations of the West in terms of their interests in Asia. To many readers, no doubt, the broad outlines of the story will be familiar, and I cannot claim to have given it a dramatically new twist. Nor would it be right for me to suggest for a moment that Japanese imperialism alone was responsible for the transformation of the political map of Asia during the past few decades. But the pace and, to some extent, the nature of that transformation were dictated by the course of Japan's policy and by the way in which the Western powers, notably Great Britain and the United States, reacted to it. The pages that follow will, I hope, demonstrate the force of this contention.

I could scarcely have written this study without the support given me in so many ways by my Oxford friends and colleagues, the Warden and Fellows of St Antony's. I must record, too, a debt of special gratitude to the Rockefeller Foundation, New York, for giving me the privilege of a period of residence at the Foundation's Study and Conference Center in Bellagio, Italy. Dr William C. Olsen, Director of the Center, the very soul of kindness, was a most helpful host. Any virtue this book may be thought to possess owes a good deal to the atmosphere created at the Villa Serbelloni by Bill and Betsy Olsen.

I must declare my warm appreciation of the wise advice and long-suffering patience of Professor Christopher Thorne and Mr Derick Mirfin. Their editorial suggestions have been invaluable, but I am solely responsible, needless to say, for the views expressed in this work.

Finally, I should like to thank, for a variety of good reasons, the staff of the International House of Japan, Tokyo; the *Shimbun Kenkyū-jo*, Tokyo University; Professor Maruyama Masao; Mr Fukada Yusuke; Dr Jean-Pierre Lehmann; Mrs Sue Henny; Miss Sarah Mahaffy; Miss Susan Dickinson; and (above all) D.L.S.

August 1978   RICHARD STORRY

Author's Note

Where the names of individual Japanese appear in the text the custom has been followed of giving the surname before the personal name: for example in Yamagata Aritomo, Yamagata is the surname.

Publisher's Note

The author and publishers are grateful for permission to reproduce the extracts from Correlli Barnett's *The Collapse of British Power* (Methuen).

1 Disaster for the West

I frankly admit that the violence, fury, skill, and might of Japan have far exceeded anything that we had been led to expect.

WINSTON CHURCHILL, secret session of the House of Commons, 23 April 1942

I

IT was four o'clock in the morning of 8 December 1941. Moored off the Bund at Shanghai lay the sole surviving representative of British naval power, the Yangtze gunboat, HMS *Peterel*. She had a reduced crew; her guns were without their breechblocks; her commander, Lieutenant Stephen Polkinghorn RNR, was fifty-seven years of age. Within a few hundred yards of *Peterel* were at least three Japanese warships. In the event of trouble *Peterel*'s commander, as the Admiralty report puts it, 'had to place his chief reliance on his demolition charges'.[1]

Lieutnant Polkinghorn received a telephone call from the shore. He was told that the International Settlement was being taken over by Japanese forces. Accordingly he rang the alarm bells, sent all hands to action stations, and set about the destruction of his cyphers and confidential books. In less than ten minutes a launch came alongside, bearing the Chief of Staff of the Japanese naval Commander-in-Chief and a civilian interpreter. *Peterel*'s commander met them at the head of the gangway. Through the interpreter the Japanese officer announced the outbreak of war and demanded the immediate surrender of HMS *Peterel*. Lieutenant Polkinghorn refused point blank to surrender his ship; and the Japanese returned down the gangway to the launch. When this had proceeded about a hundred yards one of the Japanese shot a red Verey's light up into the dark. This was the signal for gun and machine-gun fire from all sides to be opened on the *Peterel*, and in a matter of minutes she was adrift and ablaze fore and aft; for the first shell, from a Japanese destroyer, hit the stern and carried away the cable. The commander gave the order to fire the demolition charges and abandon ship. The survivors, all of whom were wounded, swam towards the Bund and were picked up by Chinese sampans which put

ST. PHILIPS COLLEGE LIBRARY

out from shore to rescue them, in spite of machine-gun fire and the presence of burning oil on the surface of the water.

The gallant conduct of Lieutenant Polkinghorn [says the Admiralty report] in defying the Japanese who called upon him to surrender his ship attracted a great deal of attention and much favourable comment in China and was widely reported throughout the country. As long afterwards as October 1944, it was found that full details of the incident were known and lauded in many places in the interior.[2]

The story of HMS *Peterel* and her resolute commander is told here for two reasons. In the first place, the episode is by no means well known; no dispatch about it was ever published in the *London Gazette*.[3] Secondly, it has a certain symbolic flavour. Just a hundred years after the Opium War 'gunboat diplomacy' – that famous instrument of Western imperialism in the Far East – reaches the end of the road at last, not ignobly, with a virtually unarmed Yangtze 'flat-iron', manned by a skeleton crew and commanded by an officer of the naval reserve in his fifties. Needless to say, she goes down fighting – like the *Prince of Wales* and *Repulse* two days later. At no time did the Royal Navy embarrass their former pupils, the Japanese, by offering to surrender.

The blows endured by the British at sea at the hands of the Japanese in the first six months of the *Dai Toa Senso*, 'The Greater East Asia War', have not attracted the general attention and interest given, naturally enough, to the savagely dramatic air assault on the American battle fleet at Pearl Harbor. Without doubt Pearl Harbor as a single event, and in terms of its effects throughout the world, is one of the benchmarks of recorded history. For it led Hitler, in an act of quixotic folly, to honour his alliance with Japan and declare war against the United States, thereby bringing that country into open conflict with the European fascist states. There were many other consequences of the 'Day of Infamy'. But it cannot be claimed that among them was the possibility of a successful Japanese invasion of the American West Coast. For one thing, the crippled fleet at Pearl Harbor included no aircraft carriers; they were at sea when the attack occurred. But even if they had been caught, like the battleships, at anchor in Pearl Harbor, American air power at home was capable of defeating any attempted invasion of the West Coast.

Consider by way of contrast the extreme vulnerability of India a few months later. Singapore surrendered on 15 February 1942. A combined fleet of British, Australian, Dutch and American cruisers and destroyers was sunk or dispersed during and after the battle of the Java Sea on 27

February. Allied forces in Java surrendered on 7 March. The Japanese occupied Rangoon on 8 March and prepared to reinforce their army with units fresh from the conquest of Malaya. In the last week of March devastating attacks by Japanese bombers and fighters drove the RAF out of Burma.

Now great wedges of silver bombers droned across the sky, and one after another the cities of Burma spurted with flame and vanished in roaring holocausts. Prome, Meiktila, Mandalay, Thazi, Pyinmana, Maymyo, Lashio, Taunggyi, largely wooden towns, all of them crumbled and burned. The Japanese used pattern bombing, coming over in faultless formation, giving themselves a leisurely dummy run or two, and then letting all their bombs go in one shattering crump. They were very accurate.[4]

As the Japanese proceeded with their conquest of Burma, advancing north up the valleys of the Irrawaddy and Sittang, the framework of government began to crumble. General Slim's comment is apposite:

It can, of course, be argued that the fact that policemen, clerks, scavengers, and minor officials desert is itself proof of something very wrong with their superiors. Nevertheless, when all is said, the real reason the Burman civilian, like his soldier brother, left his post was because he doubted that we, the soldiers and airmen, could hold back the Japanese.[5]

Indicative, also, of the disintegration of public order was the exodus of the Indian population, fleeing in many cases as much from the enmity of the Burmans as from the dangers of the approaching tide of battle.

Such was the situation in the first week of April 1942 when two Japanese fleets sailed into the Indian Ocean. The first, consisting of a carrier, seven cruisers and eleven destroyers, roamed the Bay of Bengal at will for five days. It sank twenty-three ships; and aircraft from the carrier raided Cocanada and Vizagapatam on the east coast of India with shattering effects on local civilian morale: the raids, in the words of the British official history, 'practically cleared both towns'.[6] More serious was the flight from the city of Madras, where the panic was exacerbated by news that the Governor of Madras understood that a large Japanese force was on its way and could be expected to invade the province any day after the middle of April.

The second Japanese fleet comprised five carriers, four battleships, three cruisers and eleven destroyers, commanded by Vice-Admiral Nagumo, who had struck the blow at Pearl Harbor. His carrier aircraft had followed up their success at Hawaii with strikes at Rabaul, Amboina, Timor and Darwin. In none of these operations had any Japanese vessel received so much as a scratch. This armada now approached Ceylon, hoping to bring to battle Admiral Somerville's Eastern Fleet. While quartering the ocean south of Ceylon Nagumo's aircraft attacked Colombo and Trincomalee. The main force of the Eastern Fleet escaped detection, but two heavy cruisers and the carrier, *Hermes*, were spotted and sunk by Japanese bombers. One cannot doubt that a similar disaster would have been the fate of Somerville's four old battleships of the 'R' Class (*Resolution, Ramillies, Royal Sovereign, Revenge*) had they encountered the Japanese. However, they were able to beat a retreat. In the measured words of the official history: 'As a result of the raid on Colombo, the Admiralty had suggested to Admiral Somerville that he might be finding the presence of the 'R' Class battleships more of a liability than an asset, and had given him full discretion to withdraw them to the east coast of Africa.'[7]

It was at this juncture that the Indian National Congress formally rejected 'the Cripps Offer' – the proposals, brought from London by Sir Stafford Cripps, for fuller Indian participation in the Viceroy's Council and the firm promise of self-government, with the option of complete independence, once the war was over. Churchill had been under pressure from President Roosevelt to grant Dominion status to India. King George VI was to record in his diary his surprise at being told by Churchill that the Cabinet and all parties in Parliament were ready 'to give up India to the Indians after the war'. Churchill, the King wrote, 'felt they had already been talked into giving up India'.[8] For Indian Nationalists the proposals brought by Cripps might have been a disappointment, since the possibility of independence was deferred to the post-war era; but Nehru, it is said, felt inclined to accept them. But the seemingly invincible advance of the Japanese played a decisive role. The attitude of the Congress party, when it turned down the proposals on 10 April 1942, was neatly summed up in the famous comment attributed, perhaps in error, to Gandhi: 'This is a postdated cheque on a crashing bank'.*

---

* Several years ago I was assured by the Indian scholar – diplomat, K. M. Panikkar – that it was he, not Gandhi, who deserved the praise or blame for uttering those words. In April 1942 Panikkar, as adviser to one of the Indian Princes, held discussions with Cripps in New Delhi. Asked by an Indian journalist to make some comment, Panikkar produced the famous phrase spontaneously.

The truth is that 'India's most dangerous hour' (as Wavell was to describe the month of April 1942) marked the final collapse of the old edifice of European power and prestige in Asia. In Burma, although Mandalay had not yet fallen, the end was near. In the East Indies, from Sumatra to Timor, the Dutch were either interned or compelled to carry out essential functions on the railways, in power stations, telegraph offices, and banks, under enemy supervision pending the arrival of specialists and technicians from Japan. In Indo-China the French administration operated on sufferance, that is to say by permission of the Japanese. In the Philippines only Corregidor continued to defy the Japanese. The perilous position of northern Australia was such that the Commonwealth government seriously contemplated the evacuation of the entire continent north of a line drawn westward from Brisbane to Shark Bay on the Indian Ocean.

As for Russia – the European country with the largest territorial stake in Asia – the security of the Maritime Province, and possibly of all Siberia east of Lake Baikal, depended essentially at this time upon Japanese goodwill. The Russians had survived the first great German onslaught of the summer and autumn of 1941; but the end of the spring thaw would bring a renewed German offensive, the outcome of which could not be foreseen. Hitler's attack on the Soviet Union in June 1941 had been followed by a Japanese mobilisation on a huge scale. That summer it seemed that Japan might decide (a) to attack the Soviet Union (a course of action urged by Matsuoka, the Foreign Minister); (b) to move south against Malaya, the Dutch East Indies, and perhaps the Philippines; (c) to undertake operations (a) and (b) simultaneously. For although thousands of those mobilised were kitted out with tropical gear, others were issued with warm clothing; and the Kwantung Army (the Japanese army in Manchukuo) was reinforced by some fifteen divisions. The Russians could count themselves fortunate that July 1941 passed without a Japanese declaration of war. There is little doubt that Soviet military prowess in savage battles with the Kwantung Army in 1938 and 1939 inclined the Japanese to adopt a waiting game. Thus, although Matsuoka had declared, 'We must strike while the German war situation is still unclear', it had been agreed, at the insistence of the army high command, that Japan would attack the Russian Far East only 'if the German–Soviet war should develop to the advantage of our Empire'.[9] It has been suggested by an American expert on Russo-Japanese relations that 'the United States with her soft life and lack of discipline had seemed less formidable an opponent than the USSR, particularly since the might of the Japanese navy could be brought to bear on the former more readily than the latter'.[10] But the idea of attacking the Soviet Union had not been discarded. Locked in the costly and desperate struggle with the Germans, the Soviet Union in the spring of 1942 was probably in no position to repel a Japanese *blitzkrieg* in the Far East.

Among the Western powers at this critical moment only Germany retained a certain standing in Asian eyes. In China, for example, General Falkenhausen's military mission, until its recall by Hitler in 1938, had trained the armies of the Kuomintang and helped them in their efforts (which had nearly succeeded) to liquidate the Communists. Observing the performance of their American, British and Dutch allies in the early stages of the Pacific War, Chinese officers could be forgiven if they were impressed by the apparently unshakeable strength of German power in Europe, North Africa and the Atlantic Ocean. It goes without saying that there was great respect in Japan for the efficiency of German science and industry as well as for the dynamic competence of the German military machine; although this respect was tempered by distrust. For Nazi racial theories could not be reconciled with Japan's own ethnocentric convictions.

The reputation in Asia of the United States and of the European colonial powers had been torn to shreds in a mere five months. Apologists for imperialism always claimed, when under fire from critics of the system, that in the final analysis its ethical justification was the ordered peace and security it provided for the native inhabitants of the colonies and protectorates. Thus failure to repulse an enemy invasion destroyed the *raison d'être* of colonial government. If this was true when one European empire seized by force of arms the colony of another (as occurred, for example, in the Horn of Africa during the Second World War), it was doubly so when colonial rulers were overthrown, not by their own kind, but by invaders racially akin to the ruled: which is what happened, of course, in South-east Asia from North Borneo to the Chin Hills of Burma.

It was not only the speed with which they were defeated that cost the British, Dutch and Americans so much loss of face. Rather too frequently the circumstances of the evacuations and retreats preceding surrender were such as to convince the indigenous population that the emperor had no clothes. For example, Georgetown (Penang) and Kuala Lumpur, the most important towns in Malaya outside Singapore, were emptied of their white inhabitants in conditions approaching panic. Ian Morrison, of *The Times* (London) published a first-hand account of the effects of the civilian exodus from Kuala Lumpur. Of the house of a senior British official in K.L. he wrote:

It reminded me of the *Marie Celeste* . . . a half-finished whisky-and-soda stood on the small table by the sofa in the drawing room. Upstairs a woman's dress, half-ironed, lay on the ironing-table in one of the bedrooms. Two dispatches, addressed to the Governor, typed out but unsigned, lay on the desk upstairs. In the offices on the ground floor the files were intact. The staff appeared to have downed pens in the middle of whatever they were doing and made off.[11]

The ingredients of Japanese success were surprise, air superiority, and matchless fighting spirit. Subsidiary to these, but of some importance none the less, was Japan's political warfare, the flow of propaganda stressing Japan's mission as a liberating power and emphasising the attractions, economic and cultural, of 'Co-Prosperity' for an Asia freed from the leading strings of the West.

Nationalist activities and expectations in South-east Asia varied according to different regions. The Philippines, promised full independence by 1946, already enjoyed as a Commonwealth under President Quezon a fair measure of autonomy. But there remained the memory of resistance to American arms after the overthrow of Spanish rule; and Aguinaldo, the leader of that resistance, had received comfort and support in Japan. In the East Indies Java was the centre of nationalist disaffection. Here the Japanese could amass a good deal of capital as the destroyers of Dutch hegemony. In other islands of the Indies, notably the Moluccas, such opportunities did not exist on the same scale. Malaya, British North Borneo and Sarawak had been remarkably free from serious political unrest. The Malay sultans basked under British protection and their subjects knew that the busy, acquisitive Chinese population would not be given the chance to combine its commercial acumen with political power. The Chinese might have no love for the British or Malays, but they had even less for the Japanese. But among the Indians in Malaya, whether clerks, shopkeepers, or plantation workers, Japanese agitation for the cause of *Swaraj* could be pursued with every prospect of success.

Since Vichy was not at war with Japan a degree of caution was required in French Indo-China, which had become a Japanese military base area. But Burma was a promising field for political manipulation. Here the independence movement was a significant force and one which the Japanese, especially in the early months of the war, exploited with considerable effect.

It is extremely difficult to assess the element of altruism that lay behind Japanese talk of 'Greater East Asia'; the question being complicated by the fact that most Japanese believed that what was good for Japan must be good for the rest of Asia. The idealistic view was that Japan should be the benign senior partner in a group of newly independent Asian states. Yet, in practice, the military forces in the occupied countries tended to behave as stern and suspicious masters whose commands must be obeyed without much argument. Dr Ba Maw, Burma's first Prime Minister under the British and Head of State under the Japanese, has pointed out that General Tojo's 'Asian instincts told him that only such a visionary project as a Greater East Asia composed of truly free and independent nations could endure'. But Ba Maw goes on:

However, most of the Japanese military leaders were men without a truly Asian vision. They were too introverted, lived too much within their own insular past and its legacy to be able to learn anything new or different. The result was that they refused to give up their old notions of conquering weak lands and holding on in one way or another to what they conquered. Thus for them our independence was to be just a means to win the war, a show without substance.[12]

From one who remained faithful to the Japanese beyond their moment of defeat such testimony carries conviction. Moreover, the earlier record of the Japanese as overlords in Formosa, Korea, Manchukuo and occupied China, did not suggest that they would be likely to attach the first importance to the freedom and independence of the territories they liberated from the yoke of Western rule. Of course, it may be argued that if the Japanese had won the Pacific War their hegemony in South-east Asia would have assumed in due course a liberal and enlightened form, since the predominantly militarist character of Japan's domestic structure might not have endured beyond the 1950s. But one cannot be sure of this. It is wise to be sceptical about the revisionist theory that Japan's liberating mission justified her assault on the European colonies in the Far East. A Japanese scholar has stated the real position in words that should be remembered: 'It is true that Japanese military control disrupted the control of Europe and America and resulted in weakening the power of the former controllers, but that was an inadvertent result of the transition from European imperialism to Japanese imperialism.'[13]

All the same, even an essentially bogus independence may be thought preferable to colonial status; and Javanese and Burman nationalist leaders, having tasted the ersatz product during the war years, would be satisfied with nothing less than the real thing once the war was over. Generally speaking, the Japanese military presence was so irksome as to make the people of South-east Asia – including the Thais, who had never experienced colonial rule – heartily welcome the outcome of the Pacific War. The prejudice against Japan that persisted in South-east Asia long after 1945 was fed by the memories of hard times endured under Japanese military occupation.

It is also significant that at no stage in the war did Tokyo accept the demand by Subhas Chandra Bose that the Indian Nationalist Army be recognised as an *allied* (rather than auxiliary or subordinate) force. Indeed the first commander of the INA, Mohan Singh, who fell out of favour with the Japanese, was to assert later that what the Japanese army looked for from the Indians was 'quiet submission and unconditional surrender of soul'.[14] A good many Japanese officers no doubt shared the views of Field-Marshal Count Terauchi, the Generalissimo in South-east Asia. Terauchi, it appears, rather despised the INA. He observed that his own father, when Governor-General of Korea, had no time at all for colonial independence movements. Filial piety prompted the Field-Marshal to cherish similar sentiments.

Did the Japanese ever see themselves replacing Britain as the paramount power in India? The best evidence suggests that neither government nor high command in Tokyo envisaged this as a serious possibility. But to the wilder dreams of Japanese nationalists there were few, if any, limits. Their ultimate goal was described by a military theorist (Major-General Ishiwara Kanji) as a world 'at peace under the guidance of the imperial throne'.[15] If the victories of 1942 had been followed by further military successes on a grand scale there is no knowing how far the Japanese might have been tempted to extend the tentacles of their power; although further expansion would doubtless have been preceded by a period of consolidation, lasting perhaps for some years. In any case, it was the huge, virtually empty, terrain of northern Australia, rather than the Indian sub-continent, that interested Japan. On the other hand, Ceylon may have been seen as the domain of some future Japanese governor-general; and in the backrooms of the Tokyo War Ministry there seems to have been consideration of a long-term project for the Ceylon government-general to include India south of a line from Nellore, on the Bay of Bengal, to the northern frontier of Portuguese Goa.[16]

II

In the event, the year 1942 marked the high tide of Japan's strategic offensive, even if further advances were made in 1944, on the Burma–India border and in China south of the Yangtze. Midway and Guadalcanal are the generally accepted turning-points on sea and land. But the first undoubted defeat for the Japanese on land took place in New Guinea in the last week of August 1942, when an Australian force expelled a Japanese regiment that had come ashore at Milne Bay. 'Some of us may forget', wrote Field-Marshal Slim in later years, 'that of all the allies it was Australian soldiers who first broke the spell of the invincibility of the Japanese Army; those of us who were in Burma have cause to remember'.[17]

On the eastern frontiers of India the change in the fortunes of war came much later. There was, for example, the Donbaik affair, which was peculiarly disheartening for British and Indian arms. In late 1942 General Wavell launched an operation to capture the Japanese-held island of Akyab, close to the Arakan coast of Burma. For reasons connected with military demands in Madagascar and elsewhere an attack on Akyab by sea could not be contemplated. It was necessary to approach the island down a narrow peninsula; and here, six miles from its tip, a Japanese force of about 1000 men was entrenched in 'bunkers', semi-underground defensive positions protected by logs and sited in groups so as to provide mutual support. This type of redoubt was to be encountered again and again before the war in Burma ended; and ways of overcoming it were devised. But the bunkers at Donbaik proved impregnable. Between 7 January and 19 March 1943 five separate assaults were made on the Donbaik position. The first was by an infantry company, the second by a battalion, the third by two battalions, the fourth and fifth by a full brigade. The Japanese held the position and inflicted heavy losses on the troops assaulting them.

For British military planners the shock of Donbaik lay in the realisation that the Japanese could be as resolute in defence as in attack. The defeats in Hong Kong, Malaya and Burma could be explained in terms of the strategic disabilities that the British had faced in those areas. No such reason, however, could be found to excuse the Akyab débâcle of the early spring of 1943. Indeed, so far as the British were concerned, the myth of Japanese invincibility made its greatest impact in the wake of the ill-fated Akyab offensive. The defenders of Donbaik had been ordered to fight to the last man, their resistance being an essential element in a plan of counter-attack prepared by the Japanese command. For while the British and Indian forces were checked at Donbaik a Japanese detachment was advancing undetected through deep jungle, in a wide flanking movement, to assail their enemies from the rear. This manoeuvre forced the British back to where they had started six months before. Perhaps it is not surprising that at this season a British regular officer, with expert knowledge of the Japanese army, warned senior commanders that the North-east Frontier of India might become another North-west Frontier, as the scene of intermittent warfare for many years to come.

This bleak prophecy was discredited a year later by Imphal, the longest continuous battle of the Pacific War and one of the greatest disasters suffered by any army since Napoleon's retreat across the Beresina. Yet the Japanese had the stamina to continue the fight all the way south to the Irrawaddy delta and then, having evacuated Rangoon, to keep up a rearguard action on the road to Moulmein. It was only on orders from Tokyo that the Japanese Burma Area Army surrendered. It was the same story in other regions of South-east Asia. The Japanese retreated or fought to the last: no military unit, as such, surrendered until after the Emperor's broadcast on 15 August 1945, and then not until confirmation of the broadcast was received – in many cases from a special emissary dispatched from Tokyo. In the Far East there was no counterpart on the Japanese side of Arnim at Tunis, of Paulus at Stalingrad.

Yet when it took place, the Japanese national collapse was total. For apart from the immense material ruin there was a destruction of traditional beliefs that amounted to a moral revolution. The fighting man, once the hero of everyone at home, became at best an object of embarrassed pity. The very term *gunji*, 'military', acquired overnight a distasteful flavour. It was as though the civilian population had made up its mind to bear every hardship, so long as the army and navy won the war in the end, but had turned against the two services in mocking resentment when it was demonstrated that they had indeed taken on a task beyond their power. The new heroes were the forces of occupation, in particular the Americans.

So on the face of it the West had made a comeback. While throwing their main weight against Germany, Great Britain and the United States contrived nevertheless to impose their will on the Japanese even before the end of the war in Europe was in sight. Ground lost in New Guinea, the Philippines and Burma, was regained in battle; and at Leyte Gulf in October 1944 the Japanese navy was destroyed as a fleet in being. And while the war in Europe was ending, Iwojima and Okinawa were captured at the cost of some 60,000 American casualties. The sudden and dramatic termination of the Pacific War after two atomic bombs and the intervention of the Russians has served to blur the memory of the appalling but successful air, sea and land operations in which the principal Western allies were involved during the final eighteen months of their struggle against Japan.

For Great Britain, in particular, the effort was prodigious, was indeed beyond her resources, since she was dependent on American economic support. Lend-Lease, it has been argued, transformed 'England into an American satellite warrior-state dependent for its existence on the flow of supplies across the Atlantic.'[18]

Thus the British and imperial armies which marched and conquered in the latter half of the war, in North Africa, in Italy, in Burma, in Normandy and north-west Europe; the great bomber forces which smashed and burnt German cities; the navy which defeated the U-boat; these were not manifestations of British imperial power at a new zenith, as the British believed at the time and long afterwards, but only the illusion of it. They were instead manifestations of *American* power – and of the decline of England into a warrior satellite of the United States.[19]

But if this was true, and if the British appreciated – as the Dutch and the French were to discover – that a return to the pre-war colonial pattern was out of the question, surely the same could not be said of the Soviet Union and the United States?

Here, however, most of the positions in Asia recaptured or won in 1945 did not long endure. Certainly the acquisition of southern Sakhalin and the Kuriles represented a Russian advance. But within a few years the Soviet Union surrendered the Port Arthur base and withdrew from the Manchurian railways. That the key factor in the Soviet decision was the new power of Communist China, demonstrated in the Korean War, is not to be doubted. It was Communist China, too, which checked any possibility of America maintaining in the Far East the hegemony gained in 1945 by the defeat of Japan. MacArthur was right when he told the American Congress in his farewell speech that there is no substitute for victory. The stalemate in Korea was in reality a defeat for the United States. It foreshadowed events in Vietnam twenty years later.

In China and in Vietnam, the agents of revolution, though this was far from their intention, were the Japanese. In their invasion of China in 1937 their stated purpose was the suppression of communism; they went so far as to claim that their military action was a rescue operation on behalf of the Chinese people. In fact, the misery brought to north and central China by the Japanese war was the prime cause of Mao's success. Spared interference from the Japanese, the Kuomintang government could well have maintained its prestige, and therefore its dominant position, for many years. Thus in China the Japanese created the very situation they were most eager to forestall.

In one way or another during this century in Asia the Japanese factor has been crucial. Directly or indirectly, the British withdrawal from India, the independence of Burma and Indonesia, Mao's revolution in China, Ho Chi Minh's in Vietnam, America's advance and retreat in the Far East, were the products of Japanese action. It is the purpose of the following chapters to throw some light on the Japanese factor and to show, if possible, how and why it came into play.

2 The Yellow Peril and the White Peril

If Momotaro went to take away treasure which belonged to someone else, then he was a wicked robber. If he had gone to punish the demons for being wicked and troublesome that would have been very good.

FUKUZAWA YUKICHI

I

BECAUSE of its relative remoteness, geographically, from Europe and North America, the Japanese archipelago was one of the last regions of East Asia to feel the intrusion of the nineteenth-century Western world. But in the middle years of the century American pressure, in the shape of Commodore Perry's small but powerful squadron, persuaded the Japanese to modify the strict seclusion policy established and maintained by the Tokugawa shogunate. Other nations soon followed the American example. The shogunate was obliged to sign treaties opening the country to foreign trade and granting extra-territorial rights to foreigners in those ports where they were allowed to reside.

These new, enforced contacts with strangers gave rise to much debate, during which the prestige of the shogunate was gravely harmed. Well before there appeared to be any danger from the West the legitimacy of Tokugawa rule, based on Yedo (the modern Tokyo), had been questioned by those who had come to believe that the ancient imperial house in Kyoto ought to be at the centre of affairs. The failure of the shogunate to fend off the Western intruders inevitably weakened its standing in the eyes of the warrior, samurai, class. The latter did not lose its faith in Tokugawa rule overnight. But those provincial households that happened to dislike the shogunate found it possible to raise their heads and challenge the *status quo* with increasingly less risk of consequent effective punishment.

Domestic commotion, complicated and often savage, reached a climax in the winter of 1867–8 with the overthrow of the shogunate. This event and the move of the imperial court from Kyoto to Yedo, renamed Tokyo, constituted the Meiji Restoration. In a purely formal sense the Emperor, a boy in his teens, had the governing powers restored to himself and his descendants. This was not achieved without civil war. But once the Emperor Meiji's new government, composed mainly of anti-Tokugawa samurai, had consolidated its position it embarked on a programme of political, social and economic modernisation – or 'Westernisation', as it was commonly called in those days.

Each step in this programme was taken with, as it were, one eye on the 'West', meaning of course Great Britain, the United States, France and other leading powers. For these nations were perceived to be both a menace and a model. They were feared and respected, despised and admired. How best should Japan respond to the materially advanced civilisation represented by such nations? This was the central issue throughout the 1870s and 1880s.

The answer took the form of an energetic, though selective, adoption of foreign modes and practices. Critics of Japan tended to dismiss the modernising programme as nothing more than an exercise in shallow emulation of the West, as though the Japanese were mere copycats. This misreading of the situation did less than justice to the resilience and ingenuity of the Japanese race. It was also productive of complacency. Accordingly, throughout most of the nineteenth century, Europeans and Americans, when they directed their thoughts to Japan, tended perhaps to adopt a genially patronising view. As an historian has recently observed: 'Although Japan was praised for her beauty and the charms of her people the country was not taken very seriously.'[1]

The philosophy behind all the changes that took place in the seventies and eighties was summed up in a national slogan, *fukoku kyohei*, 'a rich country with strong armed forces'. That was the goal towards which the Meiji oligarchy directed its efforts; and the slogan was well understood and amply supported by the people at large. That it would have important consequences in terms of foreign policy, especially for neighbouring countries, was in the nature of things to be expected.

II

In 1890 the Japanese Prime Minister, Yamagata Aritomo, declared that a distinction should be made between what he called his country's 'line of sovereignty' and her 'line of interest or advantage'. But the latter was essential for the preservation of the 'line of sovereignty' if Japan was to achieve a position of genuine self-reliance in the contemporary world.[2]

This concept is indeed inseparable from power politics. It was well understood by Stalin and those who succeeded him. The Brezhnev Doctrine is an assertion of the Soviet Union's 'line of interest'. Until recently at any rate the Low Countries were within Great Britain's 'line of interest'. Canada and the Carribean belong to much the same category *vis-à-vis* the United States. In the Japanese case it is not difficult to pick out the territory that Yamagata had in mind. The Kingdom of Korea, fated to be the *casus belli* in 1894 and again in 1904, would be absorbed within the 'line of sovereignty' in 1910, Japan's 'line of interest' having been extended meanwhile beyond the Yalu.

In retrospect the expansion of imperial Japan seems to follow a predictable course – penetration of Korea leading to an inevitable clash with China; further penetration, leading to an inevitable clash with Tsarist Russia; penetration of China, followed by further and more serious clashes; penetration of Indo-China, leading to confrontation and final struggle with great powers collectively too formidable to be successfully resisted, much less overcome. Many students of history have seen Japan's expansion in such terms; and the fact that this is an uncomplicated view does not render it invalid. Errors tend to occur not so much in the examination of events as in the weighing of motives. For the historian of Japan's modern imperialist age, the fifty years from 1894 to 1945, the problem is to identify a number of motives, not least those of fear and *amour propre*, and to assess the importance of each one relative to the rest.

At first sight Yamagata's analysis suggests plain ambition; especially in the light of Japanese–Korean relations during the preceding twenty years. A fierce debate over Korea between 1869 and 1873 – the *Seikan Ron* ('Conquer Korea Argument') as it was called – had wrecked the harmony of the closely knit group of Japanese that had brought their country into the modern world. The nub of the matter was not *whether* Japan should chastise Korea, but *when*. This was a dispute, in other words, not between hawks and doves, but between two types of hawk, the venturesome and the wary. The former became so furious with their cautious colleagues, who carried the day, that they withdrew from further participation in the government; and from the rift had come assassinations, local revolts, and an armed rising of civil war proportions.[3]

Yet in the matter of Korea the case for 'the line of interest' rested on more than predatory instinct. Japan at the beginning of the 1890s remained in certain respects something less than a fully independent country. In the management of her own tariffs and in the control of aliens she was still hobbled by the treaties concluded in earlier years with the foreign powers; treaties appositely described as 'unequal', since they imposed limitations on the full exercise of Japan's sovereignty within her own territory. In such circumstances it might be considered strange that a 'semi-colonial' country like Japan should seek to dominate another 'semi-colonial' country such as Korea. But in the Japanese view Korean (and Chinese) conservatism amounted to a betrayal of the one cause, that of reform and modernisation, that held any future for Japanese, Koreans and Chinese alike in face of the presence and pressure of the Western powers. To the resolute, fear will always act as a stimulant. Alarming as Western intrusion had been for the Japanese in the 1850s and 1860s, their reactions, then and later, included feelings of envy and admiration as well as those of anxiety and dislike. 'What we must do', declared Inouye Kaoru, the Foreign Minister, in 1887, 'is to transform our empire and our people, make the empire like the countries of Europe and our people like the peoples of Europe.'[4] No such aspiration was cherished by those who ruled Korea and China at the time. They can hardly be blamed for failing to perceive that (as a Japanese historian has put it) 'paradoxically the more Westernized the country [Japan] became, the easier it became to emphasize its traditional aspects'.[5]

The Japanese leadership believed that to beat the West you had to join it. 'Joining the West' meant being admitted to an élite club of civilised and powerful states. The strategy adopted to secure admission was marked by realism and caution. These were attributes that did not endear the oligarchy to the Japanese people as a whole. Public sentiment tended to be impatient and excitable, and from time to time it was swept by waves of chauvinism. The movement for 'people's rights', looking to the creation of an elected Parliament, was stridently nationalist. The principal figures in the movement were members or successors of the group that had wanted to 'conquer Korea' in the 1870s. It is a distortion of history to see Japan during the half-century before the Surrender of 1945 as presenting the spectacle of an oligarchy pushing essentially deferential and docile masses along the road of expansion and war. The educational structure, it is true, was so shaped as to indoctrinate the young with the spirit of self-sacrificing loyalty to Emperor and State. But given the general inheritance of Confucian precepts and Shinto beliefs, the strongly patriotic ethical framework of the educational system was inevitable. Moreover, almost as important during the nineteenth century as the inculcation of Confucian ethics were two decidedly European concepts, namely 'self-help' and 'the survival of the fittest'. Samuel Smiles and Charles Darwin influenced, directly or indirectly, a whole Japanese generation that reached maturity before the end of the eighties. The influence was all in the direction of competitiveness and self-assertion, and it acted as a spur to the enterprising and adventurous in an age of commercialism and technological development. At the same time, to the Japanese, brought up to respect family and group solidarity, individual ambition by itself seemed arid and unsatisfactory; and it was here that indoctrination at home and in school played a key role. Thus there was nearly always a rationalisation of egotistical aims in terms of a greater good; and this was usually the nation, personified by the Emperor. In the words of a Japanese scholar, 'it was precisely when the success motive joined forces with nationalism that modern Japan was able to embark on its "rush towards progress"'.[6]

The swell of public feeling was something that the government, for all its extensive police powers, could not permanently ignore. The spread of literacy, of newspapers, of modern communications, were factors that increased the range and impact of agitation against the government. To provide a safety valve, the promise was made early in the 1880s that a Constitution, incorporating a representative assembly, would be granted by the end of the decade. The popular demand for this concession, it must be noted, found its justification in the claim that a national Parliament (the Diet) would actually strengthen the Emperor's authority, enabling him to seek advice from a wider circle than the narrow leadership that had monopolised power since the Korean crisis of 1873. It was contended that the people should be given the privilege of 'assisting the Emperor' in the execution of his rule. Years later the concept was to be revived by Prince Konoye in the promotion of the 'Imperial Rule Assistance Association', the mass organisation into which the nation's political parties were merged.

The Constitution was granted as a 'gracious gift' from the Throne in 1889, and the first general election was held in the following year. It was a surprisingly quiet and orderly affair. But no sooner was the bi-cameral Diet convened than the government began to face stormy opposition in the Lower House. Members attacked the Cabinet on two scores – its failure to obtain revision of the 'unequal treaties', and the severity of its programme of taxation. The obstruction and uproar during the session from November 1890 to March 1891 were such as to suggest that Japan was almost on the eve of civil war. When the Diet reconvened in November 1891 the noisy scenes were repeated, and the Cabinet advised the Emperor Meiji to dissolve the Diet. In the subsequent general election the Matsukata Cabinet, having hastily put up its own candidates in every district, told local governors to make sure that government nominees were elected. This ploy failed. But gross intimidation and violence, not to mention bribery, were used in the largely vain effort to defeat opposition candidates; and in the election battles 25 people were killed, and nearly 400 injured. Predictably, the new Diet was no more decorous than the old. The opposition parties were at pains to embarrass the government for its alleged weakness in dealing with the revision of the treaties. Such was the venom engendered, that statements in the Diet brought protests from Great Britain and other powers.

The clashes between the government and its opponents represented a basically irreconcilable conflict between cool-headed realists and essentially irresponsible, passionate, jingoes. But Japan's nineteenth-century leaders, the Meiji oligarchy, were men of steel. They were not to be rushed by pressures from below, and they did not hesitate to use arbitrary and even brutal means to stifle or cow their critics. It has been claimed that 'the Meiji leaders, in fact, with the unconscious help of their political rivals, had created a public opinion more actively interested in Japan's international position than was entirely comfortable'.[7] However, the creation of this public sentiment probably owed more to the 'political rivals' than to the Meiji leadership. For the latter held to the view that foreign policy was not a proper subject for debate in the Diet, or, for that matter, in the columns of the press.

Writing (appropriately enough) in the early months of the Pacific War, a perceptive Japanese observed:

For whatever reasons there may be, it is an undeniable fact that advocacy of strong foreign policy has always been the basic stand of our public opinion. Public opinion is by nature irresponsible and emotional. When one thinks of our foreign policy, he must always think of this peculiar national sentiment. A remarkable feature of this sentiment is that persistent expansionism constitutes its core . . . and our experience in the past tells us that only a powerful cabinet can succeed in controlling and guiding such public opinion and its demand for strong foreign policy.[8]

Worth noting also is Professor Maruyama's comment:

Just as Japan was subject to pressure from the Great Powers, so she would apply pressure to still weaker countries – a clear case of the transfer psychology. In this regard it is significant that ever since the Meiji Period demands for a tough foreign policy have come from the common people, that is, from those who are at the receiving end of oppression at home.[9]

Irritated (to use no stronger term) by the taunts and abuse directed at them in the Diet, Japan's leaders could be confident, at least, that when the appropriate time arrived they could rely on enthusiastic popular support for action to establish the nation's 'line of interest' in the Korean Peninsula. And for a number of reasons the early 1890s constituted the appropriate time for such action. Industrialisation had proceeded far enough to equip the armed forces with the modern weapons and supplies needed for what was expected to be a short war confined to Korea and certain areas of China round the Gulf of Pe-chi-li. The Russians began building the Trans-Siberian Railway in 1891. Their interest, mainly devoted to Central Asia in the seventies and eighties, had shifted to the Far East. The aims of Russian expansion may not have been precise, but, however flexible, they would be greatly promoted by the completion of the Trans-Siberian line. It was generally understood that the eventual acquisition of an ice-free port in Korea or South Manchuria was high on the list of options for St Petersburg. In Japanese eyes the Russians loomed as an incalculable menace. Reporting from Tokyo in the early summer of 1894, the Belgian Minister suavely observed: 'The solicitude of Russia towards Korea remains undaunted. Japan is very much afraid of her and does not let herself be lulled into sleep by the sweet words of the Representative of the Tsar in Tokyo.'[10] A more immediate problem, however, was presented by China. By the Tientsin Treaty (sometimes known as the Li-Ito Convention) of 1885 China and Japan patched up a quarrel over Korea that had erupted in the previous year, when an attempted *coup* by Korean reformers against pro-Chinese conservatives had led to a clash between Chinese and Japanese troops in Seoul. The Tientsin Treaty provided that both countries withdraw their forces and in case of trouble notify the other party before sending them back. The real beneficiary of the treaty was China. Her influence in Korea was much enhanced. Peking's energetic representative in Seoul (self-styled 'Resident in Korea'), Yuan Shih-k'ai, became the dominant power behind the scenes, pushing forward such measures of modernisation as the Korean government could be induced to accept. The growth of China's stake in

Korea is indicated by the figures of total imports into that country from China and Japan during the years, 1885–92. They show that the value of imports from China rose from just over $300,000 in 1885 to more than $2,000,000 in 1892. In the same period, although Japan maintained her lead as exporter to Korea, imports from Japan rose (in round figures) from $1,370,000 to $2,550,000.[11] The trend was clearly in favour of the Chinese. There was a corresponding intensification of contacts between anti-Chinese Korean dissidents and various influential Japanese sympathisers, ranging from respectable figures such as the eminent writer and educational leader, Fukuzawa Yukichi, to powerful and none too scrupulous super-patriots such as Toyama Mitsuru, whose activities received covert support from the Ministry of War.

III

The prospect, then, as Japan entered the last decade of the nineteenth century was one that both disturbed and challenged the Tokyo government. At home, the creation of a national Parliament had done little to calm popular passions. The country seethed with political discontent. Abroad, across the Japan Sea, the Russian presence was becoming more obtrusive. China displayed an unyielding temper *vis-à-vis* Korea. Since her war with the French in Tongking (1883–5) China had enjoyed a period of peace and had refurbished her forces, notably the navy. It was apparent that Peking would not be passive if and when the Japanese exerted diplomatic and military pressure on the government of Korea.

However, the most urgent question was undoubtedly that of treaty revision. In 1893, as in the previous two years, it was this issue above all that excited the rancour of Diet politicians. There was a growing agitation, alarming to the government, in favour of a strict enforcement of treaty provisions. The 'unequal treaties' included clauses restricting the residence and travel of foreigners. At the time when the treaties were concluded, such provisions had been desirable in view of the possibility of attacks on foreigners by xenophobic samurai. But later, after the fall of the shogunate, it was seen that this particular risk had ceased to be a real one. In any case, many European and American residents were prepared to ignore the restrictions on travel, even if the Japanese authorities had tried to maintain them.

The demand for strict enforcement of the treaties was an effective way of embarrassing the government, but it also strengthened the latter in their negotiations with the treaty powers, of whom Great Britain was the most important. If Britain could be induced to accept revision, other countries would follow suit.

In 1893 Mutsu Munemitsu, Foreign Minister in the Ito Cabinet (Ito Hirobumi had succeeded Matsukata as Premier in August 1892) embarked on treaty negotiations with Great Britain. These were cloaked in secrecy, Japanese ministers refusing to make any statement on the issue, despite shrill demands, non-confidence resolutions in the Diet, and continuous pressure from all sides. A general election in March 1894 was fought very largely on the issue of 'strict enforcement' of the treaties, and the outcome was a Lower House hostile to the Ito Cabinet. In the turbulent Diet sessions that followed the Foreign Minister and his colleagues did not ease their own position by revealing that in fact treaty talks in London were proceeding in a hopeful, if leisurely, way. Success was finally achieved in July 1894. A commercial agreement was signed in London, abolishing consular courts and other unequal features of the existing treaty arrangements with Japan, these changes to take effect five years later, in 1899. As had been expected, other powers soon agreed to a revision of their own treaties. For the Japanese equality with the West now seemed very near.

It is unlikely that the Meiji oligarchy would have bowed to vulgar pressure and denounced the treaties if the London talks had failed. But it is probable that the danger of unilateral denunciation by Japan was taken seriously by the British government.

One would expect the foreign business community in Japan, concentrated for the most part in Kobe and Yokohama, to have mixed feelings about the loss of their extra-territorial privileges. What is perhaps surprising is that such misgivings were shared by some of those best qualified to have an intimate and sympathetic knowledge of Japanese society. Basil Hall Chamberlain, for example, was an Englishman who attained the singular distinction for a foreigner of becoming Professor of Japanese and Philology at Tokyo Imperial University. He can scarcely be accused of the kind of uninformed prejudice prevalent among at least some members of the British colony in the treaty ports. Nevertheless, in his famous, idiosyncratic, work *Things Japanese*, he has some blistering comments to make on 'the working of the new treaties'. Speaking of the old treaties, Hall Chamberlain observes that they rested on the assumption of 'the unequal status of the two contracting parties – civilised white men on the one hand, Japan but just emerging from Asiatic semi-barbarism on the other'.[12] On the revised treaty with Great Britain he declares that it puts in jeopardy the privilege of British subjects in Japan to publish newspapers and hold public meetings, 'their birthright of free speech'. He refers to 'new duties of from thirty to forty per cent levied precisely on those articles which are prime necessities to us but not to the Japanese'. And he asks whether anyone could 'imagine such terms having ever been agreed to except as the result of a disastrous war'. His summing up is worth quoting at some length:

Diplomacy is not a game of chance. It is a game of skill, like chess, at which the better player always wins. The Japanese negotiators, who, to be sure, had more at stake than their opponents, entirely overmatched them in brains. By playing a waiting game, by letting loose Japanese public opinion when convenient, and then representing it as a much more potent factor than it actually is, by skilful management of the press, by adroitly causing the chief seat of the negotiations to be shifted from Tokyo, where some of the local diplomats possessed adequate knowledge of the subject, to the European chanceries which possessed little or none, by talent, perseverance, patience, tact, exercised year by year – in a word, by first-rate diplomacy, they gained a complete victory over their adversaries, and at last avenged on the West the violence which it had committed in breaking open Japan a generation before. From the point of view of patriotic Englishmen, the residents in Japan (that is, the class which possesses the best knowledge of the state of the case) almost unanimously regard the British Foreign Office with contempt, for having allowed itself to be so grossly misled and roundly beaten.[13]

Hall Chamberlain's language may be thought extreme; but it is employed by one who accurately describes himself as being among those 'who love Japan but dislike jingoism'. Still, even if it is conceded that the British Foreign Office was 'roundly beaten', treaty revision could not have been postponed for very much longer in view of the remarkable proof of national strength which Japan was soon to display in her struggle with China. And if the Japanese Foreign Minister, Mutsu, 'overmatched' the British in July 1894, he achieved a scarcely less impressive diplomatic victory in the same month. For he obtained assurances from Great Britain and other powers of non-intervention in the event of war between Japan and China.

Although many British experts on the Far East were sceptical of China's chances of success, they never expected Japan's victory to be so rapid or so complete. Other European powers were no better informed.

The German Kaiser, for example, and his principal military and naval advisers brushed aside a prediction of China's defeat made by a minority of the General Staff that had been influenced by Major-General Jakob Meckel of the Berlin War Academy, an outstanding specialist on Japan and former adviser (1885–8) of the Japanese army.[14] In most quarters there was, to say the least, an imperfect understanding of Japan's capabilities.

Even within the Japanese army leadership there appear to have been misgivings about the likelihood of success, should war occur. Yamagata, the so-called 'Father of the Japanese army', is reported to have been reluctant at first to authorise, as an 'Elder Statesman', a strong line against China in 1894; for he thought the prospects of victory were poor.[15]

The details of the crisis that blew up in Korea in the summer of 1894 do not call for extensive examination here. Suffice it to say that two dramatic events helped to raise the temperature to boiling point. The first was the murder in Shanghai at the end of March of a well-known Korean dissident named Kim Ok-kiun. He was lured to Shanghai from Japan, where he had been living in exile for several years, by a fellow-Korean on instructions from the government in Seoul. Kim's death occurred almost certainly with official Chinese connivance; and the murder took place in a Japanese hotel in the Shanghai International Settlement. The assassin and the corpse were handed over by the Settlement police to the Chinese, who shipped both the Korea. The one was honourably received and well rewarded financially; the other was treated with ignominy, being cut up into four pieces for public exhibition in the four corners of the Korean Kingdom. All this stirred up great indignation in Japan, where Kim had many powerful and articulate friends, who gave it much publicity in the press, exploiting it as a stick with which to attack the oligarchy. The belief that the governments of China and Korea were 'uncivilised' became more firmly implanted in the popular mind.

The shock waves of the Kim Affair had scarcely abated when news came of a general rebellion in South Korea, in May 1894, headed by a group of deeply conservative nationalists known as the Tonghaks. Their aim was to preserve 'Eastern learning' (*tonghak*) and to eradicate modern thought and institutions, Japanese and Western alike. Korean government troops were at first unable to suppress the rising. So at the beginning of June the Korean King sought military help from China. This was speedily supplied; and in accordance with the Tientsin Treaty of 1885 Peking informed Tokyo of the dispatch of Chinese troops to Korea. By the middle of June these were already south of Seoul, and within a fortnight the Tonghak rebellion was no longer a serious threat to anyone.

When China sent in troops, Japan followed suit. This excited public opinion; but it does not follow that Japan from that moment was set on the road to war. The Prime Minister, Ito, was notoriously cautious. So far as one can judge, the dispatch of troops was intended to be no more than a move to establish a balance of power with China in Korea. However, it must be said that the attitude of the Foreign Minister, Mutsu, is not entirely clear. For there is a well-known story of how he and General Kawakami Soroku, Vice-Chief of the Army General Staff, deceived Ito about the strength of the military force – one brigade – that was sent to Korea early in June. It was reported that the Chinese had sent 5000 men to Korea (the actual number was 2000–2500). Kawakami visited Mutsu at his home and put it to him that Japan must commit a force large enough to deal with the Chinese contingent. Mutsu's rejoinder was that Ito would never agree to the dispatch, at that stage, of so many troops. Kawakami then suggested that Ito and the Cabinet be asked to approve the transfer to Korea of one army brigade – a proposal to which Ito would not object, since the strength of a brigade was 2000 men. However, in fact the army would send a mixed brigade, with a strength closer to 8000 than 2000 men. The subterfuge worked. The day after the Mutsu–Kawakami meeting the Cabinet authorised the dispatch of a 'brigade' to Korea.

It appears that it was not only the Prime Minister who was deceived in this matter. There is evidence that the Japanese Emperor may have been kept in the dark. He was informed at first, so it seems, that 3000 men were being sent to Korea. A week later he was told that this force numbered 8000.[16]

Who was General Kawakami? Whence did he derive his power? He had been Vice-Chief of the General Staff for an exceptionally long period. He had held the post, apart from one brief interval, for nine years, ever since 1885. The fact that he was only thirty-seven when first appointed marks him as a man of outstanding ability and firmness of will. It is also clear that he was a militarist in the full old-fashioned sense of that now rather shop-soiled term. A visit to Germany and some acquaintance with Moltke did nothing to dilute his conviction that Japan ought to be 'a military state' (*gunkoku*) and that the brains of this state must be the Army General Staff. Moreover, the aim of military training and the purpose of an armaments programme should be the expansion of Japan's power in Asia.

To further the realisation of his ideas, Kawakami organised an elaborate intelligence service. On information received from his agents, and on the basis of his own observations during a prolonged tour of China and Korea in 1893, Kawakami was convinced that the Chinese army was no match for the Japanese. So he believed that Japan (to use the oblique and muted language of his biographer) 'should not avoid the outbreak of war'.[17] To this end he had few scruples about being involved in clandestine activities. There is good evidence that he encouraged the ultra-nationalist *Genyosha* ('Black Ocean Society') to send a group of adventurers to join and stir up the Tonghak movement in Korea.

It is true that General Kawakami was often opposed and checked by powerful rivals, of the calibre of Yamagata, Oyama Iwao, Katsura, Taro, Kodama Gentaro and other famous names on the army list. But he appears to have been supremely competent and therefore irrepressible; and there is no doubt that in 1894, at the moment of crisis in Korea, he played a key role. It has been well said that he 'was responsible more than any other individual for creating a situation in which war remained the only alternative to the government'.[18]

The initial Mutsu policy of balancing Chinese strength was augmented by a further, and much more provocative, aim; namely, an insistence that Korea carry out a programme of drastic internal reform, in which the Japanese would play an important part. This was likely to commend itself neither to the Koreans nor the Chinese; and from the end of June, when the Ito Cabinet approved the Korean reform programme (largely Mutsu's work), war was certain. The Japanese leadership, the cautious men as well as the bold, had now reached unanimity. The time had come to expel the Chinese from Korea.

Hostilities began – from the Japanese side and prior to a declaration of war – at the end of July. By mid-September, the navy dominated all the sea approaches to North China; for off the mouth of the Yalu River, in the most important naval action since Trafalgar, the Japanese, without serious damage to a single one of their vessels, inflicted a crushing and decisive defeat on the Chinese fleet. Port Arthur was captured in November; and by the end of February 1895 the Japanese were in possession of the whole of Korea and of the Liaotung Peninsula in South Manchuria; and the Chinese were suing for peace. Talks started in Shimonoseki in March. They were concluded on 17 April

1895, when Li Hung-chang signed a treaty that conceded great gains to the Japanese. These were the territories of Formosa and the Pescadores; most of the Liaotung Peninsula, including Port Arthur and Newchwang; an indemnity equivalent to £30 million; and immensely valuable commercial concessions, such as the opening of Chinese ports hitherto closed to foreign trade, and the right of vessels to proceed up the Yangtze as far as Chungking.

The Chinese and Japanese, long before the treaty was signed, allowed the prospective terms to leak out to the governments of the great powers. China in defeat, intending to play off one country against another, hoped that Russia and Great Britain, not to mention other states, would object to Japanese territorial ambitions in South Manchuria. The Japanese, for their part, calculated that their stiff peace terms might be acceptable to other powers; since the latter would benefit from the commercial concessions to be extracted from the Chinese, thanks to the 'most-favoured nation' clause (a promise to each power that it would receive whatever privileges might later be given another) in their treaties with China. Nevertheless, there was great uneasiness in Tokyo about the possibility of some intervention by the powers; for it was realised that the cession of the Liaotung Peninsula must arouse Russian antagonism. Indeed, Japan's purpose in securing control of Port Arthur and Newchwang was to anticipate the completion of the Trans-Siberian Railway and to forestall Russian access to an ice-free port. It has been claimed that during the formulation of peace terms Mutsu at first insisted on excluding any demand for the cession of Chinese mainland territory.[19] But in the last days of January 1895 high command, Cabinet, and 'Elder Statesmen' agreed, with the approval of the Emperor Meiji, to include the Liaotung Peninsula in the territorial demands to be presented to Peking.

IV

The intervention of the three powers, Russia, Germany and France, occurred six days after the signing of the Treaty of Shimonoseki. It came, of course, as a bolt from the blue to public opinion, although it had been half expected by the government for more than two months.

The Triple Intervention, whereby the three powers 'advised' Japan to drop the claim to Port Arthur and the Liaotung Peninsula, could have been a Quadruple Intervention. Great Britain might have joined Russia, Germany and France. An approach to this end had been made

in London; and China, too, had appealed for help. A special meeting of
the Rosebery Cabinet on 8 April 1895 could not agree at first on what
response should be offered to these approaches. But much importance
was attached to the commercial concessions demanded by Japan; so the
Cabinet finally concluded that the Japanese terms did not justify British
intervention.[20]

This decision was one of the most important made by a British
government in modern times. It is easy to read back into the decision, in
the light of the Anglo-Japanese Alliance some years later, a far-sighted
bid for Japanese friendship. But this was hardly the case. A Tenniel
cartoon in *Punch* (4 May 1895) reflects the mood of British ministers and
British public opinion. A distressed mandarin (China) sits on the
ground opposite a smug young figure in a peasant's hat (Japan). They
have just played a game of cards across a low table, and 'Japan' is
collecting the stakes, his hands, like those of a croupier, raking in stacks
of coins away from the sad Chinese. 'Germany', 'France', and 'Russia'
(two of them are sailors, bearded 'Russia' wears a fur cap) stand behind
the players. In the background, propped against a wall, arms folded, a
clay pipe in his mouth, lounges the stout figure of John Bull in a Jack
Tar's summer rig. 'Russia', pointing at the card table, is clearly arguing
with John Bull. The cartoon caption reads: '*Russia*: "Is he to have all
this?" *John Bull*: "Well – he's played a square game – *I* don't see any call
to interfere!"' There is more than a touch of complacency in John Bull's
attitude; as though he were saying to himself, in a more modern idiom:
'let them get on with it!'

Within five years, British confidence would be shaken by the South
African War, much as in more recent times American self-esteem has
been undermined by the struggle in Vietnam. But in the run-up to the
Diamond Jubilee the British mood was self-assured and assertive *vis-à-
vis* the rest of the world. It was not clear that the Japanese would bow to
the Triple Intervention without putting the determination of the three
powers to the test. There seemed no advantage to Great Britain in
becoming involved in the dispute. If non-intervention earned a modest
dividend in the form of Japanese goodwill so much the better. But this
consideration was a minor factor; as was the likelihood of Chinese
resentment at British passivity. Quite simply, the feelings of the
Japanese and Chinese were regarded with benevolent, not to say
patronising, unconcern.

This book deals primarily with Japan, and with Japanese rather than
Chinese national sentiment. But we should note that consternation at

their country's defeat, and even more so at the terms of the Treaty of Shimonoseki, led Chinese scholar–officials into the wistful four years of the Reform Movement, culminating in the Hundred Days of 1898; when the Emperor Kuang-hsu, influenced by K'ang Yu-wei and other modernisers, issued, between 11 June and 21 September 1898, forty or more reform edicts on almost every subject from education to the organisation of the armed forces. It was China's tragedy that the reform programme should have been abruptly terminated, by the *coup d'état* engineered by the Empress Dowager, whereby she regained supreme power. But in any case the war and the peace treaty gave rise in China to 'an unprecedented outpouring of patriotic concern'.[21]

In Japan the war united public opinion. All criticism of the oligarchy was stilled. Needless to say, the peace terms were greeted with general satisfaction. The more appalling, therefore, was the shock of the Triple Intervention.

When the 'advice' of the three powers was conveyed to the Tokyo government, the latter decided quickly that Japan would have to give way if it was clear that the powers – and Russia in particular – were not bluffing. The Legation in St Petersburg reported that the Russians were in earnest. Moreover, Russian naval vessels were cleared for action, not only at Vladivostok but also in Japan's own waters, at Kobe and Nagasaki.[22] It was Russia's sea power that impressed the Japanese. The Russian army in the Far East did not exceed 30,000; and it could not be reinforced with any speed until the Trans-Siberian line was finished.

The Japanese government tried to soften the blow by offering to evacuate the Liaotung Peninsula except for Port Arthur and the nearby harbour of Talienwan. As it was precisely this region that, in Russia's view, must not fall into Japanese hands, this attempt to modify the 'advice' was unsuccessful. It was made brutally plain that nothing short of a total evacuation of South Manchuria would do. Accordingly, twelve days after the 'advice' was received, the Japanese agreed to renounce their claim to any part of the Liaotung Peninsula, provided that China ratified the Shimonoseki Treaty immediately and agreed to pay an additional indemnity. The Emperor Meiji shortly afterwards issued a rescript declaring that Japan's war aims had been attained, that the evacuation of South Manchuria was no reflection on the nation's dignity and honour, and that the Japanese people must show restraint.

No understanding of twentieth-century Japanese nationalism is possible without some comprehension of the bitterness and sense of humiliation that swept the country in the wake of the Triple Intervention. Firm measures were taken to bridle the press and dissolve public meetings; but Japan's rulers, no less than the mass of the people, were deeply affronted, despite the fact that to most of the ministers the Intervention was by no means a complete surprise. In cold fury they drew certain conclusions about their nation's future policy. These are nowhere better expressed than in an article in June 1895 in the journal, *Jiji Shimpo*, by Hayashi Tadasu, Vice-Minister of Foreign Affairs during the crisis. It was Hayashi who had received the Russian, German and French Ministers when they made their *démarche* (Mutsu was ill at the time). It was Hayashi who had to endure a double insult from the German Minister, Baron von Gutschmid, who was strongly anti-Japanese. The latter read his government's communication aloud in Japanese, from a text written in the romanised script. But Gutschmid's competence in the language was so modest as to render much of the message incomprehensible to Hayashi. He understood, nevertheless, one menacing phrase not included in the 'advice' presented by the Ministers of Russia and France. 'Japan', Gutschmid read out, 'cannot defeat the united strength of Russia, France, and Germany'. Hayashi reacted so strongly that Gutschmid backed down, agreeing to resubmit his message in more polite phraseology. It was two months after this experience that Hayashi, now Minister in Peking, wrote his article.

We must continue to study and make use of Western methods; [wrote Hayashi] for among civilised nations applied science constitutes the most important part of their military preparations. If new warships are considered necessary we must, at any cost, build them; if the organisation of our army is inadequate we must start rectifying it from now; if need be, our entire military system must be changed.

We must build shipyards for the repair of our vessels. We must build steelworks to provide us with guns and munitions. Our railway network must be enlarged to enable us to carry out a speedy mobilisation of our troops. Our merchant fleet must be expanded to enable us to transport our armies overseas. . . . At present Japan must keep calm and sit tight, so as to lull suspicions nurtured against her; during this time the foundations of her national power must be consolidated; and we must watch and wait for the opportunity in the Orient that will surely come one day. When this day arrives Japan will decide her own fate; and she will be able not only to put into their place the powers who seek to meddle in her affairs; she will even be able, should this be necessary, to meddle in their affairs.[23]

Hayashi went on to advocate an alliance between Japan and Great Britain – in order to check Russian power – and declared that 'together England and Japan can control China and keep the peace in the Far East'.[24] Five years later this decided Anglophile was to become Minister in London and would handle the negotiations for the Anglo-Japanese Alliance.

During those five years, 1895–1900, by greatly strengthening her armed forces and industrial capacity, Japan followed the path mapped out for her in the Hayashi article. She drew closer to Great Britain; and the national determination to put in their place 'the powers who seek to meddle' was greatly stiffened in the early months of 1898 by Russia's occupation (on a twenty-five year lease from China) of Port Arthur and Talienwan (Dairen), by Germany's acquisition (a ninety-nine years lease) of Tsingtao, and by France's lease (ninety-nine years) of Kwangchow Bay. This activity by the three powers almost seemed like a revival of the Triple Intervention. So Great Britain's lease of Weihaiwei was greatly welcomed by the Japanese, who feared that Russia or Germany coveted that harbour, commanding the southern approaches to Tangku, (the port giving access to Tientsin and Peking). Indeed, pending the final payment of the Shimonoseki indemnity, the Japanese themselves were occupying Weihaiwei; but they were due to leave, and the Germans at Tsingtao were not far to the south, in the same province of China. Still, the Russians posed a greater threat. So the Japanese military authorities wanted to retain Weihaiwei. However, to have the Royal Navy there was some small consolation. The Japanese left Weihaiwei the day before the British moved in.

Thus as the century drew towards its close the West looked at the rising power of Japan with curiosity, benevolence and suspicion, according to the prejudices, interests and plans of the viewer. It was left to the German Kaiser to inject a note of hysteria into the scene. In 1895 he was inspired to rough out in his own hand the sketch of a symbolical drawing that would represent the 'Yellow Peril'. Having commissioned an artist (H. Knackfuss) to complete the cartoon, he sent it as a personal gift to Tsar Nicholas II. In the famous *Kaiserbild* the 'Yellow Peril' appears to be the Lord Buddha seated on a dragon, bursting through a storm-cloud formed by the dense smoke rising from a burning city. Standing on a rocky crag, in face of this horror from the East, the archangel Michael exhorts the female personifications of the European powers to unite against the Peril. It is noteworthy that Britannia (with spear instead of trident) hangs back, although she is being urged forward by Austria.

Britannia wavers; her lovely face – a reminiscence, maybe, of sweet English girls seen at Cowes – is pensive. She knows that Peril well, you see; she has done a good deal of business with him in the past, and, naturally, feels reluctant to use her spear against an old and valued customer.[25]

But behind such expressions of racial feeling there was, of course, calculated policy – the consistent determination to keep Russia's gaze on the East, away from Europe.

Seen from Japan the Russians were supremely the 'White Peril'. But the Japanese – in 1898 as in 1895 – were as yet unready to face it. As the British Minister in Tokyo, Sir Ernest Satow, reported to London: 'They [the Japanese] have the appearance of being thoroughly disheartened, and they do not seem to appreciate the value of diplomacy except as a preliminary to the use of force'.[26] The second sentence of that passage sums up the lesson the Japanese had learned from their dealings with the Western powers. Having grasped only one important part of the true function of diplomacy, they were tempted into the error of supposing it to be the whole of the diplomatic art. *'They do not seem to appreciate the value of diplomacy except as a preliminary to the use of force.'* This was a shrewd comment, by one who was an expert on Japan and on the art of diplomacy. For Sir Ernest Satow (Minister in Tokyo, 1895–1900) first arrived in Japan (as a student interpreter) in 1862 and stayed there continuously, except for two short breaks, for twenty years. It was in 1917 that he published his famous work, *A Guide to Diplomatic Practice*, of which the fourth edition appeared in 1957. The truth of Satow's observation was to be amply confirmed as the twentieth century progressed.

3 A Question of Alliances

Since there are grounds for believing that Britain has already passed her zenith and will to some extent decline, it would be best to fix a time-limit for any British treaty.

BARON KOMURA

I

IF the 'White Peril' from the Japanese point of view was represented overwhelmingly by the Russians, it must be remembered that the closing years of the nineteenth century also witnessed a remarkable trans-Pacific advance by the United States. In 1898 there occurred not only the annexation of Hawaii but also the Spanish–American War, followed by the establishment of American control of the Philippines and the acquisition of Guam and Wake. Moreover, Washington began to contemplate the lease of a port on the China coast, namely Samsah Bay in Fukien, in the vicinity of Amoy.

But Fukien Province is opposite Formosa and was by now, in an entirely unofficial sense, a Japanese sphere of influence. Accordingly, the American Secretary of State, John Hay, thought it prudent to sound out the Japanese very discreetly on their reaction to a possible lease of Samsah. The response was not favourable, and Hay proceeded in the matter no further. However, he embarked on the 'Open Door' diplomacy associated ever since with his name. His first Notes on this policy were dispatched in September 1899.

What was meant by the phrase, the 'Open Door', was the principle of equal and unrestricted commercial opportunity for the nationals of all countries trading with China, irrespective of existing spheres of influence. In declaring its own adherence to this principle the United States sought a like declaration from the other powers. Words cost nothing; and such declarations were soon forthcoming.

Bearing in mind Satow's observation on the Japanese concept of diplomacy – 'they do not seem to appreciate the value of diplomacy except as a preliminary to the use of force' – we should not except the altruism professed in the Hay Notes to be taken at its face value in

33

Tokyo. The whole question of American intentions presented the Japanese with something of an enigma. While the United States did not follow the example of Russia, Germany, France and Great Britain by securing a territorial lease from China, this could be put down to the fact that the Americans had heavy military commitments in the Philippines, where the suppression of the independence movement was proving to be a costly business in manpower and resources. At the same time, it was difficult for the Japanese to assess the degree to which American public opinion favoured the new imperialism symbolised by the expansion of their country's power in the western Pacific. On the face of it the imperialist lobby appeared to have every advantage. But its opponents were resolute and eloquent. They could draw strength from the long tradition of American isolationism. It was significant that in 1899 a Senate resolution in Washington promising the Filipinos their independence was only rejected by the casting vote of the Vice-President. So as they watched the advance of America across the Pacific towards the China coast, the Japanese could hardly fail to note the manifestations of isolationist opposition to that advance. It became increasingly important for Japan to form an accurate estimate of isolationist strength. In later years some of those who seemed to know America best, such as Matsuoka Yosuke, were to make serious miscalculations here.

But at the turn of the century American imperialism, even in its most aggressive and self-righteous guise, was not notably anti-Japanese. Certain fears and prejudices, it is true, had begun to fester in California; but these would not attract great attention outside that state until the Russo-Japanese War. (It was in 1905 that the California state legislature resolved unanimously that Japanese immigrants were 'immoral, intemperate, quarrelsome men bound to labour for a pittance'.)[1] Before 1905 Americans who had their eyes on China were apprehensive about Russia rather than Japan. The American attitude towards Japan, outside California at any rate, was not free from the touch of condescension implicit in the term, 'little brown brother', used affectionately to describe the Filipino and Hawaiian who had grasped the helping hand of 'the elder brother', Uncle Sam.

Still, Japan's status as an acceptable if still junior member of the club of civilised powers was confirmed by the part she played in the international force sent to rescue the diplomatic missions besieged by the Chinese in Peking. This was the climax of the Boxer Rising, in which antipathy to foreigners, provoked by years of 'barbarian' intrusion, found bloody expression. The Japanese contingent was larger than any other and was remarkable for its discipline no less than for its martial ardour. Once the Legations had been relieved it was disclosed that the life and soul of their small, improvised, defence force had been a Japanese officer, Major Shiba. To the popular imagination in Britain and America in 1900 the Japanese appeared as the heroes, the Chinese as the villains, of the drama in Peking.

The reprisals that followed the Boxer Rising represented in the case of the Western powers the highwater mark of their interference in Chinese domestic affairs. The punishment imposed on China was spelt out in the Boxer Protocol, concluded at Peking on 7 September 1901 and signed by China and eleven foreign powers (Britain, the United States, Russia, Germany, France, Italy, Austria–Hungary, Holland, Japan, Belgium and Spain). From the point of view of those countries whose nationals had suffered harshly in Peking and other parts of China the Boxer Protocol was no more than stern retribution. From the point of view of the Chinese, including those hostile to the Boxer movement, it was an instrument of revenge and humiliation. A glance at the terms of the Protocol will suggest why this was so. Their severity will be apparent; and their bearing on the later resurgence of Chinese nationalist feeling will be readily understood. But for our purpose the important point is that once again the Japanese were given a demonstration of power politics in the Far East by the countries of the Western world. In particular, the Japanese were provided with a further example of how to deal with a weak, unreformed China.

The heavy indemnity imposed on Peking remains no doubt the best-known feature of the Boxer Protocol. It amounted to 450,000,000 Taels, the equivalent, at the rates of exchange then obtaining, of £67,500,000 or $317,700,000; and amortisation of the debt by annual payments was to be completed by the end of 1940. Service of the debt was to be the first charge on the revenues from the Chinese customs service and salt gabelle.

The indemnity was a serious burden. But it is arguable that it offended Chinese susceptibilities less than certain of the other clauses of the Protocol. Wounding to national pride as an indemnity might be, it could be interpreted as the necessary price to be paid for defeat in war. The same could be said of such painful requirements as the punishment, in certain cases execution or a sentence of suicide, of officials held responsible for outrages against foreigners or Chinese Christians. Much harder to bear, being more offensive to Chinese *amour propre*, were some of the other terms of the Protocol; for example, Articles VII and IX. Article VII stipulated that the Legation Quarter in Peking should be placed under the exclusive control of the foreign diplomatic missions. Every mission would have the right to maintain a permanent military garrison; and in the Legation Quarter 'the Chinese shall not have the right to reside'. Article IX specified the localities – twelve of them from Peking to the coast – to be occupied by foreign troops 'for the maintenance of open communication between the capital and the sea'.[2]

By these provisions a foreign organism was implanted in the heart of the imperial capital, thereby lending Peking a semi-colonial character comparable with that of Cairo or Seoul. Indeed, there was a general impression abroad that an inevitable consequence of the Boxer affair must be the break-up of China, the expectation being that when this occurred China would be split territorially into four regions. South China would become for all practical purposes a French sphere of influence. Central China, embracing the Yangtze basin, would be controlled by Great Britain. Germany would lay successful claim to the whole of Shantung Province. The rest of China, from Sinkiang to the sea, including Mongolia, Manchuria and Peking itself, would fall to Russia. In this scenario, it will be noted, neither Japan nor the United States were given a role.[3]

But partition required agreement among the powers. This was not forthcoming. Russia's grip on Manchuria provoked anxiety in London as well as Tokyo and created suspicion, not untouched by envy, even in Berlin. Rather more serious, at least from the British point of view (as well as the Japanese), was the seeming intention of the Russian military contingent, following the defeat of the Boxers, to behave as though North China was already well on the way to becoming part of the Tsar's dominions. Relations between Britain and France in China at that time were, if anything, less cordial than those between Britain and Russia. In Tientsin in the winter of 1900–1 the French concession was placed out of bounds to British troops; for the French contingent off duty was prone to utter cries of *à bas les Anglais*, *Fashoda*, and *Vive les Boers*. In such demonstrations the Germans were inclined to add their own voice. There were frequent riots, culminating in the summer of 1901 in pitched battle with the British and Japanese on one side, the French and the Germans on the other: there were about twenty casualties, including some deaths.[4]

When predators fall out among themselves their putative victim may survive, however weakened, and indeed virtually lifeless, his condition might appear. In any case, China was adept at playing off one imperialist power against another – the only sensible course of action open to Peking. At this critical moment in China's history the Russians claimed to be the sole guardians of her integrity; and although the claim seemed, on the face of it, unconvincing it was one which the Chinese knew how to exploit to their advantage. They recognised, for example, that the Russians themselves were not entirely of one mind as to the best strategy to be employed.

The Tsar's advisers, certainly, were broadly united in a belief in Russia's 'civilising mission' in the Far East. But in their commitment to national expansion they differed in the degree of urgency with which they were prepared to promote it. Now differences of degree can be vital, as was to be revealed in the case of the Japanese as well as the Russians. It is not so much the aims of statesmen as their methods which lead a country to disaster.

In St Petersburg there were those, typified by Sergei Witte, the able Minister of Finance, who were disposed to advance the frontiers of Russian power with considerable caution and tact. Their motto could have been *suaviter in modo, fortiter in re.* Witte was an empire-builder who saw the destiny of the Trans-Siberian Railway in political as well as economic terms, as a means of projecting his country 'southward along the road of history'. 'The absorption by Russia of a considerable portion of the Chinese Empire', he declared, 'is only a question of time'.[5] Nevertheless, Witte accepted a flexible interpretation of that 'question of time'. In any case, Russia at the turn of the century was in his view still too weak to risk a quarrel with the power that seemed to be her most formidable rival, namely Great Britain. Witte was increasingly drawn, therefore, towards a moderate course in relation to both China and Korea.

The Russian Minister of War, General Kuropatkin, was a more adventurous figure. Earlier in his career he had taken part in a military expedition that had added a sizeable chunk of Central Asia to the Russian Empire; and it was doubtless the recollection of that campaign that led him to argue that northern Manchuria, at least, must be made 'another Bokhara'. After the Boxer Rising Kuropatkin supplanted Witte as the minister with the greatest influence at court. For although tending to oscillate between boldness and circumspection, Tsar Nicholas II seems, on the whole, to have favoured a decidedly unyielding policy in the Far East. Nicholas had some first-hand knowledge of that part of the world, having travelled in the region as

Crown Prince in 1891. On 31 March of that year he had inaugurated the construction of the Trans-Siberian Railway 'by personally emptying the first wheelbarrow full of ballast for the embankment of its eastern terminal – Vladivostok, "Ruler of the East"'.[6] A month later, while touring in Japan, he was attacked and wounded by one of the Japanese policemen responsible for his safety. Such experiences were unlikely to be forgotten. At all events, Nicholas II came to listen to advisers who surpassed Kuropatkin in a readiness to take risks; and if Kuropatkin replaced Witte as the Tsar's most influential counsellor he was to lose ground to men more extreme than himself. These were new personalities on the Russian political scene and they formed a chauvinist clique, of whom the leading members were Plehve, the Minister of the Interior, Rear-Admiral Abaza, and Abaza's cousin, a wealthy ex-cavalry officer named Bezobrazov. The cast of their ideas is indicated by that fact that in all sincerity they considered Witte to be a traitor.

Thus, Russian policy in Asia from the time of the Boxer Rising in the summer of 1900 to the outbreak of war with Japan, early in 1904, followed a course which, though erratic, tended to reflect the influence of progressively adventurous imperial advisers. Even so, historians today disagree as to the extent to which Russian Far Eastern policy can be accepted as really bellicose.[7]

The Japanese picture, on the other hand, is perhaps clearer. There were broadly speaking two main schools or cliques of policy-makers. The more cautious was represented by Ito and his circle, the more venturesome by Yamagata and his followers. We must not make too much of the fact that the former were civilians and the latter military men. Nearly all Japan's leaders above the age of fifty at this time, the opening of twentieth century, had started life as samurai and had therefore absorbed the ethos of the warrior class. But thirty years and more of post-feudal society, including a decade of parliamentary politics had in some degree 'demilitarised' those in public life who had not become professional soldiers and sailors in the early Meiji era; and by 1900 there was a perceptible difference in outlook and life-style between soldiers like Yamagata and men such as Ito and Okuma who had exchanged their swords for bowler-hat and frock-coat. The 'civilians', as one might expect, were on the whole more flexible and sophisticated than the soldiers in their response to the problems of foreign affairs.

The imperial Diet had not yet acquired the corporate self-confidence, much less the power, of the British Parliament or United States Congress or, for that matter, the German Reichstag. Still, as we saw in the last chapter, members of the Diet never hesitated to attack and embarrass the government of the day. If such attacks could come from the chauvinist Right, they could emanate on some future occasion from the radical Left. Ideologically, the Diet was no doubt 'sound', in terms of loyalty to the imperial house – this could be taken for granted in the Meiji period – but the spectre of socialism was already there. Thirteen bold spirits had founded a socialist society in 1898, meeting in Shiba Unitarian Church, Tokyo. Historians have taken this event as signifying the birth of the Marxist movement in Japan. The aim of the society was 'to study the pros and cons of the application of socialist theory to Japan'.[8] Probably because it was for the moment no more than a tiny study circle the society was not banned outright by the police. But once it aspired to be an active political body – as the *Shakai Minshuto* ('Social Democratic Party') – it was suppressed on the very day that it was founded in 1901. The authorities viewed Marxism in much the same way as their forebears in the seventeenth century had regarded Christianity – namely, as a form of ethical and intellectual poison.

From such infection the armed forces had at all costs to be kept immune. To be on the safe side it was best that no civilian be allowed to have a direct say in the administration, much less the operations and training, of the army and navy. There was, too, a further consideration. Since only high-ranking soldiers and sailors could serve as ministers of war and of the navy (the Navy Minister had to be an admiral or vice-admiral), no Cabinet could survive if it persistently defied army or navy opinion. It was practically impossible for a general or admiral to ignore the considered views of his service colleagues. Having entered a Cabinet he could always bring it down by his resignation; and the collective leadership of the army or navy could prevent a general or admiral from accepting ministerial office in a new Cabinet. Accordingly, the army and navy possessed, and often exercised, a real power of veto in the political field. This was an invaluable weapon from their point of view, for it gave them an entrenched position on the highest councils of the state.

When the Boxer troubles convulsed Peking the Tokyo government was headed by a military man, Yamagata. In October 1900, however, his Cabinet gave place to one led by a civilian, Ito Hirobumi. The army's choice of War Minister in the Ito Cabinet was General Katsura, a protégé of Yamagata's and, like most prominent soldiers of the Meiji era, a samurai from Yamagata's province, Choshu. Katsura's career had been guided by his powerful mentor; and Katsura himself has been described as 'Yamagata's stooge from start to finish'.[9] The masterful Yamagata had now reached a high plateau of authority and prestige. Released from the chores of the premiership (including the need to handle a fractious Diet) he was able to operate on two levels. So far as day-to-day cabinet business was concerned he had in Katsura a reliable informant as well as a loyal tool. In addition, Yamagata would soon be recognised officially as a *Genro*, as one of the select coterie of 'retired' senior statesmen entrusted not only with the duty of recommending new premiers to the Throne, but also with the final power of decision on questions of foreign policy. On top of that, Yamagata had enjoyed an unexpected stroke of good fortune. His one dangerous rival in the army, General Kawakami of Satsuma, whom we met in the last chapter, died in 1899 at the age of fifty-two.

The change of government in Tokyo in the autumn of 1900 broadly coincided with the shift in the political balance at St Petersburg that elevated Kuropatkin at the expense of Witte, although the latter had still nearly three years of ministerial office ahead of him before he was eventually dismissed by the Tsar. The more assertive policy in Asia, symbolised by the new ascendancy of Kuropatkin, was soon to be reflected in Russian diplomacy. At the end of 1900 the draft of a treaty dealing with Manchuria, Mongolia and western China was presented by the Russians to Peking. Ignoring the principle of the 'Open Door', Russia demanded that within a huge crescent of territory, from Khotan and Yarkand through Mongolia and Manchuria to the Yalu River, the Chinese should not negotiate economic concessions, including leases of land, with foreigners without the prior agreement of St Petersburg. More than this, the Chinese were not to maintain armed forces in any part of this vast region; and the size of the police force was to be fixed after consultation with the Russians.

These terms were leaked by China; and Witte himself, unconvinced of their wisdom and concerned as always to test reaction abroad, revealed their essential features to the envoys of the great powers. Undoubtedly, the reported terms of the treaty represented Russia's maximum demands and were therefore negotiable and could be whittled down in a process of bargaining. It has been argued, too, that the terms where intended to be 'temporary', that compared with the Boxer Protocol 'the terms of the agreement contained very little of an alarming nature'.[10] But the Japanese and the British, to mention only two of the nations concerned with the struggle for power in the Far East, could be forgiven for regarding the proposed treaty as a blatant exposure of Russian ambitions.

Certainly, the repercussions in Tokyo and other capitals were sharp enough to bring the international temperature to boiling point. In this crisis the Japanese were particularly active. There was talk of war unless the Russians abandoned the proposed treaty. In their anxiety the Japanese approached Great Britain and Germany for an assurance of support. These two powers had concluded during the previous autumn an understanding, the Anglo-German Agreement on China, which committed them to uphold the principle of the 'Open Door' 'for all Chinese territory as far as they can exercise influence'. But the qualification expressed in the last seven words of that sentence emasculated any power that the Agreement might otherwise have possessed. For the Germans soon made it plain that as they did not 'exercise influence' in Manchuria they were not prepared to take part in a joint German–British–Japanese stand against the Russians. The Kaiser and his advisers were willing to see both China and Japan embroiled in a quarrel with Russia, but were not ready to jeopardise good relations with the Tsar; the position being stated very plainly by the Chancellor, Count Bülow, when he told the Reichstag that the fate of Manchuria 'was a matter of absolute indifference to Germany'.

Britain, it must be remembered, was still at war with the Boers, although the struggle was in its final stage. The war had exposed the degree to which Great Britain had won the dislike as well as the envy of other powers; for the news of her early defeats in South Africa had been greeted with *schadenfreude* in most countries of Europe. The need for cooperation against the Boxers did something to soften such asperities, but, as we have seen, once the danger to the Peking Legations was over national rivalries reasserted themselves. The exigencies of South Africa had weakened Britain's military strength in India. This made London the more sensitive to reports of fresh Russian activity and interest in the buffer states that were ranged on the outer perimeter of the Indian Empire. Thus, British concern was aroused when St Petersburg in June 1900 made a substantial loan to Persia, thereby greatly enhancing Russia's commercial position in that country. A few months later a Tibetan mission arrived in Russia. It may be that 'its purpose and achievements remained uncertain'.[11] But the authorities in India were alarmed. China claimed suzerainty over Tibet, but at this moment of national weakness it was a claim that could not be effectively enforced;

and it was feared in Simla and Calcutta that an independent Tibet might very well fall under Russian influence.

Great Britain, therefore, felt apprehensive and vulnerable so far as Russia was concerned; and Lord Salisbury's Conservative Cabinet went so far as to accept the idea of a secret Anglo-German promise to intervene on Japan's behalf, if necessary, in the event of Japanese–Russian war. But, as we have seen, the Germans refused to participate in any anti-Russian operation in the Far East. Japan, then, had to face Russia on her own.

There followed a display of firmness by the Japanese and a climb down by the Russians. Stiff notes were sent from Tokyo to St Petersburg, and a bellicose anti-Russian tone was apparent in the Japanese press and in the Diet. The Russian Minister to Japan, Izvolskii, seems to have thought the Japanese meant business when they talked of war, and the Russian Foreign Minister, Lamsdorf, was not disposed to quarrel with this view. The Chinese, in any case, rejected the proposed treaty – here they were reacting to pressure from London as well as Tokyo – and this gave the Russians a chance to drop the project, an official announcement to this effect being made on 5 April 1901.

It is by no means clear whether the Japanese would in fact have gone to war in the spring of 1901 if the Russians had declined to give way. Kato Takaakira, the Foreign Minister, favoured a decidedly stern posture *vis-à-vis* Russia; and Katsura, the Minister of War, adopted an equally resolute stand. But the Premier, Ito, was more cautious. Indeed, he may be called Japan's Witte. It is always said that the Emperor Meiji trusted Ito more than any of his advisers; and at this juncture such backing might have tipped the scales in favour of peace. In April 1901 the Russians had five battleships in the Far East. The Japanese had no more than five, even if ship for ship they may have been superior to the Russian vessels. In first-class cruisers, the Russians had six against Japan's four. Only in light cruisers and smaller craft did the Japanese possess a clear numerical advantage. Financially, too, Japan was scarcely ready for war against Russia at that time. One historian's view is probably close to the truth: 'On the whole, it seems that the Japanese leaders were preparing for an emergency but were incapable of engaging in an immediate war.'[12] Be that as it may, in this diplomatic tussle the Russians evidently did not think the Japanese were bluffing. So they backed down. This was an undoubted triumph for the Ito administration, and more particularly for the energetic Foreign

Minister, Kato. After six years some of the shame of the Triple Intervention was expunged.

The crisis appears to have convinced Yamagata of the need for an alliance with one or more powers in order to deal with further Russian pressure. His first preference was a tripartite alliance of Japan, Britain and Germany. Towards the end of April 1901 he presented the case for this in a letter to Ito. It is a famous document, its composition marking an important step along the road that led to the Anglo-Japanese Treaty of 30 January 1902. Furthermore, it states certain fundamental national aims that were to be reflected in the clauses of that treaty. For our purpose the kernel of the Yamagata letter is the following passage:

Relations between Japan and Russia have not yet suffered a major upset but sooner or later a serious collision is inevitable. . . . We should seek Britain's views and devise with her a treaty of alliance in consultation with Germany. Among its clauses we should stipulate our freedom of action in Korea. . . . It should be provided that, when one party to the alliance is engaged in fighting with another power and a third power assists the enemy, the remaining signatory to the alliance should intervene, though it is not clear how far it should be involved in the war.[13]

Yamagata's influence was much enhanced only a few weeks later, when for domestic political reasons the Ito Cabinet resigned and was replaced by a government headed by General Katsura. Those who wanted an alliance with Britain and Germany, directed against Russia, were now well placed politically to achieve their goal. However, it became clear in the course of the summer that Germany was not to be a partner after all, and with the coming of autumn 1901, serious talks with Britain were well under way.

II

To transform friendship with Great Britain into a full-blown alliance had long been the ambition of certain circles in Japan. The advantages of such an alliance had been urged, as we have seen, in 1895 by the Foreign Vice-Minister, Hayashi Tadasu. Now, in 1901, he was Minister in London. From the moment of his arrival in London the previous year he had been indefatigable in preaching the need for the alliance. Speaking English with a fluency unusual among his compatriots, Hayashi moved easily in London society. Doubtless his sincere

Anglophile sympathies were the more cordially recognised at a time when South Africa made Englishmen feel that most foreigners were hostile. But at first he did not make much headway. It was not until the spring of 1901 that the British government seemed to be giving prime attention to a Japanese, rather than a German, entente.

Even after the change of Cabinet in Tokyo, however, Hayashi and the pro-British school faced difficulties. Ito might be out of office, but he was now himself a *Genro*, high in the Emperor's confidence; and he had an important following among bureaucrats and politicians. Ito did not want his country to accept any commitment that might spoil the chance of an understanding with the Russians. For he believed they could be persuaded to come to a settlement with Japan on the basis of mutual recognition of respective rights in Manchuria and Korea. He was to fight a strong rearguard action against the conclusion of the proposed British alliance.

Yamagata and his army disciples, on the other hand, saw in the alliance a lever with which to apply effective pressure on Russia when an appropriate moment arrived. In principle, the navy, too, welcomed the prospect of having Britain as an ally, as did many civilian officials.

Even in these quarters, however, there were certain doubts, despite Britain's wealth, industrial output, naval strength and world-wide connections. Such misgivings are suggested by the caveat uttered by Komura (Katsura's Foreign Minister) that has been quoted at the head of this chapter (see p. 33 above). To those without up-to-date knowledge of the changing world, the very thought of the alliance was flattering to national self-esteem. But the well-informed noted Great Britain's decline, by comparison with the predominant status she had once enjoyed. The position at the close of the Victorian age is well described by Professor Max Beloff: 'Britain neither presented the picture of self-confident private enterprise that was turning the United States into the world's greatest industrial nation without the aid of a powerful state machine, nor approached the controlled urge to national power and expansion of imperial Germany'.[14]

Thirty years earlier the picture had been different. America was only just beginning to recover from the Civil War, and Bismarck's Germany was no more than a few months old. Within a generation, nevertheless, these two new industrial powers had demonstrated a vitality and speed of growth that could not fail to impress the eclectic and wideawake Japanese, causing them to wonder how soon the United States and Germany would overtake Great Britain, hitherto the unrivalled leader among the advanced nations of the world. There was matter for reflection, too, in Britain's poor showing in the South African War. It was taking her a long time to suppress the forces of two small farming republics.

Still, neither the Boer War nor the industrial challenge presented by America and Germany had cast a shadow on the prestige of the Royal Navy. British rule in India, too, seemed as solid as ever, its power unshaken as yet either by external pressures or internal revolt.

The Royal Navy ever since the 1860s had filled a key role in the training of Japanese sailors. Gunnery, battle tactics, modern signals, hydrography, engine-room maintenance, dockyard organisation;* the construction and repair of warships; the victualling of their crews; all these were taught in Japan, or in Britain to Japanese, by British naval officers. Etajima, the naval academy on the Inland Sea near Hiroshima, took Dartmouth as its model. In the first years of the twentieth century new battleships and cruisers for Japan were still being built on Tyneside. In the Japanese merchant marine, as well as the navy, English terms were (and are still) used in orders from bridge to deck and engine room. At the turn of the century 'old salts' from the Thames estuary and the Clyde could still be found among the Inland Sea pilots on the passage from Kobe to the Shimonoseki Straits. In nearly everything that concerned the handling of modern ships the Japanese looked up to Great Britain as their mentor or, in later years, as their *onshi* ('honoured former teacher'). This long-established naval connection provided Britain, in her relations with Japan, with an asset which, though hard to assess, was of great importance. Thus, when Yamagata and the army favoured a British alliance (although they would have wished their own *onshi*, Germany, to have been associated with it), they could expect the navy – the 'junior service' in Japan – to back them up with enthusiasm.

Indeed, considerations of naval strategy were a vital element in the thinking of both Japanese and British when they contemplated the question of the alliance. The Japanese margin of superiority at sea over the Russians was not impressive. The latter, moreover, could reinforce their Far East fleet from the Baltic. In the event of conflict Russia's ally, France, had to be taken into account; and French naval strength in the Far East was not contemptible. Russia and France together could

---

* However, the Yokosuka naval dockyard near Yokohama was built under the supervision of a French naval mission in the last years of the shogunate.

muster a fleet that the Japanese might not be able to match on their own. A prime aim of an alliance with Britain – as Yamagata stressed in his letter to Ito – was to prevent a third power (France) intervening in a Japanese–Russian war, or, should that prove impossible, to bring in Britain as a fighting partner on Japan's side. Of vital concern, then, to the Japanese were the tonnage and fire-power of Britain's China squadron; and in the negotiations for a treaty of alliance the Japanese devised a formula calculated to guarantee their own security. This stated that each ally, namely Japan and Great Britain, undertook 'to preserve in the Far East at all times a fleet more powerful than the greatest oriental squadron of any other power'.[15] In other words, the British fleet in the Far East – like the Japanese – must always be stronger than the Russian. This was a commitment little to the liking of the Admiralty.

One of the attractions for the Royal Navy of a Japanese alliance was that it seemed to offer not only added security, as a means of combating Franco-Russian naval power, but also a way of saving money. It could enable Britain to reduce her naval strength in Chinese waters, thereby giving greater protection at home for no extra cost. Furthermore, the dockyard and coaling facilities at Hong Kong, being considered in need of improvement, were calling for money. But an alliance with Japan might make this expenditure unnecessary, for a treaty of alliance could open Japanese dockyards and coaling facilities to British warships.

If her naval prestige, untarnished for a century, gave Great Britain a special place in Japanese eyes, her fame rested also on her industrial power and the control of India. Britain's industrial hegemony, however, was already a thing of the past. As for India, in the corridors of Whitehall there was an obsessional fear of a Russian threat, a fear the more acute because, thanks to South Africa, India was short of trained troops. But to Japan and the other countries of the East the Indian Empire presented a spectacle of glittering strength, of a rich and secure economic base from which stemmed Britain's multifarious political, financial and commercial activities throughout South-east Asia and up and down the China coast. All the same, some Japanese perceived that it was anxiety about the safety of India, as much as concern for spheres of influence in China, that was pushing Britain towards an anti-Russian alliance.

The reader at this point may be inclined to ask why Japan did not consider wooing the United States, as well as (if not instead of) Great Britain and Germany, in the effort to construct a counterweight to

Russian power in the Far East. America, observing the advice of its founding fathers, might shun an alliance; but since 1898 that country had become politically involved in East Asia; and the 'Open Door' doctrine gave them ample reason to oppose Russian encroachments on Manchuria and North China. The Japanese could have had reason to hope for a working agreement, short of an alliance, with the United States. During the crisis that blew up over the proposed Russian–Chinese treaty, however, the Japanese received a clear rebuff when in great secrecy they approached Washington for support against the Russians. The Secretary of State, Hay, told the Japanese that his government was not prepared to take part in any action in Asia 'which could present a character of hostility to any other Power'.[16] Tokyo took this dusty answer to mean that America intended to steer her own course free of obligations to other states.

The logic of events, then, indicated that Japan must either reach a satisfactory understanding with Russia or ally herself with Great Britain. In the past Japan and Russia had been able to come to an agreement over Sakhalin and the Kuriles. That seemed a hopeful precedent; for the agreement rested on a division of the territories in dispute, Russia acquiring all Sakhalin and the Japanese all the Kurile Islands. A commonsense resolution of the Russo-Japanese problem in 1901 would have been an explicit willingness by Russia to allow Japan a free hand in Korea in return for Japanese recognition of Russian predominance in Manchuria. (We may note, in parenthesis, that the views of King and Court in Korea and of the Chinese imperial administration hardly counted as factors in the equation.)

Accordingly, as the Prime Minister, Katsura, was to set out in a memorandum during the summer of 1901, there were two separate views: 'to make friends with Russia or to make friends with Britain'. The first view was strongly argued by Ito and many others; and it is of interest that Katsura did not dispute Ito's opinion that London's interest in an alliance showed that Britain's 'national strength was failing'. But it was always the contention of the Yamagata–Katsura school that a settlement with Russia would not last, since Russia would not stop at the occupation of Manchuria. Russia (in Katsura's words) would 'inevitably extend into Korea', and in the end Japan 'would be forced to let Russia proceed as it likes'. Katsura was not recommending the rejection of friendly overtures by Russia so long as people realised that 'there is bound to be a clash in the end'.[17]

Much the same points were made in a memorandum by Komura, the

Foreign Minister, in December 1901, when Anglo-Japanese talks were far advanced. Having warned that 'if Manchuria becomes the property of Russia, Korea itself cannot remain independent', Komura continued:

An agreement with Russia could maintain peace temporarily in the east but Russia with its aggressive principles could not ultimately be satisfied with this. Since Russia expects to bring the whole of China progressively under its control, an agreement with Russia would not succeed in guaranteeing the maintenance of peace for any length of time.

Komura touched on the central issue for Japan when he declared:

There is no means of getting Russia to agree to a solution of the Korean question in accordance with our wishes unless we link ourselves with a third power and force Russia to accept our wishes. If we link ourselves with Britain as the most suitable third power, this will greatly strengthen our hand in solving the Korean question.[18]

Solving the Korean question – it was an old phrase, and indeed a battle cry going back to the *Seikan Ron* and the 1870s. At the opening of the twentieth century, Japan, thanks to her defeat of China, dominated the Korean economy but was not quite yet the total and exclusive political master of the Korean state; but that was a position Japan was determined to achieve. That is what the anodyne phrases – 'solving the Korean question' and 'the independence of Korea' – implied.

It was undoubtedly the belief of Ito and of the 'pro-Russian' school that St Petersburg was amenable to a bargain. Their view was strengthened in the summer of 1901, when Witte let it be known that Russia was ready to agree to further Japanese political penetration of Korea if Japan acknowledged Russia's position in Manchuria. Witte also promised to persuade French financiers to arrange a large loan on behalf of the Japanese government. At the same time the leading government newspaper in St Petersburg launched a campaign for an improvement of relations with Japan. Dr Nish, the historian of the Anglo-Japanese Alliance, observes that there is no evidence that the Japanese paid particular attention to these unofficial overtures; but he admits that they explain, in part at least, why Ito decided to visit Russia.[19]

For in September 1901, Ito set off on a trip abroad, his immediate destination being the United States. There he gave a series of lectures, and he tried without success to raise a loan for the Katsura government. He then proceeded to Europe, his intention being to approach the Russians and, if possible, reach some rapid understanding with them that would obviate the need for the British alliance. Ito did not travel as an official emissary of the Japanese government. In fact before he left Tokyo he appears to have had a stormy meeting with Yamagata, who was naturally anxious that an approach to Russia should not damage the prospects of concluding an alliance with Britain. Implying that Ito might act too hastily, Yamagata warned him to report to Tokyo any Russian offer, 'so the government can first decide whether or not it is acceptable'. Ito took offence. 'I am not going abroad for my own pleasure', he snapped at Yamagata. 'If you make such fatuous requests I shall call off my trip.'[20]

Ito's mission to St Petersburg might have succeeded had the Tsar and his ministers acted with the speed shown forty years later by Stalin and Molotov during Matsuoka's visit to Moscow, when a Neutrality Pact was negotiated almost in a matter of hours. Ito reached St Petersburg in the last week of November 1901. He stayed for eleven days. His talks with the Russians, though cordial, faced certain difficulties. With Lamsdorf, the Foreign Minister, Ito spoke in bad English, Lamsdorf replying in poor German. Both statesmen had to rely on a multilingual Japanese interpreter. The outcome was a draft Japanese–Russian agreement written by Ito but not presented to Lamsdorf until the day before Ito's departure from Russia. Ito's draft did not satisfy the Russians, and they prepared counter-proposals, which they sent on to him ten days later, Ito being now in Berlin. Meanwhile, at the express wish of the Emperor Meiji, Ito while in St Petersburg and Berlin was kept informed of the progress of the Anglo-Japanese negotiations. It was during his absence that the Katsura Cabinet pressed forward on the final stages of these talks; and many Japanese argued then, and since, that Katsura was glad to have Ito out of the country, had even plotted to push matters to a conclusion at the very time when Ito would be away. This may have been so. But had Ito been able to reach a quick agreement with the Russians in St Petersburg Katsura and Yamagata would have been outmanoeuvred. Ito, in other words, took a justified risk in going to St Petersburg, and he must have hoped, in any case, that a final decision of the British alliance could be delayed until his return. But the issue was not allowed to hang fire. Komura's memorandum, to which we referred in an earlier paragraph, helped to produce that consensus among decision-makers that the Japanese in all their transactions seek to attain. Emperor, Elder Statesmen, Cabinet and armed services agreed in December that the alliance with Britain was the appropriate policy for the nation; and Ito was left to send somewhat querulous telegrams to Tokyo, pleading for delay.

The treaty with Britain was signed in London on 30 January 1902 by Lord Lansdowne, the Foreign Secretary, and a much relieved and gratified Hayashi Tadasu. It contained six clauses, only two of which – Articles I and III – need concern us here.

Article I opened the way for Japan to consolidate, at some future date, her grip on the still nominally independent state of Korea. Or, to put it another way, this clause lowered a cloak of respectability over Japanese acquisitiveness. Britain and Japan declared that they re-cognised the independence of China and Korea and were 'entirely uninfluenced by any aggresive tendencies in either country'. But Britain had special interests in China, while Japan, in addition to her interests in China, was interested in Korea 'in a peculiar degree politically as well as commercially and industrially'. Accordingly, Britain and Japan recognised that it would be

admissible . . . for either of them to take such measures as may be indispensable in order to safeguard those interests if threatened either by the aggressive action of any other Power, or by disturbances arising in China or Korea, and necessitating the intervention of either of the High Contracting Parties for the protection of the lives or property of its subjects.

Article III stated that if either country were at war (in defence of the interests described in Article I) and 'any other Power or Powers should join in hostilities against the Ally, the other High Contracting Party will come to its assistance and will conduct the war in common, and make peace in mutual agreement with it'.[21]

It should be noted that, by implication at any rate, the treaty had no force in areas outside the Far East. For Article II made reference to one or other country going to war in defence of its interests 'as above described' – as described, in other words, in Article I, namely the interests of Britain in China and of Japan in China and Korea. The treaty was to remain in force for five years and did not require ratification.

Looking back, from the vantage point of the last quarter of the twentieth century, at this treaty of alliance between the two island Empires it is plain enough that Japan got the best of the bargain; a point that did not escape the notice of at least some members of the two Houses of Parliament. It is true that in a secret exchange of notes on naval matters Britain was able to avoid giving the firm promise, so greatly desired by Japan, to maintain in the Far East a fleet superior to that of any third power. But this was virtually the only concession extracted from the Japanese.

It is surprising that London did not persist in bringing the question of India into the final negotiations. Hayashi had expected that India would figure largely in the talks, and he advised Tokyo to respond favourably, although he knew his government would be most reluctant to extend Japan's commitments beyond the Far East. India would not be excluded when the treaty came up for renewal, but in the bargaining that preceded the original treaty the question of India played no part, except in the early stages.

Nevertheless, Britain did not want the alliance to be confined to the Far East, and London pressed for some arrangements that would also cover South-east Asia. But the Japanese were adamant. They claimed that the Yangtze basin (the area of Britain's 'special interests in China') was important enough to balance Korea. With reluctance the British gave way.

On Korea, the British argued that there ought to be joint Anglo-Japanese consultation before Japan took unilateral action there. This was successfully resisted by the Japanese side. The comment has been made that the Foreign Secretary, Lansdowne, 'wanted to avoid involving Britain in what might be mere expansionism on the part of Japan but he appreciated that a guarantee over Korea was from Japan's standpoint the most tempting part of the treaty'.[22] This does not acquit Lansdowne and the British government of the charge of selling Korea down the river. Giving Japan what amounted to *carte blanche* in Korea set an evil precedent. No wonder the Japanese in 1941 failed to understand why America should refuse, on moral grounds, to behave in the same way with respect to China.

The declaration that Japan was 'entirely uninfluenced by any aggressive tendencies' (like Britain's similar statement on her interests in China) may be accepted as so much eyewash. A nation in the exercise of its foreign policy never sees itself as influenced by aggressive tendencies.

At least in the short term, Japan played better diplomatic poker than Britain, the more experienced participant in the game. For Japan, of course, the whole affair was vital, a matter almost of national life or death, whereas for Britain the Japanese alliance was important but not really crucial. So the Japanese had much more at stake. Accordingly, they handled the business with the determination and skill, the attention to detail, and the ambitious *élan*, of a football eleven newly promoted to the First Division which can yet be 'relegated' if the team fails to play at the top of its form.

Yet on a longer view the Anglo-Japanese Alliance had a certain value for the British Empire; for it delayed by several years the storm from the East that would destroy or shake loose the ties that held that Empire together. Perhaps, after all, there was a crazy validity to the Kaiser's nightmare, depicted in his inartistic gift to the Tsar. But Britannia, so far from being moved by such fears, welcomed the Rising Sun. It was a gesture of inspired common sense. More foresight, however, in hammering out the instrument that gave shape to this alliance of East and West would have made it a better reflection of the imperatives of self-interest and of the ideals of common justice.

4 'These Little People Will Fight'

Rokoku wa taikoku de gowasu kara no
(Russia, remember, is a powerful nation).
FIELD-MARSHAL OYAMA

I believe these little people will fight, if they are crowded too far.
JOHN HAY, Secretary of State to President Theodore Roosevelt

I

THE Anglo-Japanese Alliance may have taken the Russians by surprise – Lamsdorf, the Foreign Minister, was informed of the treaty by the Japanese Minister only on the day of its publication in the press – but they saved their face by issuing a declaration jointly with France that the new diplomatic alignment was entirely acceptable to both St Petersburg and Paris. Nevertheless, the Russians made haste to mend their fences with the Chinese, and within a few weeks an agreement was signed in Peking covering the prospective withdrawal of the Russian forces that had been sent into Manchuria at the time of the Boxer Rising.

This agreement, the Russian–Chinese Convention of April 1902, provided for the military evacuation of Manchuria in three stages over a period of eighteen months. The troops involved, it should be noted, did not include the Port Arthur garrison or the men seconded for special guard duty along the Russian-operated railway lines (vulgarly known as 'Matilda's guards', after Witte's second wife, a former actress and the focus of much colourful gossip).

The first stage of the evacuation was completed, as laid down in the Convention, in the autumn of 1902; and had Witte been able to retain his influence with the Tsar the evacuation would probably have been carried out eventually through all three stages. For it was not Witte's intention to risk a serious clash with Japan. He believed the lease of Port Arthur and Dalny (Dairen) and the control of the railway system to be adequate guarantees of Russian predominance in Manchuria. In any

53

case, he could argue that Russian forces withdrawn from Manchuria could be sent back into the region at some future date if necessity arose.

But when the time arrived in April 1903 for the second stage of the evacuation the Russians dragged their feet. They wanted to make the second stage dependent on the grant of certain concessions by the Chinese. Witte was still in office, although rapidly losing ground to his rivals, and so he cannot escape his share of responsibility for the new policy of imposing further demands on China before proceeding with the next stage of the evacuation. Yet this amounted, in fact, to a bargaining ploy, and in negotiations with the Chinese Russia's demands were progressively modified. However, in August, Nicholas II, like his cousin in Germany thirteen years earlier, 'dropped the pilot'. On the day that Witte was dismissed, the Tsar wrote in his diary the laconic phrase, 'Now I rule', no doubt with a sense of psychological release such as the Kaiser had known when he sent Bismarck into retirement. Through such behaviour are emperors and dynasties unmade.

Certainly after Witte's fall, Russian–Japanese relations seemed set on a collision course. China's refusal to comply with Russia's demands gave St Petersburg an excuse for halting the evacuation of Manchuria. This, in turn, created a notable stir in Japan.

Japanese public opinion, sensitively alert to issues of foreign policy since the Triple Intervention and no less excited than gratified by the new association with Great Britain, became more aggressive; and it is from the summer of 1903 that we can note a growing agitation for a hard line *vis-à-vis* the Russians. This agitation was by no means confined to ultra-nationalist circles. For example, in June 1903 there emerged from the irreproachably respectable milieu of Tokyo Imperial University a group of seven eminent academics committed to pressing the Katsura Cabinet for an immediate declaration of war on Russia. A Japanese historian makes the point that 'at a time when the prestige of university professors was particularly high, the activities of the professors, popularly called the *Kaisen Shichi Hakase* (seven pro-war doctors) were influential in unifying Japanese public opinion in support of war'.[1]

The range and intensity of anti-Russian feeling in Japan need not surprise us. What is indeed a matter of surprise is that right up to the outbreak of hostilities a small but not totally uninfluential minority of newspaper editors, writers and teachers publicly opposed the idea of going to war, on grounds that were in most cases humanist or Christian.

As we saw in the last chapter, Japan's first socialist party, the *Shakai Minshuto*, had a life of only a few hours, since it was suppressed by the police on the day it was founded. That was in May 1901. In the words of one authority, 'its democratic and anti-militarist and not its socialist posture doomed the *Shakai Minshuto*'.[2] For according to this argument the new party could never have grown to be more than a splinter political group, because its programme virtually ignored the peasantry, which then formed about three-quarters of the population. At all events, the anxiety felt by the authorities was genuine and, indeed, not unreasonable, seeing that all manner of disconcertingly unJapanese ideas inspired the founding fathers of the *Shakai Minshuto*; for they 'were strongly indebted to Lassalle, Marx, Engels, Proudhon, Ely, George, American Christian socialists, and English Fabians'.[3]

It might be supposed that having suppressed the infant socialist party the Home Ministry and police would have banned the dissemination of 'dangerous thoughts' through the printed word. But this draconian measure was not imposed until the Russian war was in its stride. Thus pacifist as well as Marxist publications appeared between 1901 and 1905. Dissenters often moved from a Christian, or humanist, position to one of uncompromising Marxism; and this created rifts in what was otherwise a bold united front against capitalism, imperialism, and the resort to war. The competing opinions of the Left found their way into print, notably in articles in specialist magazines read by a coterie of subscribers. One such journal, appearing late in 1903 when patriotic fervour was reaching boiling point, was the *Heimin Shimbun* ('The Commoners' Newspaper') designed to 'arouse the sentiments of the masses'; although, as its first editorial hastened to add, this would be done 'within the limits of the law'. Despite a tiny circulation it struggled along for rather more than a year. When it ceased publication at the height of the Russo-Japanese War the editors were imprisoned for several months – an action which at least one prominent Tokyo daily paper was courageous enough to condemn.

The most spectacular example of dissent was the famous gesture by the socialist writer and trade-union organiser, Katayama Sen, at the Amsterdam Congress of the Second International in the summer of 1904. In front of an enthusiastic audience of socialists from many countries Katayama shook hands with the Russian revolutionary, Plekhanov. Among first-hand accounts of that dramatic scene one of the more colourful was provided by Daisy, Countess of Warwick, writing to a friend in Mayfair:

You would have been struck with the dramatic *coup* of the opening of Congress on Sunday. A Jap *moved* the Resolution, in a speech of an hour in fluent and perfect English, a Russian *seconded*, a gem of oratory, in *French*, then 10,000 hands were held up, and a shout to blow the roof off of the great Concert Hall in Amsterdam went up, as Japan and Russia gripped hands, for a moment, in the universal Brotherhood of Man. It was a wonderful touch on a human stage.[4]

It is still commonly believed that the Japanese in 1904 embarked as one man on their struggle with the Russians. But, in truth, there was much more open, candid dissent on the eve of the Russo-Japanese War than was conceivable in 1941, when a far greater war was drawing near. Katayama himself uttered a memorable comment on pacifist activities in Japan at a time when the vast majority of his compatriots perceived Russia to be an undoubted menace to the further progress of their nation. 'It is perhaps the first time in the history of Japan', he wrote, 'that the cry "Down with War" has been heard in the land of the samurai.'[5] The novelist Kinoshita Naoe, a Christian convert who became a socialist, published *Hi no Hashira* ('Pillar of Fire') in serial form from January to March 1904 in the *Tokyo Mainichi*. The novel was explicitly anti-capitalist and implicitly hostile to the appeal of militant patriotism. But best remembered to this day is the *waka* poem by Yosano Akiko in which she appeals to her brother, serving in the army, not to offer his life, 'whether Port Arthur falls or not'. One passage in the poem reads:

> Do not offer your life
> The Emperor himself does not go
> To battle.

This celebrated poem, *Kimi shinitamo koto nakare* ('Do not offer your life'), was published in September 1904 when the first disastrous frontal assault on Port Arthur had already taken place. And it was Uchimura Kanzo, probably the best-known Japanese Christian intellectual of his time, who pronounced in 1904 the prophetic words: '*Those who let their soldiers attack other nations eventually will become the victims of their soldiers.*'[6] Such heretics, it is very true, were scarcely representative of public opinion. All the more impressive, therefore, is the stuff of their integrity and courage. The Meiji era, Japan's Victorian age, nurtured great rebels as well as heroic and dedicated servants of the state.

II

In an initiative, the real motives of which are still debated by historians and by Russian historians in particular, Japan in August 1903 opened negotiations with Russia for a settlement in the Far East. Ito Hirobumi, as we saw, was slow to accept the need for an alliance with England, and he still hoped that Japan could come to an accord with the Russians on the basis of a 'Manchuria–Korea exchange', or *Man–Kan kokan*, as it was called. In the approach to St Petersburg of August 1903 this was expressed in terms of a Russian acceptance of Japan's 'preponderating interests' in Korea in return for Japanese recognition of Russia's 'special interests' in Manchuria. This formula, it will be seen, was weighted in Japan's favour, since 'preponderating interests' imply a good deal more than 'special interests'; and it has been claimed that Japan's proposals were so heavily loaded against the Russian side as to make ultimate agreement impossible. The inference here is that the Japanese, realising that time was not on their side in view of growing Russian naval power and the development of the Trans-Siberian line, were insincere in their overture to the Russians, believing no real settlement to be in sight. So it is alleged that 'in view of Japan's first demands, from the beginning of the negotiations very little possibility of success existed'.[7] It is difficult, however, to accept this interpretation. On the face of it, the proposals contained little to which the Russians should have taken exception; unless, of course, they were adamantly determined to play a part in the economic and political development of Korea.

The Japanese proposals comprised five main items. The first was an obligatory genuflection to the principle of 'the independence and territorial integrity of the Chinese and Korean empires', together with the anodyne statement that Japan and Russia would support the equal commercial and industrial rights of all nations in China and Korea. The second formulated 'a Manchuria–Korea exchange' on the lines already described, although Russia's 'special interests' were somewhat narrowly defined as 'special interests in railway enterprises in Manchuria'. Thirdly, it was proposed that Japan and Russia should agree not to obstruct each other's economic enterprises in Korea and Manchuria, and Russia was asked not to oppose a possible extension of a Korean railway line into South Manchuria to link it with the Manchurian railway network. The fourth item put forward by Japan concerned military forces. It was suggested that if Japan sent troops to Korea, and

Russia sent troops to Manchuria, to protect vested interests or to suppress insurrection, 'the number of troops sent shall not exceed the number actually required', such forces to be withdrawn 'as soon as the mission for which they were sent shall have been accomplished'. Finally – a vital point for Japan – Tokyo sought 'recognition on the part of Russia of the exclusive right of Japan to give advice in the interests of reform and good government in Korea, including military assistance'.[8]

The Japanese proposals were not unreasonable from the standpoint of Russia's established position in Manchuria. But they constituted a barrier against any designs which the more adventurous of the Tsar's advisers had on Korea.

About two months went by before the Russians responded with their own counter-proposals. Tardiness persisted on the Russian side throughout the negotiations and helped to persuade cautious members of Japan's oligarchy, such as Ito, that a peaceful settlement was not going to be achieved. It is hazardous in a serious international dispute for one side to prolong the negotiations, since the other may conclude that the opposing camp is merely playing for time. A popular temper is thereby engendered that can be unhelpful to those personally involved in critical diplomatic talks. Such was the mood in Tokyo as Russian diplomacy followed its unhurried and seemingly disdainful course.

On the day (12 August 1903) that the Japanese proposals were received, a new move by St Petersburg served to impede progress in reaching an agreement. By imperial ukase there was established at Port Arthur a Viceroyalty of the Far East under Admiral E. I. Alexieff. In theory, Alexieff was given charge of all matters, diplomatic as well as military and economic, concerning Russia's possessions and spheres of interest in the territories east of Lake Baikal. There may have been sound administrative reasons for the creation of this post. It was not without precedent: there was already a Viceroyalty of the Caucasus. But undoubtedly the chief purpose of the Tsar's decree was to serve notice on Japan and China of Russia's determination to consolidate her strong position in East Asia. At the same time, the course of Japanese–Russian negotiations would now be complicated by the fact that the Viceroy, Admiral Alexieff, would have to be brought into them as a leading participant.

In any case, the Russians now insisted that Tokyo, not St Petersburg, should be the setting for the diplomatic talks. This was unwelcome to the Japanese, and they agreed only with great reluctance and after some delay. For the Russian decision implied a diminution of the influence of Lamsdorf, the Foreign Minister, whom the Japanese knew to be opposed to a forward policy in the Far East. Their misgivings increased when Witte was dismissed late in August, at a time when Komura was fighting unsuccessfully to retain St Petersburg as the venue for the diplomatic exchanges.

Ironically enough, by early autumn 1903, the Bezobrazov–Abaza clique, which had supplanted both Witte and Kuropatkin in the Tsar's favour, no longer enjoyed supreme influence at court. Nicholas II became disenchanted with certain economic ventures in North Korea in which, thanks to Bezobrazov, he had acquired a personal interest. All the same, Russia's commercial undertakings on the Manchurian–Korean border – a large timber concession along the Yalu being the most notable example – appeared to be the vanguard of political, perhaps even military, advance into Korea. Russian ex-servicemen were recruited as guards for the timber concession. Japanese propaganda made the most of this, implying that tree-felling on the Korean frontier was the first step in a process that would not be completed until the cossacks were in Fusan on the Straits of Tsushima.

Squeezed between Russia and Japan, Korea had no choice but to play off one imperial power against the other. So the Korean government authorised a Japanese timber company to start work in the same general area as the Russian concession. But in every sphere of activity Japan's penetration of Korea was incomparably greater than Russia's. This very fact, however, made any signs of active Russian interest in Korea the more alarming to the Japanese.

Japan's pervasive influence in Korea, unchallengeable except by force of arms, should have made it easier for the Russians to accept, at an early stage in the negotiations, the *Man-Kan kokan*, 'Manchuria–Korea exchange', formula. Furthermore, if it is true that the Russians had no intention of pushing things to the point of war, their handling of the negotiations showed little evidence of an urgent wish to reach a settlement. For example, they consistently refused to join in a commitment to respect the independence and territorial integrity of China, although their successive drafts always included a reference to mutual respect for the independence and territorial integrity of Korea. More disturbing to the Japanese was a clause in Russia's belated reply (3 October 1903) to Japan's proposals. This stipulated that a neutral zone should be established in Korea north of the 39th parallel into which neither Russia nor Japan would send troops. As if to underline the message that, while restrictions must be placed on Japan's actions in

Korea, Russia wanted a free hand in Manchuria, the article on the neutral zone was immediately followed by a clause that sought 'recognition by Japan of Manchuria and its littorals as in all respects outside her sphere of interest'.

The Japanese response to Russia's counter-proposals was submitted on 30 October. It displayed a readiness to make some concessions. Indeed, it now brought matters close to a fifty-fifty bargain. In the phrasing of diplomatic exchanges, as in the preparation of legal contracts, every syllable counts. It is significant, therefore, that in this second round of the negotiations the Japanese offered to recognise 'Russia's special interests in Manchuria', instead of her 'special interests in railway enterprises in Manchuria' (as proposed in the first Japanese draft). By that omission of two words *Man-Kan kokan* was surely made more palatable to the Russian side. Moreover, the Japanese did not reject the neutral zone out of hand. They said they would like it to be established further north, to extend fifty kilometres on either side of the Korean–Manchurian frontier. The Japanese declared themselves ready to give an undertaking not to construct military works on the Korean coast that might threaten freedom of navigation in the Straits of Tsushima.

Six weeks passed before the Russians replied to this second approach. By now the Japanese had begun to suspect that Russian diplomacy was designed to humiliate them. The scars of the Triple Intervention had not healed, and it was easy for the Japanese to imagine that the other side was making light of them. How far that feeling was justified it is impossible to say. But there is plenty of evidence of popular Russian contempt for the 'impudent little Japanese', once relations between the two countries had reached a critical stage. After the outbreak of war Russian newspapers – and, to some extent, those of Russia's ally, France – diverted and heartened their readers with many a cartoon caricaturing the Japanese as ugly and ridiculous dwarfs. One may ponder the degree to which such sentiments moved the Tsar and his advisers. Here it is perhaps worth quoting an observation made many years ago by an American scholar:

I believe that the contempt for the Japanese expressed in Loti's books in some measure influenced the Russians to refuse Japan's requests and led to the war of 1904. The Russian Court was open to French influence, and many Russian naval officers of high rank, following Loti's example, had discovered Madame Chrysanthème. Nagasaki too was a winter station for the Russian Asiatic squadron. . . . Like Loti, the Russian

Court looked upon Japan with contempt, and chose to believe his stories because Loti shared its prejudices.[9]

Yet at least three of the principal figures in the Russian camp – Baron Rosen, the Minister in Tokyo; Viceroy Alexieff at Port Arthur; and Kuropatkin, the Minister of War – entertained a genuine respect for Japanese strength. It is possible that the delays which the Japanese attributed to calculated Russian policy were caused in the main by the cumbersome process of trying to harmonise the far from identical views and interests of the Tsar, the Tokyo Legation, the Port Arthur headquarters, and the ministries (Foreign Affairs, War, Admiralty) in St Petersburg.

At all events, both sides were preparing for the worst as the negotiations dragged on through the autumn of 1903 and into the winter. So far from showing signs of resuming their evacuation, the Russians tightened their grip on Manchuria. Indeed, in October they reoccupied the city of Mukden.

From a strictly military point of view time was on Russia's side, but in terms of international prestige her position was deteriorating. During the spring of 1903 a particularly bloody and destructive pogrom in the largely Jewish town of Kishinev had shocked world opinion, nowhere more so than in the United States. Theodore Roosevelt's administration, which protested strongly to St Petersburg on humanitarian grounds, was becoming worried, in any case, by the prospect of restrictions (imposed by China under Russian duress) on foreign investment in Manchuria. As the months passed, much of the world came to see Russia as an oversized and rapacious bully. Japan, on the other hand, was admired as a brave, long-suffering, Boy Scout, standing up manfully not only for himself but also for two feeble and demoralised geriatrics, China and Korea. Japan's success in posing as the champion of the 'Open Door' in Manchuria and China drove a wedge between Russia and the Western powers (notably Great Britain and the United States). So the war, when it broke out, seemed in no sense one of revenge on Japan's part.

There was another factor bearing on international opinion to which the Japanese addressed themselves with remarkable skill. They perceived the unwisdom of providing ammunition for those alarmed by the spectre of the Yellow Peril. At first sight there was much to be said for encouraging China to join in a struggle against the Russians. After all, Manchuria was Chinese territory. There was no sign that the Russians intended to pull out of Manchuria, unless China made concessions that would further erode her own freedom of action. All through the Tokyo negotiations the Russians had made it clear that they would not guarantee China's independence. So the Chinese had compelling motives for taking part in a Russo-Japanese conflict on Japan's side. Two considerations, however, led the Japanese to insist on Chinese neutrality in the coming war. The first was that China's military participation would make it more difficult for Japan to inherit Russia's hegemony in South Manchuria. A belligerent China could become an assertive China; which was not necessarily desired by government and high command in Tokyo. But of almost equal importance in Japanese calculations was the recognition that military victories won by allied Japanese and Chinese forces must promote fears of the Yellow Peril, thereby possibly straining Japan's ties with Great Britain and certainly affecting Japanese relations with the United States. The Russo-Japanese War was unquestionably, in some measure, a racial conflict; and the Japanese people as a whole could hardly fail to see it as such. Their rulers were nevertheless reluctant to look at it in that light. Cherishing the English alliance, they thought it unseemly as well as impolitic to make an open avowal of the strong racial consciousness that was an operative force in their direction of the nation's affairs.[10]

Between 11 December 1903, when the Russians sent at last their reply to Japan's second set of proposals, and 8 February 1904, when hostilities began, the Japanese and Russians went through the motions of two further exchanges of proposals and counter-proposals. The final offer from the Japanese side, dated 13 January 1904, concluded with the ominous words: 'further delay in the solution of the question will be extremely disadvantageous to the two countries'. The American Minister in Tokyo summed up what seemed to him to be the mood in Japan:

The Japanese nation is now worked up to a high pitch of excitement, and it is no exaggeration to say that if there is no war it will be a severe disappointment to the Japanese individual of every walk of life. The people are under such a strain that the present condition cannot last long. Nothing but the most complete backdown by the Russian Government will satisfy the public feeling, and even then it would require the most skilful handling on the part of the Japanese Government to mollify the war spirit which is now rampant.[11]

Far from showing signs of a 'complete backdown', the Russians seemed determined to concede nothing on Manchuria, while insisting that Japan accept restraints on her use of Korea for strategic purposes. Yet the Tsar had telegraphed Alexieff saying that he wanted no war. Kuropatkin at a conference in St Petersburg at the end of 1903 had put forward in vain the drastic but sensible proposal that Russia cut her losses by giving up South Manchuria and concentrating on the north of the country. Only a week before hostilities began, Kurino, the Japanese Minister in St Petersburg, reporting on talks he had held with notable hard-liners such as Abaza and Bezobrazov, declared that he did not think Russia wanted war in the Far East: 'on the contrary, she wishes for a peaceful solution but seems to be labouring under a tremendous conceit which leads to the opinion that an agreement regarding Manchuria would be looked upon as a great humiliation'.[12]

Thus one has the impression that while, in Japan, cautious and conciliatory men like Ito had become resigned at last to the necessity for war, in Russia the more venturesome and bellicose of the Tsar's advisers were showing signs of last-minute wavering. But if the Russians were practising a form of brinkmanship the timing was ill-judged. On 4 February 1904 the Japanese broke off the negotiations. First blood was drawn four days later. Before a declaration of war was received in St Petersburg the Japanese had landed troops at Chemulpo, close to Seoul, and carried out a night attack on the Russian fleet at Port Arthur.

For that breach of accepted international practice the Russians roundly condemned the Japanese; and in Britain and America in later years a generation stunned by what happened in December 1941 was ready to accept that the Port Arthur attack was a characteristic example of Japanese infamy. Anglo–American opinion in *1904*, needless to say, viewed the matter in another light. The British and American press on the whole praised the surprise attack as a brilliant strategem, *The Times* (London) declaring that the Japanese navy had opened the war by an act of daring 'destined to take a place of honour in naval annals'.

III

The events of the Russo-Japanese War have been amply described by eye-witnesses and historians; and among the former there were some who realised that Russia's defeat was at the same time a defeat for the West. But in Europe and the United States liberal opinion rejoiced at the discomfiture of the Russian autocracy. Early in 1905 the slaughter of

Bloody Sunday in St Petersburg, when the Tsar's soldiers shot down demonstrating workers in the Winter Palace Square, chilled the admiration felt in the West for the defenders of Port Arthur who had surrendered after a siege the like of which had not been seen since the days of Plevna, back in the 1870s. Admiral Togo's destruction of the Russian Baltic fleet some four months later was greeted with special enthusiasm by Japan's ally. The Russian warships had already earned British hostility and contempt in the previous autumn for firing on the Hull trawlers in the North Sea. The completeness of the Japanese victory off Tsushima in the centenary year of Trafalgar filled British hearts with vicarious pride. Togo's battleships came from British yards. Togo himself had been a cadet on HMS *Worcester*; and his captains had either received their training in England or from instructors in Japan steeped in the doctrines of the Royal Navy. (It was a common belief in St Petersburg and Moscow that there was a British naval officer on the bridge of every Japanese battleship at Tsushima telling his eager pupils what to do.)

The first line of Kipling's 'Ballad of East and West' had become tarnished by repetition well before the turn of the century. But the discriminating reader took note of the third and fourth lines of the poem, now almost forgotten, without which the full significance of the verse is lost:

> But there is neither East nor West, Border, nor
> Breed, nor Birth,
> When two strong men stand face to face, though
> they come from the ends of the earth![13]

By defeating the Russians on land and sea Japan emerged as 'the strong man' from the other end of the earth. It is small wonder that Inazo Nitobe's *Bushido, the Soul of Japan* was among the best-selling books of Edwardian England. It appeared to provide an explanation of Japan's national character, and therefore of her astonishing success in battle. This distant country, it seemed, had indeed earned the title of 'the Britain of the Far East'.

The heroic element prominent in Japanese military operations during the Russian war received general recognition at the time. Forty years later, under the emotional impact of the Second World War, Japanese valour – the readiness to fight to the last man and the last round – was commonly described as mindless fanaticism, was thought of as something akin to the fatalism of the Mahdi's hordes. Still, whatever name is applied to the phenomenon it has been a daunting problem for those who have had to face the Japanese on the battlefield.

What has not been adequately stressed, perhaps, is the resolution with which the Russians conducted their side of the struggle. It is true that foreign observers paid tribute to the bravery and endurance of the Russian infantryman. But there emerged a myth that Russian military and naval commanders always let down the rank and file by their incompetence. Kuropatkin, for example, became the butt of much adverse ciritcism.

Kuropatkin was appointed to command the land forces in Manchuria a few days after the war began. He was relieved of the appointment just over a year later. He was succeeded by General Linievich, one of his army commanders, Kuropatkin becoming, at his own request, an army commander under Linievich. His demotion followed his defeat at Mukden, a battle that lasted from 23 February to 9 March 1905, one of the longest and most savagely contested engagements in the history of warfare up to that time. It began with a Japanese attack that pre-empted Kuropatkin's own intended offensive; it ended, for the Russians, with the loss of Mukden together with most of the military supplies stored in the city. The casualties on both sides were enormous. The Russians lost close on 40,000 men, dead or taken prisoner; and their wounded numbered nearly 50,000. The Japanese casualties were rather more than 75,000 dead and wounded. The Japanese aim at Mukden, as in earlier battles, was the encirclement of the Russian forces, on the model demonstrated by the Germans at Sedan in the Franco-Prussian War. Kuropatkin, however, avoided falling into this trap. When he retreated to new positions forty miles north of Mukden he saved the bulk of his army, at the sacrifice of a rearguard which fought with a courage only comparable with that shown by their enemy. Oyama, the Japanese Commander-in-Chief, had to conclude, like Pyrrhus, that further victories of this kind must add up to something indistinguishable from defeat.

Whatever his shortcomings as a grand strategist, Kuropatkin was a first-class quartermaster; 'In this sense', it has been well said, 'he was a soldier's general who therefore never lost the good will of the troops he commanded'.[14] In those days of acute unrest in Russia the loyalty of the ordinary soldier was unlikely to be fully maintained by a callous or stupid commander. By the autumn of 1904 the gap in the Trans-Siberian line at Lake Baikal had been closed, and troop trains were running into South Manchuria on a regular schedule. As the reinforcements came under his command Kuropatkin welded them efficiently into his armies, taking great pains to ensure that they were well provisioned and equipped.

Kuropatkin knew that he could tap virtually limitless reserves of military manpower; and he knew that behind him stretched the length of Manchuria into which he could withdraw. He possessed an admirably sanguine temperament. He realised that, provided he was not outmanoeuvred and encircled on the battlefield, he could build up in the end such strength that by sheer weight of numbers he would be able to fight the Japanese to a standstill. When that happened the tide would turn. This was sound reasoning. If the war had been prolonged into the winter of 1905–6 the Russians must have succeeded in pushing the Japanese back to the Korean frontier and the Yellow Sea.

But nothing fails like failure. The loss of Port Arthur brought shame to Stoessel who surrendered the fortress and world renown to General Nogi his Japanese opponent. During the long siege Nogi's personal demeanour had made a lasting impression on the correspondents and military observers attached to his staff. He lost two sons in the siege. He accepted this blow, and the appalling cost in lives exacted by frontal assaults on the Russian forts, with an austere Roman calm. Nogi became respected the world over as the peerless exemplar of samurai Japan–*dura virum nutrix*. His chivalrous treatment of the defeated Stoessel was matched only by Togo's visit to Admiral Rozhestvensky, wounded at Tsushima, in the naval hospital at Sasebo.

Stoessel presenting his white horse to Nogi became a favourite subject for popular artists. Distributed throughout the world was the surrender photograph of Nogi and his staff seated with the defeated Russian general and his aides. All have their swords. Japanese and Russians sit amicably grouped together, like two old-fashioned amateur rugger teams after a hard-fought but sporting game.

When the Emperor Meiji died in 1912 and Nogi (and his wife) committed suicide in traditional samurai style, this added the finishing touch to his fame. In Japanese terms he was canonised. A shrine dedicated to his spirit was built in the shadow of his Tokyo home.

By contrast with this paladin, General Stoessel cuts a rather poor figure. On return home he was put on trial and sentenced to death – commuted to a term of imprisonment – for having capitulated at Port Arthur. When the redoubtable G. E. Morrison, Peking correspondent of *The Times*, of London, visited Port Arthur shortly after the surrender he reported, in a letter to a friend, that he believed Stoessel to have been 'a poltroon and a braggart' and that 'nothing could justify the surrender . . . no one was more surprised at the collapse than the Japanese themselves'.[15]

Yet Port Arthur surrendered only after months of heavy fighting, and after the warships bottled up in the harbour had been sunk or immobilised by Japanese gunfire. Comparisons with Singapore in 1942 may not be entirely fair. The fact remains that Singapore surrendered two weeks after the first Japanese artillery bombardment of the island. The Russian defence of the forts of Port Arthur, noteworthy at the time, appears in retrospect all the more impressive.

Furthermore, Nogi's reputation as a general has not grown with the passing of the years. His repeated and extremely costly assaults on the strongly fortified Russian positions were of a character that bring to mind Mutaguchi's obstinacy at Imphal in 1944, or the slogging frontal attacks against German machine-gunners at the Somme and Paschendaele. The general opinion among the Japanese today is that the credit for the capture of Port Arthur should go to Lieutenant-General Kodama, rather than Nogi. The former, who was Chief of Staff to Marshal Oyama (the Japanese C-in-C.), was sent to Port Arthur with orders in his pocket to take over command from Nogi. This he did not do; but he had the authority to direct Nogi's operations; and so it has been argued that the final battle – that most bloody affair, the capture of 203 Metre Hill – redounds to Kodama's credit, not Nogi's. At all events, the Japanese generals at Port Arthur could have used the language of Wellington at Waterloo: 'Hard pounding, this, gentlemen; let's see who will pound hardest.'

It was the opinion of foreign military observers that Russian performance improved as the war progressed. It was said that Russian soldiers fought better at Mukden than in earlier battles. There appears to have been, correspondingly, some falling off on the Japanese side; not so much perhaps in their fighting spirit as in their administrative arrangements, notably the medical service.

Once the Russian navy was crippled and South Manchuria cleared of the Russian army, Japan's basic war aims were achieved. For Japan to have persisted in continuing the struggle could only have involved a growing risk of ultimate defeat. The financial burden, too, was becoming acute. Surprisingly, perhaps, the Russian situation here was healthier than the Japanese. When war started, St Petersburg relied on financial support from France, and when this became less secure during the summer of 1904, as a result of Japan's military successes, the Russians negotiated a substantial loan in Berlin. After their early victories, the Japanese received some help from the City of London; but the initiative for the loans came from the New York banking house of Kuhn, Loeb; whose president, Jacob Schiff, had been deeply shocked by the Kishinev pogrom.

Manpower losses and financial stringency were not the only adverse factors the Japanese had to take into account as the summer of 1905 advanced. For all the progress made in modernisation, Japan's industrial revolution remained incomplete. Since the first considerable iron-works were not built until after the turn of the century, steel production was not yet adequate for the needs of a first-class power. Until 1905 no warship larger than a light cruiser had been built in Japan. It was only in the spring of that year that the Japanese began the construction of their own battleships.

It may have been necessary to challenge Russia. It was, none the less, a gamble on a majestic scale. Although heartened by the British alliance, the Japanese were made aware of its limitations before the war began. The Russians were convinced that Japan would never have contemplated war without strong encouragement from Great Britain. It is true, of course, that British public opinion, never very friendly towards Tsarist Russia, warmly favoured Japan. But at the governmental level Japan was left in no doubt that in the event of war, British policy would be the bleakly correct one of strict neutrality. The British Premier, Balfour, believed Russia would win, short of inflicting a wholly crushing defeat on Japan. However, he expected that the Russians would overrun Korea; and this, in his view, would impose a strain on Russia sufficient to weaken her in Persia and on the Afghan border. It would also make Japan implacably set on future revenge. Consequently, Russia would be fully occupied in the Far East for many years. The outcome, in Balfour's words to King Edward VII, 'would not be an unmixed curse'; for it would render Russia more temperate and amenable both in Asia and Europe.

Russian historians, broadly speaking, have claimed that Britain pushed Japan into the war. Some Japanese historians have also taken this line. One of them has written: 'Japan's powerful ally England instigated the Russo-Japanese War in order to serve the aims of her policy in the Near East.'[16]

But there is no evidence that the British government encouraged Japan to risk war with Russia. Dr Ian Nish, the leading authority on

Anglo-Japanese relations during this period, having examined, it seems, all the relevant state papers, declares categorically: 'Japan was not pushed into war with Russia by Britain nor did the Anglo-Japanese alliance precipitate the war. Japan entered the war of its own volition, without pressure or restraint from Britain.'[17] After all, there was the hazard that in a Russo-Japanese war Britain might be sucked into the struggle: an unlikely possibility no doubt, but one that could not be entirely discounted. Strict neutrality, for Balfour and his colleagues, meant what it said. Certainly, the British alliance held the ring for Japan once war started; but when Japan embarked on the struggle she was on her own; and the world watched with sympathetic interest from the sidelines to see what would happen.

Two external factors were helpful to Japan when the time came, after Mukden and Tsushima, to bring the war to an end. The first was the attitude of Theodore Roosevelt, who was well disposed to Japan and ready to act as mediator. The second was the state of affairs inside Russia. Although their agents played a peripheral role in stirring it up, the storm over Russia was an unexpected bonus for the Japanese. It was, of course, a major element in the Tsar's agreement to discuss terms with Japan, provided these were not insufferably humiliating to Russian prestige. Despite the wave of revolutionary unrest from the Gulf of Finland to the Black Sea, the Tsar's government and high command were in no mood for peace with Japan at any price.

By the summer of 1905 a good many observers in Europe and America were bemused – despite their previous admiration for the resistance of the Port Arthur garrison – by the thought that the Russian forces might be conducting the war in the Far East with less than wholehearted enthusiasm. It was imagined that the strikes, mutinies, and street fighting in Russia must incline officers and men in Manchuria to look back over their shoulders, with contrasting hopes and fears, at what was happening in St Petersburg, Moscow and Odessa. For those who worried about the general standing of Europe *vis-à-vis* Asia the Russo-Japanese War, seen as a racial struggle, did not appear to be a fair test.

This was not how matters were understood by the peoples of Asia. Their reaction is discussed in the next chapter. Here, we may conclude by acknowledging that there were at least some in the West who grasped the significance of the war. Among them was the English socialist, H. M. Hyndman. Writing more than a decade later, about Japan's victories in 1905, he declared:

Though the truth has not even yet been fully recognised, either in Europe or America, and England and her Colonies in particular have shut their eyes to obvious facts, Japan thenceforth stood forward as the champion of Asia against Europe.[18]

Let us add as a pendant to that passage a warning uttered by Hyndman in the same year (1919). He predicted that Japan would 'follow the course of the great aggressive Empire of Modern Europe', and that if she were allowed to have her own way in Asia, 'then a war more terrible than that which is now being concluded may easily confront our successors'.[19]

5 The Necessary and Unpopular Peace

Don't you know that if you light a fire you must also know how to put it out.

GENERAL KODAMA

1

In the first days of March 1905, while the Mukden battle was still being fought out, General Terauchi, the Japanese Minister of War, gave a dinner in honour of Major-General MacArthur (the father of Douglas MacArthur) who was passing through Tokyo at the time. In the course of the evening, Terauchi drew aside one of his guests – Lloyd Griscom, the American Minister – for a private talk. Griscom was asked to send a message to President Roosevelt, conveying Terauchi's firm opinion 'as a private individual' that the war should now be brought to an end; further hostilities could only become increasingly murderous. The following evening, at another dinner party, Griscom met Katsura and Komura, the Premier and the Foreign Minister, and raised with them the question of a peace settlement. Their attitude was more guarded than Terauchi's. Komura pointed out that much would depend on the eventual fate of the Russian Baltic Fleet, then making its way to the Far East. He added that it was important that Japan should not be seen to be anxious to end the war.

In fact, the Japanese had been active behind the scenes in Washington for nearly a year, preparing the ground for Roosevelt to act as peace-maker when the appropriate moment arose. As early as March 1904 an influential but unofficial envoy, Baron Kaneko, had been sent to Washington with that end in view. Kaneko had been at Harvard with the President; and the personal relationship maintained since those days was a valuable card in Japan's hand (even if it aroused jealousy in the breast of Takahira Kogoro, the Minister to the United States). It strengthened the goodwill that Roosevelt had towards the Japanese, and it led to a series of confidential talks between him and Kaneko and Takahira. The full scope and content of these talks remain unclarified to this day. But as a preliminary oiling of the wheels the conversations performed a most useful service. They were the necessary prelude to Roosevelt's prompt and sympathetic response to an official request from Tokyo, within a week of Tsushima, that he invite, 'entirely of his own motion and initiative', Japan and Russia to enter into direct negotiations.

The Japanese demonstrated great good sense in launching these diplomatic moves at the very outset of their struggle with the Russians. For it is, or should be, a cardinal rule of foreign policy never to embark on war without making contingency plans for the peace settlement that must ensue: in other words (if one may distort the maxim of Vegetius) *qui desiderat bellum, praeparet pacem.* This was something which the Japanese, to their peril, neglected in later years, and notably in 1941.

When it was announced that a peace conference would be held at Portsmouth, New Hampshire, the people of Japan were taken by surprise. They had confidently expected after every Russian defeat – Port Arthur, Mukden, Tsushima – that the enemy would sue for peace; and each time this failed to occur popular feeling became more bellicose. A similar pattern of growing chauvinism stocked by disappointment was to be observed a generation later; when Chiang Kai-shek failed to sue for peace at the end of 1937, after he lost Nanking, or in the autumn of 1938 after the fall of Hankow and Canton.

In Japan, everyone thought that Ito Hirobumi, the Emperor's favourite adviser, would be going to Portsmouth. This was certainly the hope of the Russians, and of Roosevelt. The Russians were to be represented at the conference by Witte. He was downcast when he learned that Komura, not Ito, would be at Portsmouth. Ito was known to have favoured a Japanese–Russian understanding. So Witte tried, in vain, by indirect means (through an approach to the Japanese Legation in London) to have Komura replaced by Ito. Roosevelt, too, greatly regretted that Ito would not be at Portsmouth; for he knew that Ito and Witte were on good terms, and he felt sure that their presence at the conference would smooth the course of the negotiations. But an historian has aptly remarked that Roosevelt 'did not seem to have suspected that, had they come, they would undoubtedly have sought precisely what he wanted least – a close Russo-Japanese accord'.[1] For Roosevelt, the termination of hostilities was one thing, genuine Russo-Japanese reconciliation quite another. He explained his position with brutal and characteristic frankness to the French ambassador. 'From my point of view', he declared, 'the best would be that the Russians and

Japanese should remain face to face balancing each other, both weakened.'[2]

The Japanese, albeit victors in battle, were in urgent need of peace, as we have seen. On this there was agreement among senior military and civil leaders. But the overwhelming majority of the Japanese people believed that it was the Russians who were in no shape to carry on the war. Exhilarated by success, the people of Japan expected their delegation at the conference to obtain a heavy indemnity from the Russians, as well as territorial concessions.

When the Portsmouth talks began on 9 August, Japan's bargaining hand was strengthened by three developments. The first was the conclusion of a new agreement with Great Britain. This is often described as a renewal of the Alliance of 1902. But strictly speaking the agreement of 1905 was a new treaty or, as the Japanese themselves call it, a 'revised alliance'. As in 1902, Japan made a profitable bargain, especially on Korea; since the new treaty went much further than the old in underwriting Japanese ambitions. Indeed, it almost amounted to a death warrant so far as Korea's independence was concerned. It will be remembered that Article I of the 1902 treaty paid lip service to the independence of Korea and had contained the bland assurance that Japan (like Great Britain) was 'entirely uninfluenced by any aggressive tendencies'. The new treaty made no mention of Korean independence. On the contrary, in Article III, the treaty spoke of Japan's 'paramount political, military, and economic interests in Korea', and of Britain's recognition of Japan's right 'to take such measures of guidance, control and protection in Korea as she may deem proper and necessary to safeguard and advance those interests'. The only restriction on Japanese freedom of action was the proviso that the measures of 'control and protection' should not be contrary to the principle of 'equal opportunities for the commerce and industry of all nations'. In return for the blank cheque on Korea, Japan recognised (Article IV) Britain's right to take measures 'in the proximity' of the Indian frontier to safeguard her Indian possessions.[3]

The second development heartening to the Japanese on the eve of the Portsmouth conference was the 'Taft–Katsura understanding', the product of a prolonged *tête-à-tête* on 27 July 1905 between the Japanese Prime Minister and William Howard Taft, the American Secretary of War, then visiting Japan on his way to the Philippines. The Taft–Katsura accord was spelt out in a memorandum which was fully endorsed by the President. It pledged American support for 'the establishment by Japanese troops of a suzerainty over Korea'. Speaking for Japan, Katsura formally disavowed any aggressive intentions towards the Philippines.

This understanding was not made public in the United States for nearly twenty years. It is, therefore, neither surprising nor inappropriate that it should have been called a secret pact. Moreover, it looked very much like a horse-trading deal – a Japanese guarantee of the *status quo* in the Philippines in exchange for American acceptance of Japanese control of Korea. Naturally enough, this was not how Washington cared to interpret the matter. Roosevelt objected to the implication that his complaisance on Korea was related to some kind of bargain involving the Philippines. In October 1905 a Tokyo newspaper, generally considered to be the organ of the government, announced that this bargain – we might describe it as *Hi-Kan Kokan*, 'Philippines–Korean exchange' – had been the essence of the Taft–Katsura understanding. Roosevelt at once rejected this with the lofty disclaimer that 'we neither ask nor give any favor to anyone as a reward for not meddling with any American territory'.[4] That is all very well. But the fact is that the Japanese believed (if only because they wanted to believe) that a valuable *realpolitik* bargain had been struck; and it is difficult to find fault with them on this score.

The third development was, in the short run, of more importance than either the revised alliance with Britain or the Taft–Katsura accord. In July 1905, the Japanese launched a successful operation against Sakhalin. This little-known campaign, for possession of an island nearly 600 miles long, lasted a mere three weeks. But the Russian forces amounted to no more than some 6000, of whom about a third were convict settlers who had volunteered for military service on the promise of being given their freedom after the war. The Japanese deployed a full army division (more than double the strength mustered by the Russians), supported by a squadron of cruisers and destroyers.

Until the Sakhalin campaign the Russians could claim that they had not lost a foot of their own national territory to the Japanese. Even so, the entire island of Sakhalin had been part of the Russian Empire for barely thirty years. Before 1875 the island was under joint Japanese–Russian occupation. In fact the Japanese had penetrated Sakhalin long before the Russians. But by the Treaty of St Petersburg in 1875 Japan renounced sovereignty over Sakhalin in return for Russia's abandonment of all claims to any of the Kurile Islands.

Japanese public opinion took it for granted that the capture of

Sakhalin must mean that in the peace treaty the Russians would cede the island to Japan. Equally, Nicholas II believed that, whatever concessions were made in South Manchuria or over Korea, he and his government could never surrender any portion of Sakhalin to the Japanese. However, for Komura – and for Witte also – Sakhalin was a key bargaining counter in the peace negotiations, despite popular demands in Tokyo and autocratic obduracy in St Petersburg. For at the end of the day, Japan's failure to extract a Russian idemnity was offset to some extent by the acquisition of the southern half of Sakhalin; and Russia's surrender of that part of her territory was made more palatable by Japan's agreement to forego the indemnity. It was a solution fully satisfactory to neither side, yet acceptable to both; a characteristic example of 'old diplomacy' at its best.

But before this conclusion of the business was reached there were many anxious moments. As August progressed there were times when it seemed certain that the conference would break up. The final crisis came at the end of the month, when both Witte and Komura were ready to pack their bags and go home. There was a certain piquancy in the situation. Witte was under pressure from an unyielding Tsar, supported by a confident army command in Manchuria, to concede not an inch of Sakhalin or one kopek by way of indemnity. Komura, on the other hand, was ready on his own initiative, had he been allowed to exercise it, to terminate the negotiations. But in the final analysis it was Komura, not Witte, who was compelled (much to his personal chagrin) to play the game of bluff. On 26 August he sent two long telegrams to Tokyo, declaring (in the first) that the peace talks had reached complete deadlock, and (in the second) that Russia had no intention of being conciliatory.

Witte himself [this message ran] seems to desire peace, but the situation in Russia has undergone a drastic change. Now the pro-war faction is again in the ascendant and the Tsar is completely swayed by their influence. Thus it is clear that, in spite of his personal wishes, Witte has already concluded that he can take no other course than to break off negotiations.[5]

The reply from Tokyo was the product of agonising deliberations by the oligarchy, culminating in a session in the presence of the Emperor. Komura was informed that the Emperor had sanctioned a decision 'to reach an agreement in the negotiations at this time even if it means

abandoning the two demands for indemnity and territory'. Komura
was instructed to tell the Russians that the Japanese government, 'as its
last concession' would withdraw the demand for an indemnity on
condition that Russia recognised the Japanese occupation of Sakhalin
as a *fait accompli*. However, if the Russians were unmoved by this offer,
Komura was 'to attempt to persuade the President to recommend to us,
as his last effort for peace, that we withdraw the territorial demand'.
And if Roosevelt declined to help in this way, then Komura must
withdraw the territorial demand. 'In short', said the telegram, 'Our
Imperial Government is determined to conclude peace by any means
necessary during the present negotiations.'[6]

This important telegram from Tokyo was followed within hours by
another, giving Komura new and vital information; that Nicholas II
had agreed to surrender the southern half of Sakhalin.

Astonishingly, this unexpected concession by the hitherto obstinate
Tsar seems to have been conveyed to the Katsura Cabinet in a curiously
roundabout fashion. What happened was roughly as follows. Three
days before Komura sent his pessimistic telegrams from Portsmouth,
the American ambassador in St Petersburg was received in audience by
the Tsar for two hours, during which time the ambassador managed to
extract the Tsar's agreement to the cession of southern Sakhalin to the
Japanese. The ambassador's approach had been made, of course, on
instructions from Roosevelt. Throughout the Portsmouth Conference
Roosevelt, although in no way a participating figure, watched the ebb
and flow of the proceedings with all the assiduous attention of a go-
between handling a prospective marriage. More than once, it could be
said, he saved the situation by his advice. He warned the Russians that
they risked losing Vladivostok and the Maritime Province if their
unyielding posture led to a breakdown of the talks and a resumption of
the war. He warned the Japanese (usually through Kaneko) that if they
insisted on an indemnity – something which the Russians would never
concede – they risked losing American sympathy; for it would be said
that the Japanese were fighting purely for mercenary gain. Roosevelt
hoped to induce the Japanese at least to lower the amount of the
indemnity, if he was unable to persuade them to give up this demand
entirely. On the other hand, he pressed the Russians to agree in
principle to the payment of some monetary compensation for the
recovery of northern Sakhalin, which the Japanese were willing,
however reluctantly, to evacuate. This and other suggestions for
Russian consideration formed the substance of a message to the Tsar

which George von Lengerke Meyer, the American ambassador in St Petersburg, was instructed to deliver in person.

Ambassador Meyer, in persuading the Tsar to give way on southern Sakhalin, was able to make much of the argument that the island, especially its southern half, was after all only a fairly recent acquisition and so could not be looked upon as indisputably Russian territory comparable with the rest of the Tsar's domain in Asia. The return of southern Sakhalin to Japan – which had controlled that area spasmodically for centuries – would imply no loss of face for the Russian government. It was a reasonable contention. Accordingly, in the end Nicholas II, on this single item of southern Sakhalin, was ready to compromise.

Now one would imagine that this significant concession by the Tsar would have been notified to the Japanese immediately by the President – to Komura and his delegation through Kaneko, and to the Japanese government through the American Legation in Tokyo. But Roosevelt, it seems, failed to pass on the vital news.

The Katsura Cabinet heard of it through an official of the Tokyo Foreign Ministry, Ishii Kikujiro; who heard of it from Sir Claude MacDonald, the British ambassador in Japan, who heard of it because his embassy received a copy of a telegram, from the British ambassador in Russia to the Foreign Office in London, giving the information about Meyer's meeting with the Tsar and the latter's offer to cede southern Sakhalin. Ishii in later years was to become one of Japan's best-known diplomatists; and we shall be meeting him again. But at this time he was still on the ladder of promotion, although approaching the upper rungs, since he was a bureau chief (*kyoku-cho*). He was shown, but not given, the text of the copy of the St Petersburg–London telegram in Sir Claude MacDonald's possession. However, MacDonald, appreciating its importance for Japan, read it aloud twice to Ishii. The latter hastened to report the matter to Katsura, who brought it before the Cabinet. Some ministers found difficulty in believing the truth of the St Petersburg report; and it is said that Ishii was reminded that *hara-kiri* would be expected of him if his information proved to be incorrect.

It is an odd story. Why did the President fail to pass on to the Japanese the information received from Ambassador Meyer? Raymond Esthus, in *Theodore Roosevelt and Japan*, does not provide a satisfactory answer. He suggests that Roosevelt 'may have told Kaneko of the Tsar's concession' but admits that there is no reference to this in the diary that Kaneko kept at the time. Indeed, he goes further. He refers to a letter sent by Roosevelt to Komura on 28 August (five days after Meyer's meeting with Nicholas II) in which Roosevelt stressed the stubborn refusal of the Tsar to cede any territory. Professor Esthus can only observe: 'Roosevelt had been so intent on obtaining Russia's assent to the total compromise plan that he had neglected to inform the Japanese that he had the Tsar's commitment to cede southern Sakhalin.'[7] This is not convincing as an explanation of Roosevelt's behaviour.

It may be, of course, that Roosevelt hoped he would still be able to obtain all Sakhalin for the Japanese. His sympathies were decidedly pro-Japanese. But these did not blind him to the desirability, from the point of view of American interests, of securing a balance of power in the Far East. Supposing him to have guessed – or even to have learned from some source – that the Japanese government was ready to back down and return the whole of Sakhalin to the Russians, he could hardly have failed to perceive that this would be satisfactory in terms of the balance of power. On this supposition his neglect to inform the Japanese of the Tsar's concession makes good sense.[8] Otherwise, one has to conclude that the President's lapse was unintentional and due to pressure of other work or mere carelessness: which seems out of character.

Be that as it may, the Japanese–Russian crisis was now resolved. On 29 August Komura offered Witte the return of northern Sakhalin without payment of monetary compensation, provided Russia recognised the 50th parallel as the boundary. This was accepted by Witte; and the treaty of peace was signed at a formal session on 5 September 1905.

II

The Portsmouth Treaty comprised fifteen clauses, the substance of which can be stated, briefly, as follows. Russia acknowledged Japan's paramount political, military, and economic interests in Korea (Article II). Russia transferred to Japan, 'with the consent of the Government of China', the lease of Port Arthur, Dairen, and all rights in the Liaotung Peninsula; Russia and Japan agreeing to obtain Chinese consent to these arrangements (Article V). Russia transferred to Japan, 'with the consent of the Chinese Government', the railway from Port Arthur to Changchun, together with all railway properties, including the coal mines in the railway zone; Russia and Japan agreeing, again, to obtain Chinese consent (Article VI). Russia ceded to Japan Sakhalin south of the 50th parallel (Article IX). Russia engaged to make arrangements for Japanese rights of fishery along the coasts of the Russian possessions in the Japan, Okhotsk and Behring Seas (Article XI).[9]

It will be seen that Japan's gains were solid but not dramatic. The Russian threat, genuine or illusory, to Japan's position in Korea was now removed. Japan was once again in possession of Port Arthur and the Liaotung Peninsula. And the humiliation of the Triple Intervention was expunged. Southern Sakhalin was a real acquisition, although it could be argued that this amounted to the recovery of lost territory. Of greater significance was the Russian withdrawal from the railway zone between Port Arthur and Changchun. The South Manchurian Railway was to be Japan's economic and political bridgehead for the penetration of Manchuria and Inner Mongolia.

Compared with the assets acquired in 1895 by the Treaty of Shimonoseki – Formosa, the Pescadores, and a very large indemnity – the gains at Portsmouth were relatively modest, particularly in view of the heavy loss of life and treasure. The indemnity imposed on China in 1895 had been of great utility, providing the Japanese economy with a most invigorating shot in the arm; and it would have been no less helpful to finance and industry to have had a similar injection of funds from a Russian indemnity in 1905. Furthermore, in those days it was still thought natural and proper for victors to exact reparations in cash from the vanquished. In the eyes of the common man, not only in Japan but also throughout the world, the Russians were the clear losers in the war. Had not their fleet been wiped out in one of the greatest sea battles of that or any other age? Were they not beaten in every land battle in Manchuria? Japan, then, to outward appearance was the undoubted victor.

Yet, as we have seen, the true situation was very different. For economic and military reasons alike the Japanese simply had to call a halt to the war. But only the coterie that governed the country, the *Genro* and the Cabinet and the highest military leaders, appreciated this imperative necessity; and it was not in their tradition – it would hardly have occurred to them – to present the facts of the case to the people at large. The Meiji leadership, as was pointed out in the second chapter, did not regard foreign policy as a suitable topic for popular debate. While the Portsmouth negotiations were proceeding Komura and his staff were as reticent as clams, providing the international press with little sustenance. This was in strong contrast with the attitude taken by Witte and the Russians, who grasped the importance of public relations and handled them in masterly fashion. (Witte was accompanied on his journey to America by his friend Dr E. J. Dillon, the St Petersburg correspondent of the London *Daily Telegraph*, who gave him invaluable advice on such matters.) Japanese and other correspondents at Portsmouth came to depend on Russian sources – including Dr Dillon – for news of what was happening. 'Chinese' Morrison of *The Times*, who came from Peking to cover the conference, reported to his editor in London: 'It is impossible to get anything out of the Japanese. They have not the art of making themselves popular, and it is already noticeable how much more liked are the Russians who were hearty and friendly and jovial with everyone.'[10]

If Japanese bureaucrats were so opaque in their dealings with the foreign press, it can be imagined how arrogantly uncommunicative they must have appeared to their own nationals, who were consumed by patriotic impatience to learn what terms were being imposed on the defeated enemy.

Although no official announcement was made, it was widely known in Japan before the end of August that no progress has been made on the question of an indemnity. A mounting chorus of angry disappointment became the dominant tone of Japanese newspaper comment. Public opinion started to condemn Komura as a weakling or worse. Which was indeed ironic, seeing that he was implacably against giving way to the Russians on either the indemnity issue or the retrocession of Sakhalin. It was only on firm instructions from his government that he acquiesced in the eventual compromise.

Well-founded rumours as to the nature of the final settlement were current in Japan several days before the treaty was signed. The almost universal reaction was one of indignation; and this erupted at the beginning of September in a storm that became famous as the *Hibiya yakiuchi jiken*, or 'Hibiya fire-attack affair'. A demonstration in Hibiya Park, Tokyo, protesting against the peace terms deteriorated into mob violence, directed mainly against the police; who had been unwise enough, with inadequate numbers, to try to close the park against a crowd of some 30,000 hot and angry citizens (the thermometer that day stood at 96 degrees fahrenheit). Three days of riot and arson followed before the city could be said to be quiet again. On the second day the government proclaimed martial law in Tokyo. The scale of the upheaval may be judged from the fact that nearly three-quarters of the police stations and police boxes in the city were burned to the ground. They were not the only buildings to be attacked by the mob. The Home Minister's house, the offices of a newspaper that supported the government, several Christian churches, and a number of private houses were destroyed or damaged. There were riots in other cities, such as Osaka, Kobe and Nagoya, and some loss of life.

The shock of the 'disgraceful' peace, therefore, was comparable with the trauma of the Triple Intervention ten years earlier. Yet deep and enduring as had been the sense of humiliation in 1895 it did not explode into mass protest and violence. But a decade of increased literacy and continued urban growth produced a society more assertive than in 1895. The sacrifices as well as the victories of the Russian war gave the people of Japan renewed confidence in the invincible superiority of their race.

Some Japanese writers in recent years, with the Rice Riots of 1918 and the Security Pact disturbances of 1960 in mind, have attached a left-wing ideological label to the popular turmoil of 1905. The fierce attacks on the police might appear to lend weight to this view. That the Hibiya riots represented a spontaneous upsurge of public feeling cannot be denied. Indeed, there is a faint parallel between Hibiya and Bloody Sunday in St Petersburg at the beginning of the same year. For the workers whom Father Gapon led to the Winter Palace bore banners asserting their faith in the Tsar. Likewise, the thousands who converged on Hibiya Park carried placards appealing to the Emperor Meiji to redress their grievance against the government and the envoys at Portsmouth. But beyond that there is no similarity with Bloody Sunday. Popular fury against the police did not go further and direct its aim at the imperial house. Loyal rebellion was an old tradition with many precedents during the Restoration and early Meiji period. If an ideological significance has to be attached to the riots, they may perhaps be thought of as proto-fascist.

There is a further side to the Hibiya Affair, about which scholars still disagree. The demonology of the Tokyo mob embraced Theodore Roosevelt as well as the despised Komura and Katsura. The President, it was believed, must have leaned heavily on the Japanese to moderate their demands. This seemed to offer one possible explanation of an otherwise inexplicable failure to win the peace after winning the war. Commenting on the Hibiya riots, a modern writer has suggested that 'they were the first expression of anti-American sentiment in Japan' and that the masses 'instinctively recognized who had won the best deal at Portsmouth'.[11] But the true extent of this anti-American feeling is very hard to assess. The evidence anyway is conflicting. More than fifty years later, during the Security Pact disturbances of 1960, when it was thought prudent to cancel President Eisenhower's projected visit to Tokyo, Americans in Japan were not subjected to insult or harassment. The same is broadly true of 1905.

However, the riots, put down with an iron hand by an oligarchy outwardly unmoved by the vulgar hue and cry, had one very significant result. They killed the prospect of joint American–Japanese ownership of the South Manchurian Railway.

Only a few days before the rumpus began, a leading American financier, E. H. Harriman, arrived in Tokyo. His purpose, fully supported by the American Legation, was to negotiate with the Katsura government for control of the railway from Port Arthur north to Changchun, after the line had been handed by the Russians to the Japanese. Harriman was already famous in his own country as a 'railroad king'; and he directed the operations of an American trans-Pacific shipping company. His ambition was to establish a round-the-world freight and passenger service. For if he could gain possession, in full or as part-owner, of the South Manchurian Railway and then secure running powers over the Trans-Siberian and other Russian lines (he was hoping to buy the line across northern Manchuria from the Russians), his intention was to set up a trans-Atlantic steamship service across to the Baltic ports; and the circuit would then be complete. It was a rather magnificent dream, reflecting, we might say, the most acceptable face of American capitalism.

The Tokyo government was by no means averse to Harriman's plan for the South Manchurian line, provided that the Japanese were equal partners with the Americans in the enterprise. Since there was a severe shortage of funds the influx of American capital was welcome. About the middle of October Katsura and Harriman reached a firm, preliminary, but as yet unsigned, understanding. Harriman sailed for America with every reason to expect that he and the Japanese would work together in rebuilding, operating and expanding the railway system of South Manchuria.

Three days after Harriman's departure Komura returned quietly to Japan. (His disembarkation was so discreet as to be almost clandestine: his life having been threatened, there were well-founded fears for his safety.) He immediately opposed the Katsura–Harriman plan with the greatest vigour. It was the Hibiya Affair that he was able to use as his most telling argument. How could the government possibly consider Harriman's scheme when the Japanese people were already so dismayed by the peace treaty that they had resorted to mob violence? It was unthinkable that Japan should share with foreigners a most valuable prize gained in battle. Komura won his point. When Harriman reached San Francisco a message from Tokyo awaited him, asking him to hold matters in abeyance for the time being. A few weeks later he learned that the whole deal was off.

In the light of later history Katsura's evident readiness to cooperate with Harriman is of much interest. For it clearly suggests that the Meiji oligarchy – whatever may have been the dreams of militant chauvinists – had no plan at that juncture to control the resources of South Manchuria to the exclusion of other powers. Moreover, the *Genro* and ministers were apparently unshaken by the storm of the Hibiya riots, which erupted at the very moment when Harriman was starting his negotiations in Tokyo. It is possible that Komura, viewing the situation from America, was more impressed than his colleagues in Tokyo by the agitation throughout Japan. Yet it is unlikely, to say the least, that fears of insurrection – let alone motives of self-preservation – had much to do with Komura's opposition to the Harriman plan. It has to be remembered that he was ready to break off the Portsmouth neg-otiations. If it had been left to him he would never have signed the treaty on the terms conceded by Tokyo. He and the demonstrators at Hibiya had more in common than either would have been willing to admit. This basic sympathy enabled Komura to use the popular agitation as an effective weapon with which to demolish the Katsura–Harriman project.

One is almost tempted to believe that the failure of that project may have marked some sort of turning-point in Japanese–American re-lations; since shared ownership of the South Manchurian Railway might have created the habit of fruitful cooperation, preserving for both Americans and Japanese a salutary realism in their attitude to East Asia and its problems. For if practical economic involvement in Manchuria together with Japan could have tempered the excesses of American moralism and rhetoric, cooperation with the United States would have strengthened every rational element in Japanese society, thereby holding in check the bellicose, chauvinist tendencies that emerged with such force a generation later.

But that is doubtless to make too much of what was, first and last, a financial enterprise. It may be that racial feeling in Japan and America was too deep-seated to be mollified by arrangements of this kind. Popular sentiment in Japan was, in any event, drawn more to the national ally, Great Britain, than to the United States. This was symbolised by a successful visit paid by the Royal Navy in October 1905. In Hibiya Park, the scene of such turmoil only a few weeks before, the citizens of Tokyo regaled the sailors of the China Squadron with a convivial *fête-champêtre*, Jack Tars and geisha pledging mutual friendship with sign language, laughter and an ample supply of free beer.

Meanwhile, the government was making preparations to deal with China. For the implementation of the Portsmouth settlement depended, of course, on the consent of Peking. Accordingly, at the beginning of November Komura embarked for China on a Japanese warship at the naval port of Yokosuka.

But there was also unfinished business in Korea to be attended to. This was entrusted to Ito, who left for Seoul while Komura was crossing the Yellow Sea. Secure in the knowledge that, thanks to the Taft–Katsura accord and the new treaty with Britain, Japan had the backing of Washington and London for her policy in Korea, Ito had all the aces in his hand. The Korean Emperor and his ministers were unable to resist the Japanese demands. These gave Japan complete control of Korea's foreign relations and established the office of Japanese Resident-General at Seoul. Ito himself was to be the first holder of this appointment. Korean independence, such as remained, now hung by a thread. The most charitable interpretation of Japanese aims has been offered by an American scholar: 'It can be said that in general the leaders of the Japanese government, as of the fall of 1905, intended to have their "improvements" without annexing Korea and without resort to brutality.'[12]

However, as the next chapter must record, that worthy intention, cherished by Ito so long as he lived, was not fulfilled. For the people of Korea both annexation and brutality lay ahead.

This is an appropriate moment to consider Japan's position in the autumn of 1905 explicitly within the context of our title: *Japan and the Decline of the West in Asia*. Every student of world history knows that Japan's victories in the war against Russia made her the hero of Asia, and indeed of colonised regions lying beyond the bounds of that continent. Nehru and Soekarno have both testified to the enormous impact, on their psychological development, of the Russo-Japanese War. There is abundant evidence of this kind, illustrating the surge of confidence that swept through Asia from the Philippines to the Khyber Pass. One can, indeed, go further afield. Sun Yat-sen, travelling by sea from Europe to Japan in 1905, was impressed by the joy at Japan's victory shown by the Egyptians at Suez.[13] In 1904 there was a revolt against the French in south-east Madagascar. The Governor-General, Gallieni, attributed it, in some measure, to the example of Japan's military successes in the Russian war.[14]

If most Japanese were disappointed by the Treaty of Portsmouth their feelings were not shared by the rest of Asia, colonised Asia in particular. There the Treaty was seen as a humiliation for imperial Russia. An Asian race had won not merely a single battle but an entire campaign, crowning this with a triumph at the peace table. This was something that had not been witnessed within living memory. During the nineteenth century there were, of course, clashes between East and West in which the East was in certain areas and for a limited time successful. Britain suffered military defeat at the hands of the Afghans, was hard pressed in India during the Mutiny, faced acute difficulties in putting down the Chin Rebellion in Burma. The Dutch wrestled for years with stubborn insurrection in northern Sumatra. The French endured more than one defeat in their war with China in the eighties.

It was always an illusion, then, to suppose that an allegedly passive, quietist East would invariably bend an unresisting head to the energetic and assertive West. It was an illusion suffused with a rich Victorian glow by Matthew Arnold when, in a poem on the Roman conquest of Palestine, he wrote:

> The East bow'd low before the blast
> In patient, deep disdain;
> She let the legions thunder past
> And plunged in thought again.[15]

But in both Asia and Africa the Western powers had never failed to win *in the end*. (A single exception to this rule was Italy's ill-fated campaign against Ethiopia in the nineties.) It was this seeming inevitability of eventual Western success that had come to impress itself on Asian (and African) minds, convincing them of the overwhelmingly superior technical skill and military efficiency of the peoples of European stock. And it was the mortar holding in place the bricks of this belief that was loosened by the events of the Russo-Japanese War. The bricks themselves, of course, had yet to be dislodged. The British Empire in the East, indeed, was still expanding. In 1909, for example, a bargain was struck with Siam whereby the latter, in exchange for a loan and the surrender of extra-territorial rights, transferred to Great Britain her rights over the northern Malay states of Kedah, Perlis, Kelantan and Trengganu.

Finally, it has to be admitted that in 1905 Japan presented a somewhat uncertain face to Asia and the world. She was now a power (to use the terminology of the imperial court) of 'the junior first rank'. Only a decade had passed since Hayashi Tadayasu had encouraged his compatriots 'to watch and wait for the opportunity in the Orient' that would surely come one day (see chapter 1, p. 30). What would come next? Korea, it seemed, would probably be swallowed up. China would be cajoled or bullied into accepting the new dispensation in South Manchuria. After that what was to happen? It was evidently Katsura's opinion that it was 'better for Japan to go one mile in ten days than ten miles in one day'.[16] Extreme caution – testing the marshy and treacherous ground ahead step by step with a stick, like the bandit chief in *The Seven Samurai* – was on the whole characteristic of Japanese leadership until the 1930s, even if the attack on Russia in 1904 seems to point the other way.

6 Trouble at the Golden Gate

We must stop being content with crouching in a small corner of the earth.
OZAKI YUKIO

Open your Golden Gate!
You let no stranger wait
Outside your door!
Theme song of the Hollywood movie, *San Francisco*

THE Russo-Japanese War, it need hardly be said, constituted an affront to Chinese patriotic sentiment, since it was fought on what everyone recognised as the territory of imperial China. Further humiliation came when China's warning that she might demand damages from Japan and Russia, and a wistful Chinese request to join the Portsmouth Conference, were alike ignored. Worse was to follow. Having arrived in Peking, Komura was firm to the point of brusqueness. Japan's claim to the inheritance of Russia's position in South Manchuria was supported by Britain and the United States, accepted by Russia under the terms of the peace treaty, and backed by the presence of Japanese troops on the ground; yet the claim remained invalid, in the full legal sense, without the consent of Peking. This Komura was determined to obtain without delay. It cannot have been an agreeable experience for China's chief negotiator, Yuan Shih-k'ai to face Komura under such circumstances. He was personally disliked and distrusted by the Japanese ever since his time as 'Resident in Korea' (see chapter 2, p. 20), and he was on the worst of terms with the Empress Dowager, not least, perhaps, because the old harridan could not dispense with his services during a crisis of this kind.

The Chinese did their best to deflect and moderate Komura's demands; but the outcome could not be in doubt. The treaty, signed in late December 1905, gave the Japanese substantially what they wanted – including a promise not to build railways that might compete with the Japanese lines in South Manchuria.

Within the next two years the Manchurian kaleidoscope settled into its new pattern. The Russians withdrew their troops but maintained armed control of their Chinese Eastern Railway zone across Manchuria from the north-west, on the Siberian border, through Harbin to the south-east, to the Maritime Province roughly a hundred miles north of Vladivostok. Japanese troops were withdrawn to the Port Arthur–Dairen area (the Kwantung Leased Territory, as it was officially called), but railway guards were stationed along the line up to Mukden and beyond. The South Manchurian Railway Company was established in 1906, half the initial capital being provided by the Japanese government, the rest by corporate bodies and private individuals in Japan. The SMR was from the beginning much more than an organisation for the carriage of goods and passengers; and in course of time it would operate iron works, coal mines, and other economic ventures. It supported its own bureaucracy, ran its own intelligence service, engaged in serious economic and political research (much of it published), and was, in short, a veritable *imperium in imperio*.

Japanese–Russian relations now entered a new phase, of restrained cordiality and cooperation. The two countries signed a treaty in 1907, renewed in 1910 and 1912, agreeing to support the *status quo* and, in a secret convention (revealed by the Bolsheviks after their seizure of power), to recognise each other's spheres of interest in Manchuria. The secret convention also included Russian recognition of Japan's control of Korea and Japanese recognition of Russia's special status in Outer Mongolia. Since the year 1907 witnessed the conclusion of the Anglo-Russian and Franco-Japanese *ententes* it might be thought that Japan was now firmly embedded in one of the two rival European systems of alliance, then hardening into a posture of mutual suspicion preparatory to war. But for the Japanese the question of Germany was of minor importance. Russia, on the other hand, was crucial. The agreements of 1907 and later amounted to a tacit Russo-Japanese partition of Manchuria. For Japan at that time this was more than a solace. In terms of security it was, for some years at any rate, a gilt-edged investment.

It has been contended, nevertheless, that despite the *rapprochement* the Japanese, especially the army, could not dismiss the prospect of a Russian war of revenge. According to this view, Russian activities in east Asia continued to be treated as a threat right down to the end of the tsarist government.[1] On the face of it, genuine cooperation between Japanese and Russians did seem unlikely. Theodore Roosevelt, writing to his successor, President Taft, in December 1910, expressed an opinion held by many foreign observers. 'Japan knows perfectly well', he wrote, 'that sometime in the future, if a good occasion offers, Russia will wish to play a game of bowls for the prize she lost in their last contest.'[2] This prediction was fulfilled, of course, in the closing days of the Second World War. As Russian armies swept down into Manchuria and southern Sakhalin, Soviet public pronouncements harked back in vengeful tones to what had happened forty years earlier, in 1905.

However, another interpretation of the *rapprochement* emphasises the factor of reconciliation rather than that of continued, though covert, suspicion. A Japanese authority in this field declares that the Russo-Japanese agreement of 1907 allowed 'the Japanese to dispel their apprehension over a war of revenge'.[3] We have already seen that on the political stage in Russia and Japan there were important figures who had always believed in the possibility of cooperation based on the mutual recognition of spheres of interest in the Far East. It will be remembered that this was Ito's sincere conviction. In the decade following the Portsmouth Treaty Ito's great rival, Yamagata – Ito and Yamagata are the twin giants of the Meiji era – became increasingly attracted by the idea of a close alliance with Russia. And this end was achieved by a treaty signed in 1916 after months of persistent pressure from Yamagata.

What was the main reason for this movement towards collaboration with the old enemy? The answer is to be found in the deterioration in Japanese–American relations that occurred in the years following the Russo-Japanese War; a deterioration that arose from mutual fears about the activities and intentions of Japanese and Americans in two parts of the world, California and Manchuria.

Despite the generally favourable view of Japan taken by the American press during the Russian war, and although Theodore Roosevelt and the Eastern 'establishment' of the United States admired the exploits on the battlefield of the 'gallant little Japs', there was an undercurrent of apprehension in the popular American attitude as soon as it was clear that Russia might lose the war. Feelings ran much deeper than this on the West Coast. Here there was already a good deal of anxiety about the numbers of Japanese arriving as immigrants. The flow had greatly increased after the annexation of Hawaii in 1898; for about 60,000 Japanese lived in the islands, and any of them could now enter the continental United States without a passport. In 1899 the number of Japanese on the West Coast was more than five times what it had been only four years earlier, and this rate of momentum was sustained. The Chinese had long suffered from waves of hostility in California, as they were regarded by many urban and rural workers as inscrutable aliens who would work for pay that no white American could live on. Japanese immigrants found to their chagrin that they were often lumped together with the Chinese, becoming objects of the same racial prejudice.

By 1908 there were over 100,000 Japanese in America (excluding Hawaii), three times the figures for 1899 (35,000). For some years, from the early 1890s, emigration to Hawaii and the United States had assumed the proportions of a minor boom among the Japanese, especially those who chafed under the manifold handicaps of life in an overcrowded, authoritarian society. The exciting slogan for a Japanese country boy could well have been: 'Go East, young man!' Certain regions of Japan, notably those on the Inland Sea, reproduced on a small scale the demographic pattern of Ireland and the Scottish Highlands in earlier years. In many villages there would be scarcely a household without at least one relative who had emigrated to Hawaii or the American mainland. As in countries such as Italy or Poland, so in Japan the popular image of America was of a land of freedom, riches and unlimited opportunity. History textbooks in schools praised America for its high standard of living and absence of class barriers; and many books addressed to adults warned readers of the dangers facing Japan from overpopulation and stressed the advantages of emigrating to the United States. In such works the Japanese were often scolded for their insularity; they were urged to broaden their horizons, to extend the influence of their race, while benefiting themselves, by settling in the 'land of the free' across the Pacific. Receiving such messages, the imaginative but frustrated boy who had abandoned hope of fame and fortune in Tokyo (the Mecca, then and now, of ambitious youth) would begin to think about an exciting and profitable life in California. There cannot be statistics to tell us what proportion of young Japanese emigrants escaped all humiliation after landing in the contential United States. But it is unlikely to have been spectacularly high.

Japan's dramatic victories in the Russian war gave a new dimension to the emotions of those Americans who resented the influx that we have been discussing. Anxieties on cultural or economic grounds were now reinforced by other, rather more alarming, fears. These unassimilated, competitive Orientals belonged to a powerful and expanding nation, whose citizens, one was told, thought nothing of death in the service of their divine imperial ruler. This tinge of paranoia should be borne in mind when deploring, as one must, the offensively phrased resolution passed unanimously by the California state legislature in March 1905, calling for the limitation of further Japanese immigration, and describing the immigrants as immoral, intemperate and quarrelsome – which, by strict American Puritan standards, many of them probably were. Thanks to its choice of language, the resolution cut no ice with Roosevelt; he dismissed the California legislators as idiots who had behaved in bad taste. But a few weeks after this episode there was established in San Francisco a baleful pressure group, 'The Japanese and Korean Exclusion League', which soon had a membership running into tens of thousands.

April of the following year, 1906, was the month of the San Francisco earthquake disaster. Among overseas contributions to the relief fund none was larger than the sum given by the Japanese government and the Japanese Red Cross. In fact this contribution from Tokyo, a quarter of a million dollars, exceeded the combined total received from other sources overseas. It was the more painful, then, for Japanese readers at home to see in their newspapers reports of the Exclusion League's campaign for a boycott of Japanese restaurants in San Francisco. Even more shocking was an account of how two seismologists of Tokyo Imperial University, sent to San Francisco to study the earthquake and its effects, had been assaulted by hooligans in the streets of the city. Other, less eminent, Japanese suffered the same experience that summer, when lawlessness seemed to reign among the wrecked and burnt-out buildings.

Trouble with Japanese seal poachers near Alaska in the summer did nothing to relieve tension, but it was in the autumn that a really serious crisis blew up, when the Exclusion League persuaded the San Francisco school board to segregate in a single school all Japanese, Korean and Chinese children. This measure engendered anger and dismay in Japan, provoking much bellicose comment in some sections of the press. The Foreign Minister at the time was Hayashi Tadasu, whom we have met before. It was he who had to endure the insults of the German Minister in 1895; and it was he who had heartened his countrymen with the prediction that the day would come when Japan would not only decide her own fate but would 'put into their place the powers who seek to meddle in her affairs' (see chapter 2, p. 30). Hayashi's language was restrained when he told the Washington Embassy to deliver a sharp protest to the State Department, but it included, all the same, a hint that Japan might consider measures of retaliation if the San Francisco school board's act of discrimination was not repealed. This part of Hayashi's message was omitted, it seems, by the Japanese ambassador when he met the Secretary of State, Elihu Root.

Such was the background of the war scare that cast a shadow over Japanese–American relations in 1907, creating between the two peoples an atmosphere of mutual distrust that was never wholly dissipated until after the Pacific War forty years later. The school-board crisis was resolved, thanks to pressure from Washington. By what can be called, in the hideous jargon of today, 'a package deal', Tokyo agreed to place drastic restrictions on further emigration to the United States; and the segregation of Japanese schoolchildren in California ceased. The settlement was known, in the enlightened language of yesterday, as the 'Gentlemen's Agreement'. Once fully implemented it would be faithfully observed; in due course the inflow of Japanese to the West Coast became little more than a trickle. Which rendered all the more offensive the total exclusion of Japanese immigrants in a special clause attached to a general immigration law by the United States Congress in 1924.

The patent unfairness and stupidity of that action; a bad conscience about the uprooting of West Coast Japanese and their concentration in relocation camps during the Pacific War; general *pudeur* about the whole question of racial feeling: these have led some American historians to view this problem of the Roosevelt–Taft–Wilson era as a matter first and last of vulgar prejudice, neurotic fears and ugly ward politics. That ignorance, hysteria and corrupt politics played their part is not to be denied. But there was more to it than that. Professor Iriye of Chicago has pointed out that historians have failed to see the West Coast problem 'in the context of Japanese expansionism'; unless this larger perspective is taken into account 'much of the historical significance of the period will be lost'.[4]

Nationalist passions in Japan ran deep and were greatly stimulated, though in different ways, by pride in the martial successes of the Russian war and by disappointment with the subsequent peace settlement. A substantial chunk of the population – what proportion one can never say – had become obsessed with crude, not necessarily aggressive, dreams of the limitless expansion of their race. Such visions in the age of latter-day imperialism were by no means confined to the Japanese; but in the case of Japan they displayed a particular gusto, due partly to certain strains in the national tradition, and partly to the fact that the country was a late-comer on the stage of the modern world. For if the imperialism of Great Britain, France and America – of Rhodes, Lyautey and 'Teddy' Roosevelt – represented the top of a wave just before it breaks, Japanese imperialism was the wave itself, flowing in with little sign as yet of the curl that brings the line of surf lengthening along its crest.

This urge to expand was considered the natural, the inevitable, destiny of the Japanese race, one that could take many forms – cultural, economic, political, military. On these, and on targets and timing, there were profound and rancorous differences of opinion. Yet the most rational and cosmopolitan could be carried away by the rhetoric of the expansionist ideal. Thus, Abe Isoo, a Christian socialist educated in the United States and one of the courageous dissenters associated with the *Heimin Shimbun*, declared in a magazine article in the summer of 1907 that it would be a good thing if the Japanese population on the American West Coast could grow to a million or more; just as Commodore Perry had awakened the Japanese from their long seclusion, so the Japanese must free Americans from the thrall of racial prejudice. The Japanese, wrote Abe (revealing a remarkable capacity for self-deception) were 'singularly free of such prejudice'; so their presence *en masse* in the West Coast states would destroy racial barriers and create a new and ethnically harmonious society.[5] There is no thought here of political penetration; and the idea of ultimate military action to back up diplomatic pressure on the United States would scarcely have entered Abe's mind. Nevertheless, his words would have a disquieting ring for most Americans, for they indicate, after all, an aspiration, however benevolent, to have a say in the ordering of America's domestic affairs. If thoughtful men like Abe, with a genuine regard for the United States and its ideals, could indulge in such dreams, it can be imagined that coarser spirits expressed themselves in a much more lurid style.

Not a great many years had passed since the time when the overland routes through the Rockies were still far from secure. California and Oregon in 1907 had not long emerged from conditions of turbulent frontier life. There is perceptible in some of the more sensational popular writing of the late Meiji era a belief that America's Far West ought to be considered debatable territory – rather like Sakhalin, perhaps, in the days when Japanese and Russian trappers and traders coexisted, both parties claiming rightful possession of the island.

American leaders such as Roosevelt drew an important distinction between the Japanese governing class (including, of course, army and navy officers) and the labouring masses – or 'coolie class' as they were sometimes described. But petty businessmen, too, were frequently viewed with disfavour, since there were reservations about the probity of their methods and aims.

This brings us to a brief consideration of an important phenomenon; namely, the generally antipathetic reaction of most North Americans and Europeans to the presence of Japanese in large numbers outside Japan. It was not only on the West Coast of the United States and Canada that this reaction was to be observed. It was the same story in China, Manchuria and Korea, so far as concerned Western diplomats, businessmen, missionaries and journalists resident in those countries. Their reports and memoirs rarely fail to dwell on the alleged dishonesty, rough methods and arrogant posture of Japanese settlers and traders. Senior Japanese officials would openly admit that many of the worst elements of their society sought profit and adventure on the continent; and some of these, we may be sure, travelled east and ended up in the backblocks of San Francisco and Los Angeles.

Aside from all this, linguistic, psychological and cultural differences imposed barriers, behind which the Japanese seemed very much a race apart. To those totally unacquainted with the nature or history of their society, the Japanese often appeared secretive, clannish, unpredictable, so alien and opaque as to seem at times almost beyond human understanding.[6]

That regrettable phenomenon, as well as the Japanese drive to extend the frontiers of their economic and cultural influence, must be remembered when one thinks about the persistent anti-Japanese sentiment on the West Coast. The sentiment was so widespread as to be a factor in domestic politics too strong for Roosevelt to ignore, however sharply he might condemn its extreme manifestations. These erupted again in May 1907 in the form of an anti-Japanese riot in San Francisco. In Japan the reaction seemed in many ways more strident than in the previous autumn, at the time of the school-board crisis. Protests, warnings and threats appeared in the newspapers. Political groups in the Diet added their own expostulations: chambers of commerce joined in the chorus, and there was a demand for a boycott of American goods.

All this led to a war scare which Roosevelt himself took only half seriously. Still, he chose this moment for a demonstration of his policy of the soft speech and the big stick. It was announced that the American battle fleet would be transferred from the Atlantic to the Pacific.

The Panama Canal had yet to be built. To move the battleships from the Atlantic to the Pacific was an expensive undertaking, not one to be contemplated lightly. But by the transfer of the fleet Roosevelt hoped to kill three birds with one stone. Being fitted out in a British yard was the recently launched HMS *Dreadnought*, the new kind of battleship that made all others seem out-of-date. Roosevelt, in the teeth of congressional opposition, was pressing for an enlarged 'big ship' programme; and the appearance of the American battle fleet in the Pacific – the 'Great White Fleet', as it was known later – would surely have an impact on public sentiment helpful to the campaign for a bigger navy. Secondly, the presence of the fleet would be reassuring to the West Coast and could be expected, therefore, to provide a certain political dividend in the presidential election year, 1908. Last but not least, the 'Great White Fleet' was meant to impress Japan.

In a letter to the German ambassador, an old friend of his, Roosevelt reported that he was worried about relations with Japan. The Japanese, he said, had 'unknown possibilities both as regards their power and as regards their motives and purposes'.[7] Writing to the Secretary of State, Elihu Root, a few days later, he declared: 'In France, England, and Germany the best information is that we shall have war with Japan and that we shall be beaten. . . . It was evidently high time that we should get our whole battle fleet on a practice voyage to the Pacific'.[8] Those letters were written in July 1907. Yet the sixteen battleships of the fleet did not sail from their Atlantic base until the middle of December. This suggests that despite many alarms Roosevelt had no expectation of imminent war with Japan. Was he correct in supposing that the transfer of the fleet would impress Japan?

An American scholar has speculated that 'in some deep, subconscious way the President relished the crisis with Japan, which fed his half-suppressed fantasies of martial glory'.[9] There is a good deal in this. One can see that there was a Churchillian touch to Theodore Roosevelt (which is doubtless one reason why Churchill's persona was so endearing to many Americans). Like Churchill, he was both impulsive and shrewd. These are two traits which the Japanese admire and understand. For the first is a sign of sincerity – the prompt translation of ideas into action – while the second is proof of intelligence. The right balance between them, seen as an ethical as well as a practical problem, has always gripped the imagination of the Japanese. An assessment of the President's real mind, therefore, presented Japan's civil and military leaders with an intellectual challenge that in many ways they could have relished. There was no disposition to contemplate an open breach with the United States. The immigration question, irritating and indeed provocative as it was, could not be allowed to rupture the links with America, a country of key importance to Japan both as a market and as a supplier of much-needed capital.

There was in fact not much substance to the idea, canvassed in some American newspapers at the time, that the Japanese government adopted 'a low posture' as soon as it heard of the plans for the American battle fleet. There was, for example, no noticeable hurry to implement the Gentlemen's Agreement – this was not resolved to American satisfaction until early the following year – and Hayashi, the Foreign Minister, firmly rejected American proposals for an official immigration treaty. Furthermore, he rebuked the ambassador in Washington, Aoki Shuzo, for having proposed off his own bat, in a private talk with Roosevelt, a Japanese–American declaration of friendly intentions, which would dispel rumours of impending war. Soon afterwards Aoki was removed from his post. Although personal enmity was involved, Hayashi's treatment of Aoki and, in particular, his quick repudiation of Aoki's initiative show that he appreciated the importance of not appearing in the eyes of the world to be needlessly conciliatory under foreign pressure. He had not forgotten the Triple Intervention.

Yet the plans for the battle fleet did have a sobering effect on those whom American and British diplomats described, in loose but suitable language, as 'extremists' – as opposed to 'moderates'. (The distinction was perceived to be vital in the 1930s and later.) But a vivid example of a change of heart was provided by Okuma Shigenobu, a former and future prime minister, a somewhat unpredictable political stormy petrel, veteran of many a clash with the Elder Statesmen, the *Genro*, to whose select company he seemed qualified, by reason of age and experience, to belong. This colourful old man had been justly blamed by Ambassador Aoki, in telegrams from Washington, for inflaming anti-American feeling in Japan. But in November 1907 Okuma issued a statement to the press urging the Cabinet to cooperate fully with the United States on the immigration problem; and Okuma's statement suggested that further Japanese emigration to America was now undesirable. It seems likely, as Professor Esthus claims, that this change of front was prompted by the impending movements of the American fleet, 'not by a new insight into the immigration question on the part of the aged stateman'.[10]

Okuma and his contemporaries, it should not be forgotten, were boys approaching manhood when Commodore Perry's 'black ships' first appeared off the Japanese coast. About a decade later this generation, now fully adult, witnessed the superior power of Western navies in the Inland Sea and elsewhere. Yamagata, for example, commanded a body of men that fought in vain in 1864 against British, American and other foreign sailors who captured and dismantled the forts at Shimonoseki. Nothing so craven as straightforward fear found a conscious place in the make-up of the true samurai. Respect for a dominant opponent was another matter. Thus the bombardment of Kagoshima in 1863 had laid the foundations of the long association between the navies of Great Britain and Japan. As the Japanese proverb has it, *shippai wa seiko no moto* ('failure is the basis of success').

Almost a year after Okuma's volte-face Roosevelt's 'Great White Fleet' anchored off Yokohama, on its way round the world. The fleet had already enjoyed an enthusiastic welcome in New Zealand and Australia, much to Roosevelt's gratification, for he hoped that welcome would convey a certain message to London. He had not been pleased by Sir Edward Grey's refusal to be involved in any kind of joint diplomatic action on the immigration issue. Grey, convinced of the overriding importance of the Japanese alliance, had deftly avoided making common cause with the Americans.

The Japanese reception in October 1908 for the American warships and their 14,000 officers and men was no less cordial than the greeting accorded the Royal Navy in the same season three years before. During a week of festivities, as Admiral Charles Sperry, in command of the fleet, reported in a letter home, 'there was literally nothing in the way of comfort or convenience that was not provided'.[11] Whatever may have been the effect of the announcement about the movement of the fleet a year earlier, the ships themselves on their arrival certainly impressed the people of Japan.*

By this time there had been a change of Cabinet in Japan. Katsura was back in office. Komura had returned to the Foreign Ministry. In a bid to improve relations with America, Komura instructed Aoki's successor, Takahira, to approach Roosevelt with a proposal very similar

---

* It is an interesting thought that it was just possible for a man or woman to have seen within their lifetime three American armadas at anchor below the Hommoku cliff at Yokohama – Perry's in 1854, Sperry's in 1908, and Nimitz's in 1945.

to Aoki's brain-child of the previous year. The first moves were made as the American fleet departed on the next stage of its voyage, and they culminated in a formal exchange of diplomatic notes on 30 November 1908, commonly but (to be pedantic) erroneously called the Root–Takahira Agreement. It did not touch on the immigration question, and indeed its content was not elaborate. The Root–Takahira exchange was a prime example of declaratory diplomacy; it stated that the United States and Japan would respect each other's possessions in the Pacific, while encouraging 'the free and peaceful development of their commerce' in that region. The two governments agreed to maintain the *status quo* in the Pacific, and they affirmed the independence and integrity of China, together with the principle of equal opportunity in China for the commerce and industry of all nations.

The Root–Takahira exchange of notes, like the Taft–Katsura accord and the Ishii–Lansing exchange of notes of a later date, meant much more to the Japanese than the Americans. The former naturally endeavoured to obtain the maximum mileage from such agreements. For all three, by a sanguine interpretation, could be taken to imply American acquiescence in the consolidation, if not the enlargement, of Japan's position on the Asian continent. Admittedly the Root–Takahira exchange makes no reference to Japan's Korean protectorate or to Japan's position in Manchuria. But what was unsaid seemed to be understood. 'The United States accepted Japanese expansion on the continent of Asia, while Japan recognised the impossibility of expansion into the white-dominated areas of the Pacific.'[12] That, in a nutshell, appeared to be the position at the end of the Roosevelt era.

The real situation, however, was far less promising. We must leave to the next chapter a brief discussion of American efforts to participate in railway operations and construction in Manchuria. Since Japan and the United States had quite different views on the 'Open Door', American rhetoric on 'equal opportunity', not to mention 'the integrity of China', was often misinterpreted as nothing but a cover for commercial greed. American businessmen were decidedly assertive in their desire to open up the China market; which included, of course, Manchuria. Fears about American economic ambitions in Manchuria probably carried more weight, for the Japanese oligarchy, than the emotions roused by the racial discord in California.

Yet the troubles in California and the war scare left a permanent mark, especially on the American side. The war scare died down, but the embers fired in 1907 smouldered on. The matter is well summed up by Professor Iriye: 'All factors – political, economic, racial, cultural – combined to create a particular attitude toward Japanese expansion, which was never to leave American consciousness until the end of World War II.'[13]

7 Japan, China and the First World War

There are many things going on in many places that I do not like: it is an inevitable consequence of being engaged in a huge war.

SIR EDWARD GREY

I

WE have now to consider a decade, 1909–19, of the utmost significance for Japan and the West in Asia; for during those ten years the balance of power, already affected by the Russo-Japanese War, shifted firmly in Japan's favour. On the world stage the great events of the decade were without doubt the World War, the Russian Revolution, and the Paris peace settlement. The Far East, in the same period, witnessed the annexation of Korea, the Chinese Revolution of 1911–12, Japan's 'Twenty-One Demands' on China, and the leading part played by the Japanese in the Allied intervention in Siberia.

Within Japan itself there was a striking contrast between 1919 and the situation ten years earlier. The First World War (like the Korean War of 1950–3) provided the economy with a golden opportunity for recovery and expansion. The Japanese financial and economic condition on the eve of the First World War was neither stable nor healthy, despite some substantial growth. Between the end of the Russo-Japanese War and the outbreak of war in Europe there was an unfavourable trade balance. The population was growing fast, the net increase being in the region of six million in ten years; and the nation had ceased to be self-sufficient in food supplies, was indeed importing rice along with other foodstuffs, although in earlier years Japan had been a food-exporting country. (The first deal ever negotiated by the Mitsui trading company after it opened its London branch had been for a shipment to Britain of Japanese rice.)

By Armistice Day 1918, the scene was transformed almost beyond recognition, thanks to insatiable Allied requirements and to new openings for exports in overseas markets that could no longer rely on their European suppliers. During the First World War, Mitsui, Mitsubishi and other trading houses, in the words of a Japanese economic historian, 'even advanced into trade between third countries (trade not involving Japanese imports or exports) and, as a result, they made huge profits, establishing themselves as powerful international traders'.[1] Not only light industry but heavy industry also achieved a great leap forward. It was during this period that the foundations were laid of the fully industrialised Japanese economy of the second half of this century. In short, Japan's military competence, demonstrated in the Russian war, was now matched by commercial and industrial strength.

The previous chapter discussed the rift in Japanese–American relations caused by the immigration issue. A further source of trouble was Manchuria. It will be remembered that Harriman, the American 'railroad king', was thwarted in his ambition to purchase a half share in the control of the Manchurian railway system. Soon after that disappointment, he died. But in Wall Street and Washington there was keen interest in financing railway development in Manchuria and China; an interest which seemed to reflect the aims of American foreign policy no less than the aspirations of private entrepreneurs. Several plans were put forward, the most startling being a proposal from Taft's Secretary of State, Philander Knox, for what was described as the 'neutralisation' of the Manchurian railways. This project, first aired in 1909, envisaged the transfer by Russia and Japan of their respective lines in Manchuria to an international consortium centred on four New York banks. When Britain was approached by the State Department, the Foreign Office had little hesitation in rejecting a scheme which it regarded as clumsy and ill-timed. Indeed, the project never got off the ground. But it perturbed the Russians and Japanese; the result being that they drew closer together, and Japanese distrust of American intentions was sharply enhanced.

It had now become clear that the Japanese looked upon South Manchuria as their own exclusive sphere of influence and would tolerate no foreign economic activity that might compete with their own ventures in the area. Although, as we have seen, Katsura was ready, just after the Russian war, to accept foreign participation in the economic development of South Manchuria, this attitude was not sustained. The army, in particular, would not brook intrusion by outsiders. Lip service to the 'Open Door' was maintained. Practice followed a different course. Not without good reason from their point of view, the Americans strenuously objected to Japan's virtual monopoly of economic as well as political power in South Manchuria. But the Russians and British accepted the *fait accompli*; as for the Chinese – the most interested party of all – being impotent, they were compelled to follow suit.

In any event, China in 1911 entered a new stage of her history. Insurrection shook and then overturned the Ch'ing monarchy. For control of the state two contenders emerged, Sun Yat-sen and Yuan Shih-k'ai. We need not dwell here on the complicated series of events that produced the final ascendancy of Yuan Shih-k'ai. What concerns us is the Japanese response to the revolution in China, a revolution which, so it seems, took the Japanese by surprise and found them, therefore, bewildered and unprepared.

Even today in some circles in Japan there is a conviction that geographical propinquity and the elements of a shared cultural past confer a unique insight into the Chinese mind. In this belief such Japanese delude themselves; for the history, national temper and ideals of the Japanese make them in many important respects utterly different from the Chinese. But the delusion flourished with peculiar strength in the last years of the nineteenth century and the first four decades of the twentieth. There was some excuse, it must be said, for this particular Japanese attitude towards China and the Chinese. For many years before the Revolution of 1911–12 the Japanese – as government officials, military men, traders and private adventurers – had dabbled in the affairs of China. Furthermore, after the Russo-Japanese War more Chinese went to Japan for study than to any other country; and Japan provided a refuge, a source of funds, and of disinterested as well as Machiavellian encouragement, for Chinese political dissidents, of whom Sun Yat-sen was the most famous.

The one sure bond between Chinese, such as Dr Sun, and their Japanese friends and backers was their shared intention to diminish (to put it mildly) the power of the West in the Far East; a motive powerful enough, indeed, to cement any partnership. Yet, as we saw earlier, the Japanese leadership – thanks in great measure to the English Alliance – was not eager to acknowledge that racial factors played a part in the shaping of Japan's national policy. Outside high government circles, however, it was another matter. The patriotic societies, for example, had for many years preached Japan's 'sacred mission' to liberate Korea from the dead hand of the past. Associated closely with this aim was another – the liberation of China from the fetters of the West; and here much emphasis was placed on a supposed community of racial feeling with the Chinese.

Difficulties, at least from the Chinese point of view, arose when thought was given to the way the Japanese might see the future, once Western imperialism had been expunged. Equality of status, one of the fundamental principles of modern international law, is far from being a basic tenet of the Confucian outlook on life. Except for a small minority of enlightened souls it was not in the nature of the Chinese or the Japanese to see each other as being on a truly equal footing. So those Japanese most nearly concerned with Chinese affairs perceived Japan to be China's mentor as well as friend. That was, we might say, the respectable, idealist, view. But many factors – impatience, disappointment, ambition, or plain greed – could turn aside the promptings of altruism; and so it often happened that those who hoped to guide and teach became, sooner or later, manipulators, puppet-masters, the agents of the Japanese imperial dream in whatever form this might be clothed.

For the Japanese a question never totally resolved was what type of régime in China was most desirable. From the viewpoint of the oligarchy, the radical groups led by Sun Yat-sen were an uncertain quantity, since they were backed by the firebrands of the Japanese patriotic societies, the implacable ultra-nationalist critics of the Tokyo 'Establishment'. If the Americans were stirred by the appearance of a 'sister republic' across the Pacific, Japan's leaders were less enchanted by this indication of possibly farreaching political and social change; so they hesitated to give official support to Sun's revolutionary movement. The conservative veteran, Yuan Shi'kai, seemed a safer bet, in spite of the fact that he was generally distrusted by Japanese officials. When, by 1913, it was evident that Yuan Shi'kai was firmly in the saddle, while Sun Yat-sen was once again a refugee in Japan, caution seemed to have been justified. At the same time, strictly unofficial Japanese activity was directed not only to sustaining Dr Sun but also towards clandestine manoeuvres in Manchuria and Inner Mongolia, looking to a possible restoration of some form of Chinese monarchy.[2]

The Chinese for their part could not have been heartened by the final extinction of what was left of Korea's independence, when Japan annexed the country in August 1910. To be sure, it may well have appeared inconceivable to most Chinese that a like fate could overtake their own vast territory. Yet Korea, as we have seen, was swallowed up in stages, its fully colonial subjection being preceded by a phase (lasting only a few years) during which it was a Japanese protected state – Korean foreign affairs, defence, and internal security being under Japanese control. Not quite five years would pass after the annexation of Korea before China, too, would face a state of affairs that could have made her, in all but name, a Japanese protectorate. For that must have been the result of China's acceptance of all 'Twenty-One Demands' presented by Japan at the beginning of 1915. However, before discussing that remarkable ultimatum, which had enduring consequences for both China and Japan, a word has to be said about Japan's reaction to the outbreak of war in Europe in August 1914.

It is interesting to note that when war broke out Great Britain did not expect her Japanese ally to take an active part in the struggle. The Anglo-Japanese Alliance had been renewed in 1911 for a further ten years, certain alterations being made to ensure that the treaty terms would not apply if either power became involved in a dispute with the United States. All the same, it seems that officials in London hardly thought the treaty would call for Japan's participation in Britain's war with Germany. The possibility indeed was (in the words of Dr Nish) 'remote from their thinking'.[3] Later on, the British naval Commander-in-Chief in the Far East was to admit, in a letter home, that 'nothing was further from anyone's thoughts than that Japan would be asked or even allowed to step in'.[4]

As soon as Britain was at war, however, the Admiralty, at least, realised that it was essential to have Japanese help in dealing with German commerce raiders in Far Eastern waters. Yet the Foreign Secretary, Sir Edward Grey, was unenthusiastic. At the end of a telegram to Tokyo, instructing the British ambassador to ask for Japanese naval assistance, Grey declared: 'It means of course an act of war against Germany but we do not see how this can be avoided.'[5]

Having sent these instructions, Grey remained uneasy. Reports reaching him from Washington, Peking and Hong Kong showed that the prospect of Japan entering the war disturbed the Americans and the Chinese; for Japanese operations against the German base at Tsingtao would surely lead to subsequent Japanese penetration and probably control of much of Shantung Province. Australia, New Zealand – the Netherlands, too, for that matter – were apprehensive; their worries concerned the German islands in the Pacific, the Carolines and Marshalls. If Japan were to seize the islands she would be inclined to retain them for ever.

The Japanese lost no time in assuring Grey that they were preparing to declare war on Germany, that having done so they were not thinking of restricting their operations in any way. Which meant, of course, that they intended to attack Tsingtao. This response alarmed Grey; and he now tried to discourage Japan from entering the war. This naturally gave offence to Tokyo, without in the least deflecting Japan's determination to take part in the war.

Altogether, Grey's handling of the matter was far from adroit and may be said to have damaged British prestige in Japanese eyes. This was the more unfortunate since the Foreign Minister was Kato Takaaki, a former Japanese ambassador in London, a very strong personality, who enjoyed Grey's friendship. But the historian in his study must be fair: it is right to remember that in the early days of August 1914 the Foreign Secretary was faced with a multiplicity of pressures. He could hardly be expected to devote much time for calm reflection on the consequences his action might have on the susceptibilities of an ally far from the storm centre in Europe.

The Germans were given an ultimatum by Tokyo. They were 'advised', in language not unintentionally reminiscent of the Triple Intervention, to withdraw or disarm their naval and other vessels in the Far East. They were also 'advised' to surrender Tsingtao and the Kiaochow leased territory to Japan, 'with a view to the eventual restoration of the same to China'. The ultimatum was to expire on 23 August 1914. No reply having been received by that date, Japan declared war.

Opinion in Japan as to the likely outcome of the war in Europe was by no means unanimous. On the whole, the army favoured Germany's chances of success; while the navy with its pro-British bias took the opposite view. There was, in any case, a good deal of inter-service jealousy, even rancour, which the course of the European war did nothing to assuage. The army's rather low estimation of Britain's military capabilities compared with those of Germany, seemed confirmed by the operations at Tsingtao. The siege of this German outpost in China was not an exclusively Japanese affair; for a token force of British and Indian troops took part in it under Japanese command. This force consisted indeed of no more than one Welsh battalion and a half-battalion of Sikhs. The fighting qualities of this small contingent appears not to have measured up to the expectations of the Japanese; damaging reports, doubtless exaggerated, of the poor showing of their ally circulated in the press; and a British consular report spoke of adverse comments on British army officers made by Japanese officers to

Chinese officials. The Japanese, it is said, remarked that British officers 'come from wealthy families and are therefore unfitted for the hardships and dangers of a campaign'.[6] It would have been wiser, perhaps, for London not to have pressed for British participation in the siege. As for the German garrison at Tsingtao, it resisted with vigour for some two weeks before surrendering early in November.

In those first months of the war the Royal Navy was not so dramatically successful as to fulfil the expectations of its opposite numbers and former pupils in Japan. For example, there was no close blockade of Helgoland Bight and the North Sea exit of the Kiel Canal. In the Russian war the Japanese had run serious risks in their close blockade of Port Arthur; but submarine and mine technology had advanced since that time. Nevertheless, the fully justified caution shown by the Admiralty seemed inconsistent with the 'Nelson touch', or indeed with the aggressive spirit long associated with Sir John Fisher, who had been called back to duty as First Sea Lord. Furthermore, there were such setbacks as the destruction by U-boat on a single September morning in the North Sea of the three cruisers, *Aboukir*, *Hogue* and *Cressy*. Then, five weeks later the Royal Navy suffered off Coronel on the coast of Chile its first defeat in a sea battle for well over a hundred years. This was redeemed, it is true, a month later at the Falkland Isles. But in terms of prestige something had been lost – the bloom, perhaps, on a reputation for invincibility?

As the Australians, New Zealanders and Dutch had feared, Japan took possession of nearly all the German islands in the Pacific. Yet this was not inevitable. Britain and the Dominions were in the war some three weeks before the Japanese; and a little more energy and dispatch on the part of the Australians would have enabled them to occupy most of the islands ahead of the Japanese. Indeed, Australian forces quickly captured German New Guinea and Samoa but appear to have assumed that this meant that Australia now had a legal claim to the German islands to the north; so there was no hurry to proceed further. In any case, London at first apparently 'did not envisage that the Japanese navy would extend its operations into the German Pacific Islands'.[7]

The price of complacency was Japanese occupation of the German islands north of the Equator, a gain retained after the war. Nominally League of Nations mandates entrusted to Japan, the Carolines and Marshalls provided the Japanese navy with anchorages and training areas of great strategic value a generation later.

II

It was during these early months of the First World War that the Japanese prepared the extraordinary *diktat* known as the 'Twenty-One Demands'. These represented the work of many hands, reflecting a variety of military, diplomatic, financial, commercial and other interests. The military attaché in Peking, for example, was involved in some of the planning; but the text of the Demands was drafted by a bureau chief in the Tokyo Foreign Ministry; whose predecessor, as it happened, had been murdered by a young Japanese patriot, who had then committed *hara-kiri* kneeling on a large map of China. For ultra-nationalists commonly regarded the Foreign Ministry as timid to the point of cowardice in its attitude to Yuan Shi'kai's regime. This condemnation of the Foreign Ministry found favour with Sun Yat-sen, whose hatred of Yuan Shi'kai was such that he wrote to Count Okuma (Prime Minister from the spring of 1914) promising generous commercial concessions to Japan in return for help in overthrowing the Peking government. It is not surprising that Sun Yat-sen has been described as 'at times, an apologist for Japanese aggression, and even an instrument of that aggression'.[8]

But the driving force behind the whole exercise was the Foreign Minister, Kato Takaaki. The Prime Minister, Okuma, in earlier days formidable (indeed he was one of the makers of the evolving Meiji state), was now no longer a dominant figure. The strong man in the Okuma Cabinet was Kato. It was indicative of his independent character that he broke with the custom of consulting the *Genro*, the Elder Statesmen, on important questions of foreign policy. This turned out to be unwise. Yamagata, the leading *Genro* since Ito's assassination by a Korean in 1909, did not forgive Kato for this offence.

It is the view of one historian that the origins of the 'Twenty-One Demands' 'extend back to the last year of Kato's period in London as Japanese ambassador'.[9] That is perhaps putting it rather too strongly. Nevertheless, it is true that before relinquishing his post in London, Kato discussed very frankly with Sir Edward Grey Japan's long-range aspirations in South Manchuria. There were two meetings with Grey in January 1913 at which these particular discussions took place. They were informal and were not, it seems, fully documented. But it is at least clear that Grey did not object when Kato told him that Japan wanted a free hand in negotiating an extension of the leases in South Manchuria – Port Arthur, the Kwantung territory, and the South Manchurian

Railway zone – which were due to expire in 1923. Kato and Grey, as we noted earlier, were on close personal terms. Grey always believed that Japan would have to expand, and he considered expansion in northeast Asia less harmful to British interests than expansion elsewhere. It is most unlikely that Grey could have encouraged Kato to suppose that Japan could rely on British support for demands on China beyond those relating to South Manchuria. Still, Kato seems to have persuaded himself that Britain was ready to give him *carte blanche* in any future negotiations he would conduct with the Chinese. Is it possible that British complaisance in the matter of the Korean protectorate (not the annexation, of which London expressed mild disapproval) helped to promote this wishful thinking?

At all events, once war broke out in Europe, Japan's opportunity in China had clearly arrived. Nobody could tell how soon the war would be over, but in the autumn of 1914 few thought the struggle could last more than another year at most. The preoccupations of the European powers gave Japan an opening not to be missed.

The Demands having been drafted, the Japanese Minister in Peking was told to present them at a moment to be chosen by Tokyo. The moment came in January 1915. President Yuan Shi'kai was given the ultimatum under conditions of strict secrecy which he was adjured to observe. There were sixteen 'demands' and five 'desires', set out in five groups. The first of these concerned the captured German leased territory in Shantung. The Chinese were asked to assent to any future Japanese–German agreement on the disposal of Germany's rights and interests; and Japan was to be granted additional commercial benefits in Shantung. The second group of demands extended the Manchurian leases to ninety-nine years, and further rights were to be granted in Inner Mongolia as well as South Manchuria. The third group called for Chinese consent to monopoly rights for an existing Japanese industrial complex in the Yangtze valley. The fourth required the Chinese to promise 'not to cede or lease to any other Power any harbour or bay or any island along the coast of China'.[10]

Those four groups seem farreaching enough even if the fifth group of 'desires' had not existed. But Kato evidently believed that when bargaining with the Chinese you must always ask for more than you expect to get. This, perhaps, was why the fifth group was included in the ultimatum. Yet it is worth quoting what Kato wrote, concerning these 'desires', in his instructions to his representative in Peking:

As regards the proposals contained in the fifth group, they are presented as the wishes of the Imperial Government. The matters which are dealt with under this category are entirely different in character from those which are included in the first four groups. An adjustment, at this time, of these matters, some of which have been pending between the two countries, being nevertheless highly desirable . . . you are also requested to exercise your best efforts to have our wishes carried out.[11]

The fifth group (the 'desires') called upon the Chinese government to engage 'influential Japanese' as political, financial and military advisers; to allow Japanese hospitals, temples and schools in the interior of China to own land; to place police administration under joint Sino-Japanese control 'where such arrangements are necessary'; to purchase war material from Japan; to authorise Japanese construction of certain new railways; to admit no foreign capital for railways, mines and harbour works in Fukien Province without prior consultation with Japan; to grant 'to Japanese subjects the right of preaching in China'.[12]

It will be seen that acceptance of Group V would have brought China more than half-way under Japan's direct political supervision. The inept attempt to bind Yuan Shi'kai to secrecy only made matters worse. When the news was leaked a shock wave swept through China and the Chinese communities overseas, spreading to affect American public opinion, which was greatly disturbed. Official and business circles in Britain and the Dominions were also alarmed.

Kato's folly in overplaying his hand was compounded by his lack of candour in his initial dealings with London; for his first communication to Grey on the matter omitted all mention of the 'desires' (Group V). Knowing nothing of this fifth group, *The Times* brought out a leading article cordially supporting Japan, dismissing reports of commotion in Peking as being of no significance, and declaring that Japan's demands 'do not in any way threaten the integrity of China'.[13] But once the full story was known in London the reaction was sharp. Kato was warned that Group V could not be reconciled with the terms of the Anglo-Japanese Alliance.

As an exercise in *realpolitik*, brutality in the handling of foreign relations is only effective when it achieves its goal with speed and precision. But the crisis of the 'Twenty-One Demands' was not quickly resolved. Yuan Shi'kai showed masterly skill in the tactics of procrastination, delaying any kind of decision for nearly six months. His final throw was to send a trusted emissary (a Japanese) to Yamagata, appealing for help against Kato and the Okuma Cabinet.

Yamagata was convinced that by creating a storm of protest in China, including a damaging boycott of Japanese goods, Kato's policy had done Japan much harm. So in May he and his fellow *Genro* intervened, meeting the whole Cabinet and urging Kato to drop the 'desires' embodied in Group V. Yamagata was to say later that this fifth group, if forced upon China, would have disgraced the honour of Japan.

The Cabinet withdrew the offending 'desires'. But the harm was done. Chinese mistrust of Japanese intentions now matched the wildest fears expressed on the American West Coast. In any case, China was compelled, under the direct threat of armed action, to accept the first four groups of demands; a severe humiliation, even though some of these had been modified in the course of earlier negotiations.

If on a short view Japan extracted some profit from this affair, the cost in terms of the alienation of Chinese opinion was incalculable. In America, too, the adverse effects were serious and lasting.

It might be asked whether there was no protest by Japanese radical dissenters on ideological, if not ethical, grounds against their nation's aggressive China policy. Public opinion, however, was driven on the whole by impulses of primitive chauvinism. The infant socialist movement of earlier days had suffered a mortal blow in 1911, when the police uncovered an anarchist plot to murder the greatly venerated Emperor Meiji. A trial *in camera* had been followed by the execution of those said to have been most seriously involved. Left-wing thought was, for the time being, anathema. The authorities could now nip in the bud every overt manifestation of socialist opinion. In their vigilance they were able to bank on the cooperation of the great majority of the people, thanks to the shock of the anarchist conspiracy. Such was the situation in 1915, before rising prices and events in Russia introduced an altogether new mood.

Yuan Shi'kai died in 1916, not long after an abortive effort to make himself the first emperor of a new dynasty. China now lapsed into the confusion of the warlord era, the nominal government in Peking being underpinned by Japanese money, in the form of 'loans' granted ostensibly for China's economic development. Marshal Terauchi, Okuma's successor as Prime Minister, was one of Yamagata's henchmen; and the policy was to control China by bribes rather than threats.

III

The end of the war in Europe in November 1918, like most events in that continent, took the Japanese by surprise. The army could hardly believe that it was Hindenburg who had pressed for an armistice. Even less credible was the news that the German army would have to withdraw from Russia and Poland as well as from Belgium and the occupied areas of northern France.

Thoughts in Tokyo had to concentrate rapidly on the prospective peace conference in Paris, on the gains to be consolidated and, if possible, enlarged. The Japanese delegation had one prime objective; namely, the recognition of the claim to the inheritance of all German rights and possessions in Shantung and the Pacific islands. A secondary aim was to obtain from the powers represented at Paris a declaration that they accepted the principle of racial equality. Both prime and secondary objectives encountered serious opposition at the conference table. Japan wanted the declaration of racial equality to be written into the Covenant of the newly created League of Nations. Today it appears bizarre, to say the least, that this demand should have been rejected. In this matter Britain was unhelpful to her ally. For the views of the Australians carried weight, being voiced in trenchant style by their forceful Premier, Billy Hughes. In search of a compromise, the Japanese delegation agreed to drop the word 'race', proposing that the Covenant should 'recognise the principle of equality of nations of just treatment of their nationals'. The League commission accepted this by a majority of eleven to five; but it was now that President Wilson displayed the jesuitical ingenuity not uncharacteristic of high-minded academics who venture into the political arena. As chairman of the commission, Wilson ruled that a resolution on a matter of principle required a unanimous vote. So even the compromise proposal was defeated.

It was only with difficulty that the Japanese received satisfaction in the matter of Shantung and the Pacific islands. The Chinese, as might be expected, were adamantly hostile. Yet their attitude was more rigid and united than the Japanese anticipated. China's delegation at Paris embraced two competing parties, representing the official government in Peking and a rival Kuomintang administration at Canton. In September 1918 the Peking government had been induced, in return for a railway loan, to sign a secret exchange of notes with Japan, confirming in effect the Shantung settlement imposed by the 'Twenty-One Demands'. When negotiating the 1918 agreement the Chinese

Minister in Tokyo was incautious enough, in a communication to the Japanese Foreign Minister, to write: 'I beg to acquaint you that the Chinese government gladly agree.' This was just what the Japanese needed; they could now counter the argument that the Shantung settlement of May 1915 had been accepted by China under duress. They played this card soon after the Paris conference opened. It took even some of the Peking delegates by surprise, for the secret had been well kept.[14]

Pressure of public opinion at home, pressure from the Canton delegates, and their own suspicions of Japan induced the Peking plenipotentiaries to join forces temporarily with their Canton compatriots in resisting Japan's Shantung claims when these came before the conference. Their stand was supported by President Wilson and the Secretary of State, Lansing. Accordingly, the Japanese played two more of their cards; aces, both of them. The Japanese revealed that in 1917 they had obtained through secret treaties signed with Britain, France, Italy and Russia, a pledge by those countries that they would support Japan's claims to Germany's rights and possessions in Shantung and the central Pacific. Secondly, they let it be known that if Chinese objections to the Shantung claim were upheld, Japan would withdraw from the conference, and therefore from participation in the League of Nations.

1917 was one of the two great pivotal years in the history of this century so far (the other, of course, being 1945). But if 1917 is remembered above all because of the Bolshevik usurpation of power, other events of that year were of more than usual significance – such as America's entry into the war in April, and China's in August. In the winter of 1916–17, however, American belligerence was still in doubt; and the season was a grim one for the British Isles. Losses from U-boat action had become critical. So in January 1917 Japan was pressed to send a destroyer flotilla to Malta; for this would enable Britain to transfer destroyers from the Mediterranean for convoy and U-boat hunting duties in the Atlantic. It was realised in London that Tokyo would expect something in return for agreeing to this request. There was no surprise, then, when Japan sought a guarantee of support for the Shantung and Pacific claims, and there was no real hesitation to giving the guarantee.

It cannot be said that the Japanese drove a hard bargain – such as the one clinched a generation later by Franklin Roosevelt, when he secured from Britain in her extremity the lease of West Indian bases in exchange for fifty superannuated American destroyers. In fact, Japanese naval assistance – a cruiser and two destroyer flotillas for Malta – was granted very readily, before any *quid pro quo* was arranged. The Japanese made only one condition. Their ships were not to operate under British command.

In view of this British commitment of 1917, and because of similar commitments to Japan by France and Italy, Wilson and Lansing, for all their concern to give the fullest support to China, faced an impasse. It was the Japanese threat to leave Paris – as Orlando of Italy had done – that shook President Wilson, persuading him, much to Lansing's chagrin, to accept Japan's case in the matter of Shantung. Without Japan the League of Nations would be crippled from the start (Russia, convulsed by civil war, could play no part for the moment in any such organisation). Lansing was quite sure that Japan was bluffing, that she would never miss the chance of being one of the great powers on the League Council. Back in the United States after the conference Lansing continued to criticise Wilson's policy on such lines. But he was wrong. The Japanese at Paris were not bluffing. If they received no satisfaction they were prepared to go home.

In a way, that might have been preferable to what happened; namely, China's angry refusal to sign the peace treaty and, more important, America's failure to ratify it; which meant a League minus the United States. For it was the Shantung settlement (Articles 156–8 of the Versailles Treaty) that proved to be Wilson's Achilles heel when the treaty came before the United States Senate.

Lansing's resolute pro-Chinese stance at Paris was peculiarly galling to the Japanese. For they had attached altogether too much importance to the vague American–Japanese understanding symbolised by the Lansing–Ishii Notes of November 1917. These had been exchanged in Washington when Ishii Kikujiro (a former Foreign Minister) had arrived in an effort to place relations with the United States on a more friendly footing. Ishii's mission was not an outstanding success; but in the exchange of Notes at Washington the State Department declared that America recognised that 'territorial propinquity creates special interests between countries and, consequently, the Government of the United States recognises that Japan has special interests in China, especially the part to which her possessions are contiguous'. Ishii on his side went on record with a long declaration of respect for the 'Open Door' and the integrity of China.[15]

As was to be expected, in the Lansing–Ishii Notes it was the phrase, 'special interests in China', and the term, 'propinquity', that gave particular satisfaction to the Japanese. At Paris the Americans could argue that since Shantung was not 'contiguous' to Japan's possessions the Lansing–Ishii formula did not apply. But Tokyo could not or would not see the merit of this contention. Just as Kato convinced himself that he had won Grey's full backing in the London talks, so Ishii imagined that he gained Lansing's tacit consent to Japanese plans in Shantung. For he appreciated that Lansing, unlike Wilson, was a realist; although Ishii would have been astonished, no doubt, to learn that at one stage during the war years Lansing actually favoured the idea of transferring the control of the Philippines to Japan, because he believed the colonial status of those islands weakened the United States in its dealings with the Japanese.[16] The so-called 'Lansing–Ishii Agreement' did more harm than good to American–Japanese relations, since it raised expectations on both sides that could scarcely be fulfilled. Another cause of friction and suspicion was the Siberian imbroglio; but this must be left for discussion in the next chapter.

Thus Japan emerged from the First World War with her material standing greatly enhanced. Japan's tactics at Paris, moreover, could be described as masterly. Yet the unswerving pursuit of advantage in Shantung repeated the blunder of the 'Twenty-One Demands' and was therefore on a long view counter-productive. It led to a further deterioration in relations with the United States at the very moment when the Chinese boycott and the Bolshevik Revolution created new problems for Japan. There was a new spirit abroad in 1918 and 1919, compounded of Wilsonian ideals and Marxist ideology. This new spirit was a factor of immense significance with which the old world in Japan, as well as in the West, would have to wrestle in the years ahead.

8   The Nineteen-Twenties

Now the world is thirsty for happiness and security in individual life, and for peace and friendship in international relations.

SHIDEHARA KIJURO

I

AMONG the great majority of the Japanese people the ending of the war in Europe aroused little interest. In fact there seem to have been areas of the countryside in which at least some people were not even aware that the struggle had taken place. A British army language officer, recording an encounter with such folk, tells us that they were incredulous when he assured them that there was war in Europe and that Japan was taking part in it. 'Their incredulity was based on the fact that the young men of the village had not been called up for service. If Japan was really at war, they argued, surely all the male youths of the country would be summoned to the colours.'[1]

The event of 1918 that made the greatest impact on Japan was not the November Armistice on the Western Front but the Rice Riots, the explosion of social protest that occurred in August of that year. A combination of exorbitant prices and well-founded rumours of profiteering brought crowds out into the streets all over Japan, to attack the shops and warehouses of rice-dealers. Order had to be restored by the army. The disturbances were on a far larger scale than those of 1905, at the time of the Portsmouth Treaty. More than a hundred lives were lost; and there was widespread arson. No town seems to have escaped its share of violence. The patience of the working class in city and countryside had been strained beyond endurance, and it snapped abruptly, with shattering violence.

These alarming events took place at the very moment when the government decided to send an expeditionary force to Siberia. It was a decision reached only after severe and prolonged debate within the oligarchy, and it was announced as an operation designed to comply with the desires of the United States. For in July 1918 the American government, reversing its policy of non-intervention in Russian affairs, had invited Japan to join in a limited expedition, intended (in Lansing's words) 'to aid Czechoslovaks against German and Austrian prisoners'. It is easy with hindsight to dismiss those words as a threadbare cover for other designs of an economic and political character. As it turned out, the German and Austrian prisoners-of-war in their Siberian camps were never a real threat to the Czechs or anyone else. Moreover, by August 1918 the Czechoslovak corps, on its anabasis from the Eastern Front to the Pacific, was in conflict on the Trans-Siberian line with Bolshevik forces rather than with armed prisoners-of-war (even if the latter included, as a major element, bitterly anti-Czech Hungarians). There was talk of 'rescuing' the Czechs, but by August they showed they were well able to look after themselves. Indeed, strung out along the line from the Urals to Vladivostok, they were manifestly the best-organised military force in that vast and politically chaotic area. Military help for the Czechs necessarily involved some kind of confrontation with the Bolsheviks.

To see the situation as it was perceived by the Allies at the time, two factors have to be borne in mind. In the first place there was the disturbing impression made by the Treaty of Brest-Litovsk, the peace agreement dictated by the Germans in the spring of 1918, whereby the Bolshevik government seemed to have beecome almost a puppet regime manipulated by Berlin. There were genuine fears in Paris and London that the German army, having occupied a huge region of European Russia, would sooner or later push further east. Secondly, the weight of the German offensive on the Western Front in 1918 had been such as to threaten the very survival of France; and the peril facing Britain appeared almost equally grave. It had looked at one time as though there would be a breakthrough to the Channel ports. By the summer, it is true, the German thrust was held. But in early August the tide had not yet turned. So the reconstitution of some kind of Eastern Front in Russia was generally accepted as a vital aim. The main reason why allied help was given to anti-Bolshevik Russian forces in 1918 was that the latter, unlike Lenin's regime, were ready to carry on the war against Germany.

Well before the Bolshevik seizure of power Britain and France had been pressing Japan to send troops through Siberia to Europe, to the Eastern Front. But the Japanese had no thought of committing land forces to a theatre of war so far from home. After Brest-Litovsk, however, and with the rapid spread of Bolshevik influence east of the Urals, voices were heard in Japan calling for intervention. Vladivostok, closer than Tokyo to the cities of Hokkaido, was a tempting prize for believers in Japan's destiny to expand beyond the seas. Revolutionary Marxism, needless to say, was feared as a menace to Japan's traditional values, not to mention Japan's capitalist structure. Finally, during the earlier period of the European war Japanese businessmen had done well in the eastern regions of Siberia; so there were investments to be protected; and not only against Bolshevik confiscation. American competition in Siberia appeared to be an imminent threat. Kerensky's Provisional Government in 1917 had encouraged the Americans to send a team of specialists to modernise the Trans-Siberian line, and there was a notable growth of American interest, economic as well as philan-thropic, in Russian affairs. The replacement of a monarchy by a republic has tended, until recent years at any rate, to inspire alert American observers with feelings in which altruistic goodwill mingles with calculations of the commercial advantages to be gained in the new environment of freedom and democracy. Such had been the response to the Chinese Revolution of 1911-12. Such was to be the reaction to Japan's docile compliance with MacArthur's directives during the Occupation of 1945-52.

Remembering Harriman and Philander Knox, the Japanese feared that American competition, quashed successfully in South Manchuria, would rear its head in eastern Siberia. The good work by Japan in mending her fences with Russia after the Portsmouth Treaty seemed to be in jeopardy. It was not difficult for advocates of a strong line to find good reasons for military action in both the Siberian Maritime Province and northern Manchuria.

Still, for a long time there was no consensus. The generals and admirals seemed, if anything, more cautious than some of the civilian leaders. But once the die was cast, in response to the invitation from Washington, the commitment was much larger than anyone, especially the Americans, had expected. Japan was asked to send about 7000 men. Her contribution was to rise to ten times that figure. The Americans interpreted their own military role in Siberia in a limited, almost passive, sense; so much so that the Japanese, when they thought about it, could be forgiven for regarding the Dough Boys as so many missionaries and merchants in uniform. On the American side, there were the gravest suspicions about Japanese activities and plans. For the mixed bag of anti-Bolshevik Russian officers, armed and financed by the Japanese, included certain Cossack commanders whose treatment of prisoners and the civilian population was barbaric in the extreme.

Soon masters of the railway from Vladivostok to Baikal, the Japanese also occupied localities at the mouth of the Amur. The military action was chiefly directed against Russian partisans, uncoordinated groups of armed peasants who had taken to the forests, usually in protest against the mobilisation of men and requisitioning of supplies by White commanders. The Japanese forces, unlike the Czechs did not do battle with the regular Red Army. Thus they were no more than half-hearted allies of the White Russian armies of Kolchak (the Supreme Ruler at Omsk) which thrust forward west of the Urals in the spring of 1919.

When the Kolchak offensive was first repulsed and then transformed into a retreat, the Siberian partisans, encouraged by news of the Red advance, stepped up their assaults on the Japanese, Czechs and Cossacks along the Trans-Siberian line. The situation, always confused, became a nightmare. A British historian of the Russian Civil War sums it all up in this passage:

Campaigning in Russia was a grim and unpleasant business with the killing cold of the winter, the quagmires of the spring thaw and autumn rains and the plague of mosquitoes in the swamps and forests of the northern summer. And, in the Civil War, there were factors that made for all manner of beastliness in its conduct – the vindictive hatred of the fanatics on either side, the absence of control that opened the way for thugs and sadists, the lust for reprisals that early atrocities let loose. . . . At the top, on both sides, were men of middle and lower middle class origin (the very rich and noble were, throughout, more prominent in the drawing-rooms of the emigration than in the field). In both 'democracy' was tried; found not to work; and dropped.[2]

As the advance of the Red Army gathered pace through the autumn and into the winter of 1919, a tide of humanity flowed eastward by rail and road ahead of the retreating White forces. There was train after train of Czechs (who had now stopped fighting) hoping for embarkation at Vladivostok. There were trains containing Kolchak and his government and the Russian State Gold Reserve. There were trainloads of wounded men. But the major exodus was along the *trakt*; in summer a broad unpaved road parallel with the railway, in winter a ridged ribbon of frozen snow. All was chaotic. Local governments rose and fell, with *coup* and counter-*coup*. Kolchak resigned, was arrested, was almost rescued, was shot; and his body was thrown through the ice of the river at Irkutsk. Meanwhile, the refugees poured into Manchuria and the Maritime Province. The Japanese were able to observe at first hand the disintegration of a European society.

That was, no doubt, an instructive if unedifying spectacle. In any case, control of the Maritime Province brought little profit and no fame to the Japanese. The venture became unpopular. Troop trains in Japan departed with nobody on the platform to wave a flag; an unheard-of break with established custom. The number of young men dodging the draft rose to over a thousand in one year, 'a record figure in Japanese army history'.[3] Another sign of the times was the fact that many officers, conscious of their unpopularity, ceased to wear uniform when off duty in large cities like Tokyo and Osaka. When at last the Japanese pulled out of Siberia in 1922 the general reaction seems to have been one of indifference. 'The army had fought a purposeless war in the frozen wastes of Siberia among a hostile population and had finally been forced to withdraw without achieving anything – and what was worse, the people of Japan did not even seem to care.'[4]

This must appear to conflict with what was stressed in an earlier chapter, on popular backing for a strong foreign policy. The Siberian Expedition, however, presented some special features. There was no great clash of arms; there were few opportunities for spectacular, battlefield heroics. Secondly, the gross profiteering of the war years, which spawned a new class of prominently rich entrepreneurs, had produced the Rice Riots. Among the urban working class a mood had developed pregnant with what the police called 'dangerous throughts'. Marxism started to have a new appeal for a growing number of younger intellectuals. Such stirrings were, to an overwhelming extent, an urban phenomenon. Yet during the early 1920s the banned Communist Party in one or two rural areas of Japan managed to capture and control the local youth associations set up by the government to promote patriotic and ethical education. Industrial disputes increased, with labour unions active in a series of strikes; most of them, it is true, short-lived. But in 1919 alone there were nearly five hundred. Only a few, perhaps, were organised by men (and women) aware of solidarity with workers in other lands. Nevertheless, the two revolutions in Russia, together with the overthrow of monarchies in Vienna, Berlin and Munich, encouraged Japanese radicals as much as they worried the holders of power. There was, then, a degree of ideological opposition, much of it necessarily covert, to the Siberian adventure. Lastly, there was the revulsion against what was known of the Siberian winter. Despite the prolonged snowfalls regularly experienced in northern Honshu, the Japanese people, it seemed, never quite adapted themselves to such conditions. Their housing, dress and diet remained geared to hot rather than cold climates. Hokkaido was scarcely colonised at all before 1868 (even today its population is not enormous). It is not surprising that the very thought of having to serve in Siberia chilled the heart of the recruit. Considerations such as these – to which must be added constant diplomatic pressure from America and the lack of genuine support from any of the Russian people apart from a few cossack officers – impelled the Army General Staff to wind up the affair. Japan was not ready psychologically to challenge the full force of the Red Army.

A face-saving solution for the Japanese was provided by the establishment of the Far Eastern Republic, allegedly Wilsonian in its principles and blessed with a paper Constitution resembling that of the United States. The evacuation of Vladivostok in 1922 was negotiated with this regime – the Japanese, however, retained a grip on North Sakhalin until 1925 – and not long afterwards, the pretence of an independent buffer state having served its purpose, the Far Eastern Republic allowed itself to be absorbed by the Moscow government.

Japan's Siberian Expedition was a strange, confused, but important undertaking, which has been somewhat neglected by other than Soviet historians. In the context of the Decline of the West, there can be little doubt that for those Japanese officers and men who took part in it, in North Manchuria or along the railway from the Pacific to Lake Baikal, the experience shattered what remained of their feelings of keen, if often reluctant, respect for European civilised values.

II

It will be recalled that the Anglo-Japanese Alliance was renewed in 1911 for another ten years. During and after the First World War the alliance was criticised in several quarters in Great Britain and Japan. In Britain those particularly attached to China, for reasons of sentiment as well as commercial profit, were sceptical of Japan's good faith and believed the alliance to be damaging to Britain's whole future relationship with the Chinese. There was much concern, too, about the effect of the alliance on Anglo-American relations. It was seen as an unfailing source of American suspicion; and this aspect assumed greater importance in 1919, with the outbreak of serious trouble in Ireland and India. In Japan, the army was at best lukewarm towards the British connection. Businessmen were often openly hostile in their criticisms of Britain; and sections of the press reflecting these views launched from time to time sharp attacks on the alliance.

However in the spring of 1921, the year when any further renewal of the treaty was due, the omens seemed on the whole favourable. At the end of May 1921 the British Cabinet, when agreeing that President Harding of the United States should be invited to summon a Pacific conference, agreed also that it must be made clear to everyone that London intended to renew the alliance, although for a shorter period than ten years, on terms consistent with the League Covenant and so phrased as to give no offence to American susceptibilities. The Prime Minister, Lloyd George, told his colleagues that he hoped nobody would contemplate 'dropping' Japan. It was an aspiration with which they heartily concurred. (Japan was much in their minds, the Crown Prince, Hirohito, having left England the previous day after a much-publicised three weeks' visit.)

Yet within seven months, for all the firm talk in Downing Street, Britain effectively 'dropped' Japan. The alliance was buried at the Washington Conference, the undertakers being (from the Japanese point of view) Charles Evans Hughes, the American Secretary of State, and Lord Balfour, leader of the British delegation.

No serious historian accepts the theory that the whole operation was an Anglo-American ploy, from the early stages of which Japan was carefully excluded. But that is how it is interpreted by many commentators in Japan to this day. The fact is that just as the Anglo-Japanese Alliance mystified, dismayed even, the Americans (and Canadians), so the easy, club-like, association between the British governing class and the East Coast 'Establishment' made the most Anglophile of Japanese conscious of being an outsider. Therein lay the roots of much envy, perplexity and suspicion.

The Washington Conference of the winter of 1921–2 was preceded by a gathering of British Empire leaders in London during the summer. There it was soon clear that Australia favoured, while Canada opposed, a further renewal of the Anglo-Japanese Alliance. Because of the American connection, Canada carried more guns than Australia; and American pressure was unwearying and ingenious. For example, the British Embassy in Washington learned from the State Department that a decision to renew the Japanese alliance might prompt Congress to recognise the Sinn Fein leadership, still locked in a guerrilla war with Britain, as the government of Ireland.

Nevertheless, the Australian Premier, Billy Hughes, fought hard against his Canadian opposite number, Arthur Meighen. Hughes knew that in a war between Britain and Japan his country would be endangered by Japanese sea power, and he did not believe that American intervention was something on which Australia could rely: only the Royal Navy could protect Australia and New Zealand if Britain and Japan were enemies. Being a realist and, therefore, a pessimist, Hughes thought it wiser to keep Japan as some kind of friend than to risk insulting her, thereby transforming her sooner or later perhaps into a formidable opponent. But Smuts, for South Africa, urged the need to propitiate the United States.

The Japanese were well aware that the alliance was being debated by the imperial conference in London. It was realised that Canada would follow the line taken by the United States. What was not foreseen was the way in which Great Britain would bend her policy in response to North American pressure. Only a few Japanese observers of the contemporary world grasped the extent to which the United States had already replaced the British Empire as the leading actor on the international stage. This was a fundamental change in the balance of power which pro-British circles in Tokyo, if only for reasons of sentiment, found it difficult to accept.

These were the heady years of the idealism which, like the icing on a cake, covered the half-baked, uncertain substance of the League of Nations. By contrast with the hopes voiced with compelling eloquence at Geneva, talk of 'the balance of power', or 'national interest', sounded faintly indecent: such terminology belonged to the bad old pre-war years. In June 1920 London and Tokyo had made obligatory obeisance to the League in a joint Note to Geneva, stating that if the Anglo-Japanese Alliance were to continue after July 1921 it would be in a form consistent with the Covenant. Early in July 1921 a similar joint Note was sent again to Geneva. The fact was that Britain was now marking time. Ways and means were being sought to satisfy the League and the United States, while preserving in a necessarily attenuated form the special relationship with Japan.

When it suited them, British foreign secretaries in the nineteenth century genuflected to the altar of public opinion. But after the First World War and the creation of the League, mass opinion in Britain was a genuinely operative, if spasmodic, factor in the shaping of foreign policy. Now Japan's popular reputation in 1921 in Britain was a mixed one. On the credit side there was the good impression made by the Crown Prince's state visit, which rekindled memories of wartime cooperation against Germany. Against that had to be set certain debit entries. There was awareness of the heavy-handed colonial regime in

Korea, which had put down with harsh brutality spontaneous dem-onstrations of Korean national feeling in 1919. But of greater sig-nificance were the anti-Japanese sentiments of the 'China hands', the Lancashire textile manufacturers, the Labour movement, and of nearly all who listened sympathetically to the voice of American opinion. There was much criticism, it may be, of the alleged cockiness of Uncle Sam. American culture had by this time penetrated English society at so many levels that some reaction, usually expressed in complacently mocking tones, was inevitable. Nevertheless, most Englishmen believed – quite wrongly – that America was a society composed largely of their own kith and kin; that Americans therefore cherished not only a particular friendship for Britain but also accepted, and in their hearts admired, the British Empire. So if presented with the crude choice between Japan and the United States, the man in the street would have given without a moment's hesitation only one answer.

That has to be remembered in an assessment of the decision, one of the most crucial ever taken by a government in London, to liquidate the twenty-year old treaty of alliance with Japan. The way this was done impressed the Japanese as a chilling illustration of British diplomatic expertise. Britain's enemies and critics in Japan felt their distrust fully confirmed. Britain's friends in that country were profoundly shocked and disheartened.

Yet on the face of it, looked at rationally, seen through the eyes of most politicians at Westminster, what transpired at the Washington Conference was no more than the adjustment of a long-standing relationship to the demands of the post-war world. On this view the alliance with Japan was not scrapped so much as merged in a larger grouping, embodied in the Four Power Treaty of 13 December 1921, the first fruit of the Washington Conference on Naval Disarmament and Far Eastern Affairs. The four countries concerned – the United States, Britain, France and Japan – agreed 'as between themselves to respect their rights in relation to their insular dominions in the region of the Pacific Ocean', and to consult with one another if those rights were threatened by any other power. Once the new treaty was ratified, the Anglo-Japanese Treaty of 1911 would come to an end. Balfour, justifying the Four Power Treaty, spoke at the conference of the need to annul an 'ancient and outworn and unnecessary agreement' and to 'replace it with something new, something effective'. This was making the best of a bad job – an exercise to which the rulers of Britain in this century have perforce become accustomed.

The Japanese were not deceived. Neither, perhaps, was Balfour himself; for he had one of the sharpest minds of his generation. A journalist, watching the session at which the terms of the Four Power Treat were announced, recorded that as the last clause was read out Balfour's head fell on his chest, as if the spinal chord had been severed: 'It was an amazing revelation of what the Japanese Treaty had meant to the men of a vanished age. . . . The head of stereotyped diplomacy had fallen forward – the vital chord severed – and new figures hereafter would monopolise the scene.'[5]

The leading European scholar in this field, Dr Nish, points out that the Japanese alliance did not fit in with Britain's need for American goodwill and understanding. 'Britain', he writes, 'did not consciously "abrogate" the alliance; it almost slipped away unnoticed, and she was happy at dispelling some American ill will'. He condemns as inappropriate the term 'abrogation', generally used about the ending of the alliance. 'Abrogation', he observes, suggests a conscious act of 'repealing'; 'but this was very different from the spirit in which Britain and Japan signed the successor-treaty'.[6] That well expresses one strand, and probably the main one, in British thinking then and later.

All the same, it cannot be denied that at Washington, Great Britain had to choose between Japan and the United States. It is equally undeniable that British public opinion had little doubt about what the choice should be. But was it the right choice?

That it was the wrong one has been forcefully argued by a British writer, Corelli Barnett, in the following words:

What guidance could the traditional wisdom of past English foreign policy offer? As super-powers had successively risen towards domination of the Western World, from Spain to Imperial Germany, England had thrown her weight into the opposite scale, along with other powers of lesser might than the super-power. . . . To side with the weaker against the stronger was doubly wise; it prevented the strong becoming over-mighty, while it preserved England herself from the fate of those states who were misguided enough to ally themselves with powers much greater than themselves. For example, Holland's alliance with England in the wars against Louis XIV cost her her independence of action and began her decline; while Austria in the Great War ended up as the helpless satellite of her great partner, Germany.

Traditional English policy therefore might have suggested that the correct choice for England was to renew the Japanese alliance. For Japan's total national power – military, naval and industrial – made her a state of about England's own weight. The United States on the other hand . . . was clearly the super-power of the future, and able and willing to outbuild the Royal Navy.[7]

It was, of course, America's proposed naval building programme that impelled Great Britain and Japan to negotiate with the United States the terms of the Five Power Treaty on disarmament. And it was Balfour's belief that America would not agree to naval limitation (a prime need in the British view) if the Anglo-Japanese Alliance were to be renewed.

Nearly all the arrangements for the Washington Conference – the original impetus for which had come from London – were monopolised by the Americans, who in this matter outmanoeuvred Britain and the Dominions. Curzon, the Foreign Secretary, had expected to be one of the hosts in London at a preliminary conference on the Far East, attended by the United States and other Pacific powers; and he went some way in preparing for this event, without always consulting his Japanese ally beforehand. An obdurate refusal by the United States, quite late in the day, to accept this plan upset Curzon. Indeed, it made him lose face. But this the Japanese failed to realise. To them it looked as though the British from first to last were working hand in glove with the Americans.

Again, it had been Balfour's hope, after he reached Washington, to persuade the United States to join forces with Britain in turning the Anglo-Japanese Alliance into a three-power agreement. Had he been sucessful Japanese feelings would still have been ruffled, but to a milder extent than was the case when France, on American insistence, was added to the agreement. It is small wonder that a Japanese diplomat remarked of the Four Power Treaty: 'We have discarded whisky and accepted water'. Balfour's preliminary talks with Hughes, the Secretary of State, were conducted without advance consultation with the Japanese. So it appeared to the Japanese that they were faced once again with the phenomenon of Anglo-American collusion. That this happened to be a misconception is beside the point. A vital if intangible element of trust was destroyed.

All in all, it is hard to disagree with the view that 'the right course for England was to cleave to the Japanese alliance'.[8] Which is not to say that the right course was one that in terms of domestic politics it would have been easy to adopt. A later parallel may illustrate the dilemma. In the spring of 1939 Britain hastened to give guarantees of military assistance in case of attack to Poland, Rumania and Greece. This was gallant and indeed honourable but, on a cool calculation of national interest, almost an act of folly. Yet in the climate of British public feeling after Hitler's rape of Bohemia, neutrality *vis-à-vis* Eastern Europe would have been politically most hazardous for a government that wanted to stay in office.

History, however, is an unforgiving mistress. A second chance is rarely on offer to those who ignore her lessons. The decline of the West in Asia was accelerated by the ending, however unavoidable this may have seemed, of the Anglo-Japanese Alliance, even if this particular consequence was not fully apparent in the years immediately following the Washington Conference.

III

Despite the hard feelings engendered by the loss of the British alliance, informed opinion in Japan was ready to give a guarded, lukewarm welcome to at least some of the arrangements arrived at in Washington. The state of the economy was such that cuts in public expenditure were imperative. For the boom had collapsed. Japan was once again a debtor nation, exports being substantially exceeded by imports of raw materials. Here the United States played a key role: American iron and steel, for example, were still needed by the Japanese shipbuilding industry. In the plans of the navy the United States might rank as Japan's most likely enemy; but cool-headed officers suspected that on financial grounds alone the prospect of war with America was so distant as to be invisible.

This was certainly the opinion of Admiral Baron Kato Tomosaburo, chief naval delegate at the Washington Conference and Navy Minister in the Japanese government of the day. Baron Kato cannot have been totally dissatisfied with the main clauses of the Five Power Treaty – the famous 5–5–3 (United States, Britain, Japan) ratio for capital ships (vessels of over 10,000 tons or carrying guns of more than 8-inch calibre), and the agreement by the three powers to construct no new naval bases or fortifications west of Hawaii and north of Singapore. The treaty represented for Japan a huge saving in yen, without affecting her naval hegemony in the western Pacific; indeed, the British and American assurances on fortifications could be said to strengthen it. That Britain was no longer the old reliable ally had to be taken into account by planners. But the balance sheet in strictly naval terms could be seen, all things considered, as fairly satisfactory. However, if that was

Kato's view his principal naval colleague at Washington thought otherwise, as we shall see in a minute.

There was also the important Sino-Japanese agreement concluded at Washington whereby Japan undertook to evacuate Shantung in a matter of months; a promise that was duly fulfilled. This came too late to efface the memory of the 'Twenty-One Demands', but it wound up some of the unfinished business at Paris and appeared to set relations between Japan and China ön a new course.

As for the Nine Power Treaty (the big three plus France, Italy, Holland, Belgium, Portugal and China), also signed at Washington, this was no more and no less than a declaratory document of the sort much favoured by men in public life. The treaty had no 'teeth' – meaning sanctions – of any kind. The high-sounding guarantee of China's territorial integrity was, of course, commendable, even if it lacked real substance. On the other hand, Article III stated that the powers would 'use their influence for the purpose of effectually establishing and maintaining the principle of equal opportunity for the commerce and industry of all nations throughout the territory of China'. The Chinese, although signatories of the Nine Power Pact, disliked it on account of that clause. (Some years later, Germany, having been admitted to the League of Nations, offered to adhere to the Nine Power Pact; but China objected, on the grounds that her relations with Germany since 1918 had been on a basis of equality; Germany's adherence to the pact could imply an aspiration to the rights and privileges still enjoyed by the other eight countries.)

Finally, during the Washington Conference Japan announced the intention of withdrawing from Vladivostok and the Maritime Province. This was designed to ease American–Japanese tension; and indeed it was hoped that friction between the two countries would now be a thing of the past.

But such euphoria as existed could not disguise the fact that Japan was to some extent isolated at Washington. The diplomatic triumph was America's. There were few laurels to be fitted on other brows.

The really ominous feature at Washington was the attitude of Vice-Admiral Kato Kanji, Admiral Baron Kato's naval adviser. Kato Kanji was a believer in big fleets, and he distrusted the Americans. He could not reconcile himself to the 5–5–3 ratio. Sickness sent him home before the conference came to an end. His relations with his senior, Baron Kato, were far from cordial, and he returned to Japan an embittered patriot. Not many years later, as we shall see, Kato Kanji was to be at the centre of a storm created by another disarmament conference.

The improvement in transpacific relations was furthered by the practical generosity and sympathy shown by Americans when the frightful Kanto disaster occurred in September 1923; this was the earthquake and fire that razed Yokohama to the ground and destroyed much of Tokyo. Less than a year later, however, a new crisis caused immense harm to America's reputation in Japan. In the spring of 1924 the United States Congress passed an immigration bill which among its provisions excluded the Japanese from the new quota system. The exclusion clause in the bill was not only insulting to Japanese pride, it was also unnecessary, for the 'Gentlemen's Agreement', whereby the Japanese severely limited emigration to America, had worked well.

It was small consolation for the Japanese to be told that the State Department deeply deplored the action taken by Congress. 'White imperialism' now came under mass attack in the Japanese press and in street demonstrations. There was a sudden proliferation of right-wing societies. In the grounds of the United States Embassy in Tokyo a patriot committed *hara-kiri*. So just at a time when Japanese–American relations had been restored to a condition approaching cordiality, provincial bigotry – California was the prime mover behind the exclusion clause – put the clock back. Critics of the Washington agreements, such as Kato Kanji, now found a receptive hearing for their views.

For the time being such currents of strong nationalist feeling did not greatly affect government policy. Japan in the 1920s, like most industrialised states, tended to put considerations of peaceful international commerce above any other factor in foreign affairs. In the words of Professor Iriye:

So long as the United States continued to supply Japan with raw cotton and capital loans, purchase its silk, and act within a cooperative framework in China, the immigration question could be regarded as a regrettable blunder by an otherwise progressive nation, not as something to necessitate an entire re-orientation in Japanese policy and thinking.[9]

'An entire re-orientation in Japanese policy and thinking' is a dryly apt characterisation of the turn which events were to take in the next decade. But throughout the twenties the general trend of foreign and domestic policy, although at times erratic, suggested that Japan was moving towards its own type of parliamentary democratic government. The pervasive political influence of the army and navy, derived from their entrenched constitutional position, appeared to be on the wane. During the 1920s, for example, the army's strength was reduced by four divisions; and about two thousand officers faced premature retirement. The vote was given to all males of twenty-five and over; a fourfold increase in the electorate. In the exploration of ideas editors in their journals, and professors at their lectures, sought and were allowed a new freedom, provided it found expression in language too sophisticated for common folk to understand. The twenties were the heyday of *Ero, Guro* and *Nansensu* – 'Eroticism, Grotesquerie and Nonsense'. The Three Wise Monkeys of Nikko, it seemed, had dropped their paws and were prepared to speak, see, and hear almost anything. But the road to freedom was like the game of 'grandmother's steps'. There was one stride back for every two forward. Much of the money saved from the disbanding of the four divisions went into aircraft and tank research and development. The generous extension of the franchise was matched by a Peace Preservation Law that prescribed ten years' gaol for anyone advocating a change in Japan's 'unique' national structure or the abolition of private property.

In the handling of foreign affairs the pattern was broadly the same. There were several indications of a new spirit of forbearance and compromise. By a convention signed in Peking in 1925 Japan recognised the Soviet Union and agreed, in return for coal and oil concessions, to evacuate North Sakhalin. Japanese policy towards China in the twenties is usually associated with the name of Shidehara Kijuro, Foreign Minister from June 1924 to April 1927, and from July 1929 to December 1931. Shidehara, while Japanese ambassador to the United States, had attended the Washington Conference. He was liked by the Americans, and the sentiment was reciprocated. 'Shidehara diplomacy' became a term of praise or abuse according to the predilections of those using the phrase. Admirers praised 'Shidehara diplomacy' for being temperate and conciliatory. Detractors described it as abject and 'weak-kneed'. Something he wrote in 1924 illustrates Shidehara's general outlook:

In our restricted islands we suffer from a population increase of 700,000–800,000 annually. There is, therefore, no alternative but to proceed with our industrialization. It follows from this that it is essential to secure overseas markets and this can only be done by adopting an economic diplomacy. If we try to cure our economic problems by territorial expansion, we will merely destroy international cooperation.[10]

About 25 per cent of Japan's total exports went to China, and the Chinese market was thought to have almost boundless potentialities. While Shidehara was Foreign Minister Japanese intervention in China – until the Manchurian crisis of September 1931 – was minimal. This made good economic sense. For the Chinese had shown how very effective a trade boycott of foreign goods could be. China in this period was shaken by the rivalries of competing warlords, as well as by the competition of rival ideologies. The northward advance of the Kuomintang, with the impetus it gave to patriotic resentment against extraterritorial rights and imperialism in general, appeared for a time to threaten the vested interests of foreign powers, including Japan. But to the disappointment of the British, and to the bitter chagrin of many Japanese army and navy officers, Shidehara pursued a policy of strict non-involvement, even when Japanese lives were at risk. Britain might muster a Shanghai Defence Force, with reinforcements from the home country as well as India, but Japan adopted a remarkably passive stance, refusing to be alarmed by the appearance of the Kuomintang in the Yangtze valley. Chiang Kai-shek had not yet turned against the Communists in his own ranks, and the Kuomintang, especially at Hankow, was thought to be a dangerously radical as well as anti-foreign movement.

Shidehara was unmoved by a British appeal for cooperation in defence of the common interests of the powers. When the British ambassador asked him what he would do if communism were to spread throughout China, Shidehara replied (a) that this was unlikely to happen, (b) if it did, foreigners would discover within a year or two that they could still go on living and trading in China; this was proved by the experience of Japanese traders in Russia, once diplomatic relations had been established with the Soviet regime. 'Consequently', remarked Shidehara, 'even if China should become a communist nation, we do not have to be too afraid of it.'[11]

IV

That level-headed Japanese approach, symbolised by the unruffled Shidehara, did not prevail after the Wakatsuki Cabinet, in which he was Foreign Minister, gave way in April 1927 to the government of

General Tanaka Giichi. An acute crisis in the banking world had brought down the Wakatsuki Cabinet; but there was also, it must be said, a good deal of dissatisfaction with Shidehara's China policy, even though he received more support from the press and the business world than is often realised.

General Baron Tanaka took over the Foreign Minister's portfolio as well as the premiership, holding the two offices from April 1927 to July 1929. Tanaka was a jovial figure, driven by his emotions, but gifted with organising ability and a strong, if primitive, intelligence. Always ambitious, he became president of the conservative Seiyukai parliamentary party after a successful military career, which included two spells as Minister of War.

General Tanaka was one of the last in a succession of army officers whose promotion owed much to Marshal Yamagata; for he was raised in Yamagata's province of Choshu, the nursery of the Meiji military leaders and a spiritual focus for all true believers in Bushido. The town of Hagi, Tanaka's birthplace, had been the home of the most famous of all latter-day samurai 'saints', Yoshida Shoin (1830–59). Those who grew up in that environment were indoctrinated by parents and teachers not only with the martial virtues but also with a belief in Japan's 'sacred' mission to lead Asia and indeed, eventually, the whole world. The story goes that Tanaka Giichi as a boy, having been expelled from his primary school, was told by his father (a samurai of low rank) that he ought to commit *hara-kiri*. The child was only prevented by his mother's intervention from plunging a knife into his body.

In 1910 Tanaka took the leading part in the creation of the Imperial Military Reserve Association, which in later years, especially in the thirties, exerted a moral and political influence that can hardly be overestimated. This national body of ex-servicemen was no mere semi-charitable organisation designed to help widows, orphans and old comrades. Always energetic in propaganda, the Reserve Association during the critical 1930s supplied the army with invaluable popular support, particularly throughout the countryside. Tanaka took a continuing interest in the Association, regarding it with justice as a bastion against the spread of subversive ideas.

So it is not surprising that as Premier he was at pains to root out 'dangerous thoughts'. Thus, in the spring of 1928, and again a year later, thousands of Marxists and Marxist sympathisers were summarily arrested. Most of those brought to trial received stiff prison sentences – the Peace Preservation Law was of great utility here – and some of those imprisoned, rejecting every effort by the authorities to reconvert them to a patriotic frame of mind, languished in captivity until after the Surrender of 1945.

However, it is Tanaka's foreign policy, specifically his China policy, that is of greater concern to us here. If Shidehara's name is associated with a respect for China's rights, Tanaka's is linked with a much more aggressive stance, although this image has been somewhat distorted. Although he was strongly nationalist (as his upbringing alone would suggest), Tanaka was aware of the need to conciliate world, especially American, opinion; and his reservations about the Kuomintang were not based on distrust of Chiang Kai-shek (with whom, indeed, he established some understanding) so much as on a genuine fear that Chinese nationalism would take a Marxist course. Moreover, Tanaka, like many Japanese military men, believed that the Chinese could be induced by force or the threat of force to abandon such anti-Japanese activities as the trade boycott.

He had views, also, on Manchuria and Inner Mongolia that were bound to lead sooner or later to conflict with the Chinese. Whereas the Wakatsuki Cabinet, with Shidehara in charge of foreign policy, recognised that Manchuria and Inner Mongolia were integral parts of China, Tanaka was convinced that Japan's rights in South Manchuria would be in jeopardy if Manchuria fell under the control of the new Kuomintang regime. Therefore it was desirable to check the Kuomintang's northward advance.

To this end, Tanaka sent troops into Shantung on three occasions, and there were some bloody skirmishes with the Chinese. These interventions offended Chiang's Chinese opponents no less than Chiang Kai-shek himself, and they provoked a widespread anti-Japanese boycott. Tanaka's operations also failed to discourage Chiang's forces from advancing on Peking. That city, still the nominal capital of China, was in the hands of Marshal Chang Tso-lin, the Manchurian warlord, who could say that he owed his life to the Japanese Premier. (During the Russo-Japanese War Colonel Tanaka, as he then was, captured some Chinese guerrillas, Chang Tso-lin among them, who had been fighting on the Russian side. He could have had Chang shot. Impressed by the man's demeanour, however, Tanaka spared his life. Thereafter he liked to refer to Chang as his 'younger brother'.) Chang Tso-lin, indeed, had long enjoyed Japanese support (in this context, the South Manchurian Railway Company), but he was not a Japanese puppet. He had ambitions to rule all China, and he was in his own way a patriot as well as a warlord. He objected to Tanaka's interventions in Shantung, even though these were directed against his own domestic enemies, the Kuomintag.

By the middle of May 1928 the Kuomintang forces were poised to threaten Peking, and its fall appeared imminent. Tokyo formally warned both Chang Tso-lin and Chiang Kai-shek that if hostilities reached the Peking–Tientsin area, thereby menacing the peace of South Manchuria, the Japanese government would take appropriate action. There was a simultaneous and significant move by the headquarters of the Kwantung Army (the Japanese garrison of South Manchuria) from Port Arthur to Mukden.

At this juncture the American government sent a cautionary message to Japan. Washington asked for advance notice of any intended action in Manchuria. This effectively nipped in the bud a plan concocted by the Kwantung Army, in cooperation with the authorities at home, to disarm Chang Tso-lin's forces while at the same time seizing control of Manchuria.

Meanwhile, Chang Tso-lin in Peking was under irresistible pressure from the Japanese to withdraw to Manchuria. His troops were, in any case, already retreating in their tens of thousands to the north of the Great Wall. Finally, at the beginning of June, Chang agreed to leave Peking. He departed in a heavily guarded train for Mukden. Several hours later, when approaching the outskirts of that city, the train was wrecked by a bomb explosion, and Chang Tso-lin was fatally injured.

Unconvincing attempts were made by the Kwantung Army to place the blame on the Chinese. But almost from the start it was an open secret that the Japanese themselves had planned and carried out the assassination; although the truth was not to be made public for another two decades.

An engineer unit of the Kwantung Army, commanded by a colonel, had organised the affair, the hope being that Chang Tso-lin's death would force their superiors – in defiance, if need be, of orders from Tokyo – to take over Manchuria. That part of the plot misfired. The Kwantung Army did not move. On the contrary, Chang's murder caused a political scandal of the first magnitude.

There were demands in Tokyo for a full inquiry. Tanaka himself sought the punishment of those involved, for he seems to have been thoroughly shocked by the assassination. He was certainly dismayed by the subsequent uproar, and he was put out of countenance by the Emperor's unmistakable displeasure.

The military authorities conducted their own confidential inquiry into the background and circumstances of the 'grave Manchurian incident' (the anodyne title the Japanese press felt obliged to use when referring to the affair). The ringleader, the Kwantung Army colonel, was put on the retired list. But that was all. Closing its ranks, the army insisted that for reasons of professional honour and national morale no further action could be taken and nothing at all publicly revealed. It was a vivid illustration of the army's ability to shrug off pressure, not only from liberal opinion as voiced in the Diet and in the press, but also from the last of the *Genro*, old Prince Saionji, and from the Palace itself. Nevertheless, in the end the rumpus brought down the Cabinet. The main opposition party, the Minseito, took office, with Hamaguchi Osachi as Premier and with Shidehara back at the Ministry of Foreign Affairs. There was an almost palpable sigh of relief from enlightened opinion in Japan.

Posterity has judged Tanaka harshly; but one persistent accusation deserves to be refuted. He was not the author of the famous 'Memorial' that bears his name. Like the 'Protocols of the Elders of Zion' or 'the Cliveden Set', the 'Tanaka Memorial' is one of those potent myths that seem to possess an indestructible life of their own. Even now, writers on the Far East occasionally refer to the 'Tanaka Memorial' as a blueprint for conquest, the Asian equivalent of *Mein Kampf*.

The 'Tanaka Memorial' is supposed to be a top secret petition submitted to the Emperor in July 1927, setting out in some detail Japanese plans for expansion in Asia and beyond. There is very strong evidence to suggest that the document was a forgery. But 'mystery cloaks the memorial's true identity – its conception, its authorship, its pre-publication movements'.[12] What cannot be denied was its utility as a weapon of propaganda in the hands of the Chinese. Furthermore, spurious as it certainly seems to have been, the 'Tanaka Memorial', from the perspective of the 1940s, did appear to map out Japan's course of conquest in Asia.

V

The Hamaguchi Cabinet had not long been in office when the New York stock market collapsed in the early autumn of 1929. The dire impact of the Great Depression, aftermath of the Wall Street crash, is a theme reserved for the next chapter. We must conclude this one with a brief consideration of the crisis that erupted in 1930 over the London Naval Limitation Conference of that year.

The purpose of the London Conference was to extend to the building of cruisers and auxiliary craft the kind of limitation, based on an agreed ratio, fixed at Washington in the case of capital ships. Hamaguchi and Shidehara readily accepted the conference invitation from the MacDonald Labour government, and a powerful delegation headed by ex-Premier Wakatsuki and including the Navy Minister, Admiral Takarabe, was sent from Tokyo. Before its departure the delegation had been briefed on the fundamental position agreed between the Cabinet and the Navy General Staff, sanctioned by the Emperor, and announced in the press. This, reduced to its simplest terms, was that while Japan accepted a strength in cruisers lower than that of Britain and America, the ratio *vis-à-vis* the United States must be 70 per cent. The Chief of the Naval General Staff attached the greatest importance to this point; as one might expect, for he was Admiral Kato Kanji, who never forgot his experience at the Washington Conference.

In London it soon became clear that the Americans would not agree to the proposed ratio. To break the deadlock the Japanese delegation eventually accepted, after much heart-searching, a compromise that fell short by a slight margin of the desired 70 per cent for cruisers *vis-à-vis* the United States. The Hamaguchi Cabinet considered the London proposals satisfactory. The compromise settlement could not be said to endanger Japan's security; it was desirable on grounds of economy and in the interests of general international goodwill; and it was the only way out of an impasse that could have wrecked the conference.

But the London Treaty of 1930 had an extremely rough passage on its way to final ratification by Japan. In a complicated as well as bitter quarrel the two sides, the supporters and the opponents of the treaty, were led by, respectively, the Prime Minister, Hamaguchi, and the Chief of the Naval General Staff, Kato Kanji. Both were men of unyielding, obstinate character.

Admiral Kato fought the treaty tooth and nail, and in this he had the passionate support of many in his service. He had urged the naval representatives at London not to yield an inch, even if the conference broke up. Japan, he told them, would attract world sympathy in that event, and 'even America itself would be ashamed'; but if the Americans did expand their navy to a size many times that of Japan the result would be a Japanese–English *rapprochement*, with America becoming 'another Germany'.[13]

Kato and his school, members of what was known as the 'Fleet Faction', were not motivated by an exceptionally aggressive or bellicose spirit. The 70 per cent ratio had long been accepted as orthodox doctrine, on respectable technical grounds, by Japan's professional defence planners. Their fears, it may be said, were exaggerated and, in some quarters, not a little neurotic. But American admirals, too, could be obsessed by nightmares. Many of them believed the London Treaty had made excessive concessions to Japan.

The Navy Minister, Admiral Takarabe, may have had reservations about the London compromise, but he was prepared to make the best of it, as were the officers serving in his Ministry. Thus, there was a widening of the classic rift separating the man at the desk from the man on the deck. But the really serious nature of the London Treaty crisis arose from the constitutional situation in Japan, in which the Chief of the Naval General Staff enjoyed direct access to the Throne as the only legitimate adviser on the Emperor's exercise of the supreme command; which covered operations, but not administration.

But did the tonnage and armament of the fleet come under the General Staff? Or were they the responsibility of the Navy Ministry? Hamaguchi and his cabinet colleagues believed – although they were reluctant to spell it out in public – that naval strength, as opposed to naval operations, was the concern of the Navy Minister, working in agreement with the Cabinet as well as with his own service colleagues. So Hamaguchi had no hesitation in recommending the London compromise to the Emperor; for in the absence in Europe of the Navy Minister the Premier had temporarily assumed Admiral Takarabe's portfolio. Accordingly, when advising the Emperor, Hamaguchi wore two hats – that of Navy Minister as well as Premier. Similarly, Hamaguchi recommended the London Treaty to the Privy Council, which had the task of reviewing it – a procedure required prior to ratification.

The battle raged for several months, before the treaty was ratified; and Hamaguchi earned his nickname of 'Lion' in face of the furious attacks he had to endure in the Diet and from angry naval officers, high and low. Admiral Kato Kanji resigned, and so did the Vice-Chief of the Naval General Staff. But Hamaguchi persevered. He won in the end; but it cost him his life. In the autumn he was shot in the stomach by a nationalist fanatic; several months later he died. Shidehara was acting Premier until it was clear that Hamaguchi would not recover. Wakatsuki then became Prime Minister for the second time.

The London Naval Treaty of 1930 was the last success of those in pre-war Japan who put their faith in an international order regulated by the industrialised democratic powers. Such men were to be known in later years as 'Old Liberals'. It is possible that but for the World Depression they might have been able to build on their success in outfacing Admiral Kato and the 'Fleet Faction'. In which case, the history of Asia would have taken a different course. But caught between the radicals of the Right and Left, baffled by the economic typhoon that hit their country, the Old Liberals, reasonable men in a time of mounting unreason, faced eclipse. This was a tragedy; for they were a civilised and civilising force in Japanese public life.

9 The End of the Road

Once again the crust of civilisation has worn thin, and beneath can be heard
the muttering of primeval fires.
JOHN BUCHAN, *Augustus*

I

JAPANESE historians usually refer to the period from the beginning of
1931 to the end of 1941 as 'the Dark Valley'. It is an apt description
which no reassessment of those ten years will easily undermine.

Those who suffered from the heavy hand of police censorship and
surveillance, and from the malevolence or stupidity of fanatical
'patriots', were not merely the relatively few committed revolutionaries
of the extreme Left. A much larger category was involved; namely, the
free spirits, the open-minded, the cosmopolitan, and the sceptical – in
other words, the enlightened minority that is the leaven in any society.
Thus, it has been the common practice among Japanese writers and
other intellectuals to attach the label of 'fascism' to the decade of the
1930s.

Now it is true that to anyone familiar with what happened in Italy,
Germany, and indeed the Soviet Union, in the thirties it must seem
inappropriate to describe Japan during the same period as a fascist
state. In Japan there was no all-powerful dictator, exercising through
his myrmidons a form of justice outside the scope of the established
courts of law. In Japan the Constitution was not set aside. It is also
worth stressing that the worst horrors of the Third Reich and of Stalin's
Russia had no counterpart in the islands of the Japanese homeland.
Nevertheless, if the adjective, 'fascist', is to be eschewed so far as Japan is
concerned, the use of the term, however erroneous, is at least forgivable,
in view of the drift of Japanese opinion and the course of Japanese
foreign policy.

After 1930 there was a groundswell of discontent, stridently nationalist and at the same time class-conscious, directed against those who

138

upheld like caryatids the existing order. These were the upper classes, by birth, bureaucratic status, inherited wealth or achievement in the business world. (It is significant that after the Tokyo military revolt in 1936 the Emperor charged the new Premier, Hirota, with the duty of ensuring that the position of the nobility was not endangered.) After 1930 there was a series of unsuccessful *coups d'état* designed to establish a radical totalitarian state under military leadership. Furthermore, the cult of Japan's ethnocentric mythology was promoted on an altogether new scale. Finally, and especially after the mid-thirties, great emphasis was placed on uniformity in political belief and social behaviour.

The seed-bed for most of those developments was the World Depression. That disaster produced as one of its results the collapse of the American market for Japanese silk. Japanese exports in general, needless to say, were hit hard by the Depression; but the effects on the silk trade were deadly. After the First World War silk had been the largest single item of export from Japan, and nearly 90 per cent of the annual export of silk went to the United States. The collapse of the American market brought ruin to many thousands of households, especially in the extensive region known as the Tohoku, the six northern prefectures of Honshu, the main island. For what made all the difference in the Tohoku between hard living and downright penury was the raising and care of silk-worms, which brought in a small but essential supplementary cash income. When this source dried up the results were devastating indeed.

The Tohoku had long been a reservoir from which industry drew a never-failing supply of young unskilled workers of both sexes. But when, thanks to the Depression, the fall in demand for manufactured goods led to lay-offs, the unemployed – the girls especially – tended to return to their families. So there were more mouths to feed at the very moment when the farmer's income was being cut to the bone. There is a Japanese saying: 'A crying face is stung by a hornet' ('Troubles never come singly'). The Tohoku region experienced in the autumn of 1931 the horrors of a crop failure. Relief organisations could not save the lives of all the children suffering from malnutrition. Many a household faced actual starvation.

When conditions of this kind had developed in western Europe – in Ireland, for example – emigration to the New World had provided one means of escape. This option, as we have seen, was no longer open to the Japanese; even if it is true that Brazil continued to accept immigrants long after North America had closed the door. But for farmers in Japan there could be one or more realisable assets in the shape of the daughter(s) of the household. Before the Depression such girls could find work in the textile mills of the big cities. When this avenue was closed there remained, as a very last resort, what was known as *mi-uri*, 'selling oneself for a term of service'. Every urban area in Japan at that time contained official and unofficial houses of prostitution, some of the 'licensed quarters', such as the Tokyo Yoshiwara, having a history celebrated in art and drama, going back two or three hundred years. There were also the geisha quarters, where the long training of the entertainers called for an intake of girls hardly out of childhood. In the evil years of the early thirties brokers for such establishments roamed the Tohoku in search of prey, ready to offer for each recruit a lump sum in cash to her parents.

The dominant theme of the thirties in Japan is the ever-increasing assertiveness and power of the army. Here again we must speak of the Tohoku. For that region shared with Kyushu the reputation of supplying the best soldiers in terms of moral stamina and physical endurance. The frightful conditions in the Tohoku were recognised as a national scandal; but what particularly impressed the military authorities was the rise in the number of young men from the Tohoku who had to be rejected for military service because they suffered from the effects of malnutrition.

The surprising thing perhaps is that there was no eruption of mass protest, no 'Peasants' Revolt'. A stabilising element, however, in the countryside was the Imperial Military Reserve Association (see p. 131). Its members enjoyed great respect in their localities, for they had done their stint in the Emperor's service. They were the actual or potential leaders of their own communities. Generally speaking, farmers did not fear or resent the army. On the contrary, they admired its spirit, were indeed grateful for the way in which it clothed, fed and educated their sons. Compared with politicians or businessmen, soldiers were seen as sympathetic figures, true patriots with no axe to grind. In the promotion and maintenance of this attitude the ex-servicemen played the leading role. It was otherwise in the vastly more sophisticated environment of cities such as Tokyo, Kyoto and Osaka. There the rising power of the army was less welcome.

So when in the autumn of 1930 the Ministry of War financed a series of lectures throughout the Tohoku area on Japan's position in Manchuria, the popular response was cordial, not to say enthusiastic. For the lecturer – a Tohoku man, Dr Okawa Shumei, long active in

right-wing politics – pointed out that Manchuria was a huge, unde-
veloped region to which sturdy young Japanese farmers ought to
emigrate. The lecturer warned his hearers that Japan's position in
South Manchuria was threatened by the Kuomintang government,
whose authority the Manchurian leader, Chang Hsueh-liang (Chang
Tso-lin's son) had recognised. Alas, the timidity of Shidehara and the
Foreign Ministry encouraged Chang in his impudence. When Chang
had seized the Russian-controlled Chinese Eastern Railway in 1929 the
Soviet army had promptly intervened. The lesson for Japan was clear.
Only firm measures would protect and advance her interests in
Manchuria.

Such was the message; and it was well received. The lecturer himself
was soon to be involved, together with two or three highly placed
generals, in a conspiracy to overthrow the government by a *coup d'état*.
This venture, planned for March 1931, was abandoned when the senior
general designated to head the new government refused to countenance
the plot. The whole episode, known as 'The March Affair', was hushed
up. Those who had flirted with insurrection received no punishment. As
in the matter of Chang Tso-lin's assassination, the generals closed their
ranks.

Meanwhile, across the Yellow Sea a handful of staff officers of the
Kwantung Army, with the connivance of certain sympathetic seniors
in Tokyo, were preparing for action in Mukden, to take place in
September. There was to be an explosion on the tracks of the South
Manchurian Railway, for which Chinese soldiers would be blamed.
This would be the signal for an assault on the local Chinese garrison, to
be followed by the occupation of Manchurian territory beyond the
railway zone.

Shidehara got wind of this plot rather late in the day, in early
September, from consular sources in Mukden. There was alarm in the
Foreign Ministry; and the Cabinet was alerted. But the latter had to be
satisfied by an assurance from the War Minister (Lieutenant-General
Minami) that a special envoy would be sent to Mukden with orders for
the cancellation of any projected operation against the Chinese. Since
the officer chosen for this task (a major-general) had been actively
involved in the conspiracy at the Tokyo end, it is not surprising that he
travelled to Mukden with no sense of urgency and did nothing when
he got there on the evening of 18 September 1931, the night the *coup*
occurred.

What followed took the world by surprise. Only ten days earlier,

Lord Cecil of Chelwood, speaking for Britain at the League of Nations in Geneva, had declared: 'There has scarcely ever been a period in the world's history when war seemed less likely than it does at the present.'[1] Certainly at that particular period most countries seemed absorbed, to the exclusion of foreign affairs, in dealing with their own domestic economic and social problems. From the point of view of a Japanese advocate of 'armed diplomacy' the time could hardly have been more propitious. Moreover, at this moment Britain's friends in Japan, notably among the senior ranks of the navy, were temporarily dumbfounded by the news of the mutiny at Invergordon.

Having quickly disposed of the Chinese in Mukden, the Japanese, soon reinforced from Korea, pushed on to Kirin and other areas. Chinese resistance, on the whole, was not impressive. But Chinese diplomatic activity was vigorous, as was their handling of public relations. The Kuomintang government at Nanking, aware that it had a good case, appealed with confidence to the League of Nations and to the goodwill of the American people.

Japanese diplomacy, directed in the main by officials of the Shidehara school, had the unrewarding duty of giving assurances which were rapidly belied by the actions of the Japanese army in the field. Ambassadors in Washington, London, Paris and elsewhere stressed the need for patience, while earnestly denying allegations of calculated aggression against China. They said in so many words: 'Give our government time. Be patient. Condemnation of Japan will only rally public opinion behind the army, which our "moderates" are trying to control.' This appeal was received with some understanding. The Chinese at Geneva discovered that the League powers were in no hurry to pass judgement on Japan.

However, within the next six months the climate of opinion began to harden in the West, and in Japan too. At the end of 1931 Wakatsuki and Shidehara and their colleagues resigned, being succeeded by a Seiyukai party Cabinet under Inukai Tsuyoshi. By this time the advances made by the Kwantung Army had fired the imagination of the Japanese, especially that bulk of the population that got its livelihood from farming and fishing. The warfare in Manchuria was less severe than the weather conditions. Much territory was gained at little cost. The popularity and prestige of the army, on the decline in the twenties, were now restored.

Suddenly, in January 1932, Sino-Japanese relations took a further turn for the worse. The Japanese navy at Shanghai became embroiled with the Chinese 19th Route Army, which fought with such determination and success that army reinforcements had to be rushed from Japan. In 'rescuing the navy', the army launched a major attack, the fighting being on a scale altogether more costly and dramatic than anything seen during the previous months in Manchuria. After five or six weeks, during which the Chinese were eventually forced to retreat, both sides were willing to accept a truce at the mediation of the British and other foreign diplomatic missions. But by the time the guns fell silent public feeling in Britain and America was set in an anti-Japanese mould.

The reasons for this are easy to understand. It was not so much the notable fight put up by the Chinese 19th Route Army (although this made a particularly strong impression in America) that stirred opinion in the West. What upset the world was the spectacle of a great city under heavy shell-fire and air bombardment; for it was at Shanghai in 1932 that the newsreel cameraman, as the recorder of the horrors of war, came into his own. A large cosmopolitan population lived in the Shanghai International Settlement and French Concession. The Japanese, careful to avoid those enclaves, concentrated their bombing and naval gunfire on Chapei, the 'Chinese city'. The results were seen, from a ringside seat as it were, by the correspondents and photographers who converged on Shanghai after the fighting began. Sympathy with China became a genuine popular emotion in most parts of the world.

It was during the Shanghai battle that Stimson, the American Secretary of State, attempted to exert moral pressure on Japan. Stimson's view of China, it has been well said, was 'of a protégé destined to grow in one's own likeness'.[2] In this he faithfully represented the general outlook of the American people, whose avuncular sentiment for the Sister Republic across the Pacific, sharpened by the bombing of Chapei, was roused further by the creation of Manchukuo in March 1932. By that month the Japanese Kwantung Army controlled virtually the whole of the three provinces comprising Manchuria, a huge region broadly equivalent in size to the land area covered by the Low Countries, France and the Iberian Peninsula. The Kwantung Army lost no time in accepting what was alleged to be a spontaneous demand by the five races inhabiting Manchuria – the Manchus, Han Chinese, Koreans, Russians and Japanese – for the establishment of an independent Manchurian state.

Stimson, in Notes addressed to Japan, made it clear that the United States would not recognise this alteration of the political map of China.

Maintaining the pretence that the birth of the new state was the concern exclusively of the 'Manchurians' themselves, even if the Kwantung Army had acted as midwife, Tokyo's response to American protests was one of pained surprise. But as reflected in the Japanese press, public opinion was more outspoken. Adverse comment abroad served only to stoke the fires of *Yamato damashii*, 'the Japanese spirit', set alight by the exciting news from Manchuria and Shanghai.

On the other hand, there was as yet no open breach with the League. This body had postponed reaching any verdict on the Sino-Japanese dispute by appointing a Commission of Inquiry, under Lord Lytton, to investigate on the spot in Manchuria the background to the conflict, and to recommend a settlement. This was doubtless a wise move on the part of the League powers, since they were reluctant to alienate one of their own number, Japan, if by delay some tolerable or at least face-saving solution to the Far East imbroglio could be found. In this matter France faced a rather piquant dilemma. There was something to be said for the argument that a weak, disunited China was very desirable from the point of view of the French administration in Hanoi. (Who could have foreseen that in ten years' time it would be the Japanese army, not the Chinese or Vietnamese Nationalists, who would control the government of Indo-China?) So the French felt they had no reason to fall out with the Japanese. Yet any weakening of the League's prestige must undermine French security, since in the French view the prime function of the League was to guarantee the *status quo* in Europe. Hitler had not yet moved to the centre of the stage; but he was visible in the wings.

The British view also was schizophrenic. Particularly among older Conservative politicians there was goodwill towards Japan, coloured by misgivings about the way the Japanese alliance had been allowed to lapse ten years earlier. There were mixed feelings in these quarters about the rise of Chinese nationalism, which British businessmen in Shanghai and Hong Kong were inclined to see as a somewhat deplorable, if inevitable, phenomenon. Yet the Conservatives, in power with a huge majority at Westminster, included genuine believers in the principle of collective security who sympathised with China as the victim of Japanese aggression. Supporters of the League, idealists and therefore optimists, seized on the hope that the Far East crisis would lead to active and permanent participation by the United States in the proceedings at Geneva.

The Macdonald–Baldwin government in London accordingly adopted a policy of extreme caution. In carrying this out, the Foreign Secretary, Sir John Simon, failed to win the understanding of the Americans. Thus was born the myth – not fully dispelled, perhaps, even now – that the United States was ready to 'stop Japan' in 1932, and might have done so had it not been for the way in which Britain dragged her feet.

But the Hoover Administration in Washington, so far from contemplating military sanctions of any kind, was not prepared to use America's economic muscle against Japan. Moral force, exemplified by the 'non-recognition' policy, was the only weapon; and if one can scarcely, in fairness, blame Stimson for making use of it, especially in the year of a presidential election, the fact remains that it exacerbated nationalist feeling in Japan, was of no practical help to China, and advanced America's own interests in no way at all.

II

On 15 May 1932 in Tokyo a posse of naval officers and army cadets, having shot their way into his official residence, assassinated Premier Inukai. This was the third political murder that year, the previous victims being a former finance minister (Inouye Junnosuke) and a prominent industrialist (Baron Dan). Those murders were the work of radical ultra-nationalists, some of them from a rural background while others belonged to traditional right-wing groups.

The assassins in those three incidents attracted a remarkable measure of public support. Indeed, they were seen as heroes. It is worth quoting at length a comment by Professor Edwin Reischauer on the implications of this sombre phenomenon:

Reflecting the values of an earlier age, public opinion, instead of being outraged at each attack on the duly constituted representatives of the people and the officials of the emperor's government, tended to sympathise with the 'pure motives' of the young assassins, who were permitted to turn their trials into fierce indictments of the alleged corruption and selfishness of the politicians, bureaucrats, and businessmen they had attacked. Each incident was interpreted . . . as proof that greater harmony and unity must be achieved in both government and society. In turn, the need for unity, instead of being interpreted as requiring a broader and more representative leadership, was used as justification for the reduction and eventually the total elimination of the politicians' role and subsequently for the diminution of the civil bureaucracy's share in leadership, as the military moved step by step toward control over the whole government.[3]

If the majority of the Japanese people still lived and worked in farming and fishing villages, a high proportion of the urban population was, at most, one generation removed from the traditional life of the countryside. Farming and fishing were group activities, in which the individual for mere survival had to subordinate his own plans and wishes to those of the community; hence the tremendous importance attached to 'unity and cooperation'. But these were, none the less, 'the values of an earlier age'. It was to these values that so many returned, under the stress of economic hardship and the excitement of the Manchurian drama.

Inukai's son, in evidence at the Tokyo War Crimes Trial after the Pacific War, declared that his father was planning to secure an imperial command ordering the Kwantung Army to withdraw to the South Manchurian Railway zone, and that was why he was murdered. This may be true. Only a direct imperial command could have put the Manchurian operation into reverse. An imperial rescript, countersigned by the Cabinet, might have been effective. It was seen to be so in August 1945. But a much more probable outcome in 1932 would have been defiance by the Kwantung Army, which could have justified its resistance (in the style of the die-hards of 1945) by claiming that the order to withdraw did not reflect the Emperor's 'true mind'. It seems doubtful, in any case, whether Inukai would have succeeded in carrying all his colleagues with him in so hazardous a project. If, as his son testified, Premier Inukai contemplated some such plan, that would have been ample reason for his enemies to secure his murder.

The Lytton Commission visited Japan, Manchuria and China during the summer. Few thought that its findings would be palatable to Japan. But when the Report was published later in the year the expected condemnation of Japanese actions was phrased so carefully, and was hedged by so many qualifications, that no fair-minded reader in Japan could have taken offence. The verdict all the same was unmistakable: acceptance of the Report by the League Assembly would amount to a vote of censure on Japan.

The Report came out in October. Five months later, in March 1933, after the final debate and the casting of votes at Geneva, the Japanese delegation, finding no support from any League state, walked out of the Palais des Nations, headed by their voluble leader, Matsuoka Yosuke, vice-chairman of the South Manchurian Railway Company. The rupture was permanent. Matsuoka on his return to Tokyo was greeted as a popular hero, but Japan now faced diplomatic isolation.

By this time the Kwantung Army, pressing beyond the traditional frontier of Manchuria, had advanced into Jehol Province on China's side of the Great Wall. The Chinese were now compelled to accept a demilitarised zone between Peking and the Wall. This was part of the truce arranged in the spring of 1933, clinching Japan's military success and enhancing the army's political influence at home. Manchukuo would soon be a monarchy with Pu Yi, the ex-Emperor of China, on the throne. In the Empire of Manchukuo each department, bureau and section of the governmental structure was headed by a Manchurian (usually a Han Chinese) with a Japanese deputy at his elbow, who in most cases did all the work and in every case had all the power.

The development of Manchukuo was a task that should have absorbed Japan's energies for many years. The wise course – it must have seemed so even then – would have been to avoid at all costs any further dispute with the Chinese. Given time, the breach with the League could have been repaired. In 1936, after all, Britain and other League states were to recognise the King of Italy as Emperor of Ethiopia. America's non-recognition doctrine might be tiresome, but it amounted to little more than an irritant. Chinese rancour was a more serious issue but scarcely represented a grave military threat. The Soviet Union, perhaps, was the one power that Japan had reason to fear. Nevertheless, Japan would be able to purchase, at a bargain price, from the Russians the Chinese Eastern Railway. In any case, if Russia was in truth some kind of menace, that was all the more reason for concentrating the nation's efforts on the development of Manchukuo.

Japan's failure to adhere to this policy was due in part to the new alignment of forces in Europe but arose also from the disunity (when 'unity' was the national slogan) caused by ferocious quarrels within, as well as between, the army and navy. There was another factor, too; namely, '*the values of a past age*'. For these values embraced not only the ideals of harmony and unity, but also the profound conviction that the Japanese race possessed unique qualities (such as courageous self-sacrifice) that entitled it to be sooner or later both the leader and the liberator of Asia.

Hitler, it will be recalled, came to power early in 1933. German rearmament, Germany's withdrawal from the League, the Abyssinian crisis and Britain's seeming weakness *vis-à-vis* Italy in the Mediterranean, Germany's reoccupation of the Rhineland – such events, suggestive of a permanent change in the European balance of power, could not fail to make an impression on the Japanese, at a time when they felt themselves more than usually friendless in the world. It was the army, with its traditional pro-German leanings, that brought Tokyo and Berlin together late in 1936 with the signing of the Anti-Comintern Pact. This could be interpreted, of course, as a defensive measure against Soviet military as well as ideological power. But the influence of the Nazi connection contained a more aggressive element. For European fascism seemed to teach the lesson that dynamic nationalism was the wave of the future, that the day of the 'have' nations (to use the jargon of the time), such as Britain, was past. The Third Reich, it could be seen, would not rest content with tearing up the Treaty of Versailles. Why should Japan be content with the acquisition of Manchuria?

If that question presented itself to the 'hawks' among the Japanese officer corps, it was accompanied by another; namely, what should be the next step? Here there was much debate and acrimonious disagreement. There were those who asserted that since a struggle with Russia was inevitable, preparations to this end must dominate every aspect of national policy. This 'northern advance' school, as it came to be called, opposed further military penetration of China south of the Great Wall, while favouring an advance into Inner Mongolia. The advantages to be gained from a conflict with Russia were strategic rather than economic. Developments in the range of aircraft in the twenties had given Vladivostok a new importance in Japanese eyes; air-raid exercises in Japan were always conducted on the supposition of bombing attacks from bases in the Maritime Province. The acquisition of that region and North Sakhalin would plug dangerous gaps in the defence perimeter.

The rival school of military opinion argued the case for a drive to the south. China still seemed to offer great opportunities; the dream behind the 'Twenty-One Demands' could still be realised. If a puppet government could be made to work in Manchuria, why not in North China and, later on, further south?

The navy favoured the 'southern advance', believing that control of the China coast, and of the Yangtze up to the Wuhan cities at least, would be enough to ensure Chinese compliance with Japanese political and economic demands. In the long run, however, what was of chief concern to the navy was assured access to the oil, tin and rubber of South-east Asia. The United States was the theoretical enemy when it came to the planning of sea manoeuvres and the construction of new ships; but the logic of a southern advance must involve a clash with Britain sooner or later, and this was something to which the navy in the mid-thirties began to apply its mind.

Both schools of thought, especially the advocates of the northern advance, included an influential body of 'Young Turks'; who might be very junior officers, or even cadets (such as those who helped to murder Inukai). Or they might be captains and majors, or even colonels. Some of these firebrands, with their detestation of businessmen and politicians and their distaste for foreign modes, liked to imagine that they were the spiritual heirs of the samurai heroes who had overthrown the Tokugawa shogunate in 1868. It was fashionable for young officers of this type to advocate a 'Showa Restoration'; in which the capitalists would 'restore' their riches, and the politicians their powers, to the reigning Emperor (Showa *Tenno*). From this would emerge a national socialist state ruled by the armed forces in the Emperor's name. Although there were numerous cross-currents, it was broadly the case that the most radical young officers, namely the supporters of a Showa Restoration, belonged to the 'northern advance' school.

Divided it might be by factional strike, but the army was wholly united in its resolve not to allow the new mood of patriotism to die away. The rift with the League, in any case, gave scope for a multitude of press and magazine articles by nationalist scholars and ex-officers on the need to eradicate unwholesome foreign ideas, while building up the country's armed strength. The army itself went into the publishing field with widely read pamphlets on the virtues of the military spirit. And it has to be said that rearmament was good for business. Within five years of the outbreak of fighting in Manchuria, economic recovery was well advanced, even though the Tohoku was stricken by a second calamitous crop failure in 1934.

III

For rather more than four years, from the spring of 1933 to the summer of 1937, there was peace of a kind between China and Japan. But there was no abatement of Japanese interference, economic and political, in the affairs of North China. And at a Tokyo press conference in 1934 a Foreign Ministry spokesman enunciated what appeared to be, despite later disclaimers, a Japanese 'Monroe Doctrine', warning foreign powers to keep their hands off China.

At home the nation was convulsed by a baleful, highly unedifying rumpus. An elderly scholar, Professor Minobe Tatsukichi, reckoned to be the greatest living authority on the Constitution, came under attack in the House of Peers, of which he was a member, for a work he had published twenty years earlier; in which he had described the Emperor as 'the highest organ of the state'. Professor Minobe, in other words, had been guilty of using the terminology of political science rather than the language of theology. Urged to recant, Minobe refused. A national agitation was worked up by and through the Imperial Military Reserve Association. Ex-servicemen up and down the country held meetings and wrote indignant letters to the press, protesting against Minobe's 'blasphemy' and calling on the government to 'clarify the national polity'. The War Minister of the day did much to promote this campaign; for senior officers had distrusted Minobe from the time of the London Naval Treaty, when he had come out in support of Hamaguchi's stand.

The Emperor and the Prime Minister (Admiral Okada) keenly sympathised with the harassed scholar. Yet with a lack of moral courage that would find its parallel in the prudent silence of highly placed Americans in the fifties under the blast of MacCarthyism, no public figure in Japan spoke up in Minobe's defence. He had to resign from the Upper House; he was interrogated, though not indicted, by the Ministry of Justice, and two of his books, long recognised as standard works, were removed from public sale and from library shelves open to school and university students.[4]

As this affair revealed, it was no longer safe to question the concept of the Emperor as a 'living god'. The quiescence of liberal opinion made the Minobe affair a true turning-point. Notice was now served on the intellectual community that any deviation – not just Marxism – from a decidedly nationalist, irrational interpretation of the Japanese polity would incur condemnation and probable punishment.

The Minobe storm had barely died down when another 'incident' excited public feeling. This was the murder of a lieutenant-general in the Ministry of War by a lieutenant-colonel, who had travelled to Tokyo from his unit by the Inland Sea with just this purpose in mind. When the assassin was on trial he turned his defence into a well-publicised harangue on the iniquity of corrupt, self-serving officials whom he charged with bringing shame and ruin to Japan.

Then, on 26 February 1936, there occurred the most sensational event in Tokyo's modern history; an insurrection of junior officers, at the head of some 1400 troops, and their murder of two former premiers, and a senior general. This bloody operation was intended to be the curtain-raiser for the 'Showa Restoration'. Everything was done in the Emperor's name. For twenty-four hours the nation held its breath. But the Emperor disowned the insurgents, roundly condemning the self-styled patriots who had attacked his own advisers. And the navy showed its teeth. Ratings from the fleet were put ashore on the Tokyo wharves. Rather belatedly the Army General Staff and Ministry of War decided that the young officers must be treated as mutineers. Martial law was declared and a cordon thrown round the area held by the rebels. A battle seemed unavoidable; but at the eleventh hour the mutineers surrendered without a fight.[5]

A number of generals were known to be in sympathy with the aims of the insurrection. The mutiny certainly discredited – temporarily at any rate – these senior officers; who belonged for the most part to the 'northern advance' school. They were duly purged. Those conducting the purge were, in the main, believers in the 'southern advance'. They proceeded to consolidate their hegemony not only over the army but also over the nation as a whole. The upshot was that the army became more than ever the driving force in politics. For in the aftermath of the rebellion the army leaders as good as dictated the composition of the new Cabinet (under the former Foreign Minister, Hirota Koki) and had their way on such decisive matters as the national budget (the proportion devoted to the army and navy rising to almost 50 per cent), the reform of educational textbooks, and the 'guidance' to be given to industry, agriculture and commerce by the central bureaucracy. The pattern that now prevailed was that of a 'semi-wartime economy'. Against those attempting to resist or modify its pressure the army applied moral blackmail, arguing that further insurrections could be avoided only if civilian officials and politicians accepted its demands.

As for the navy, it had abrogated at the end of 1934 the Washington and London Treaties, and it withdrew from the London Naval Conference of 1835. Its expansion, Kato Kanji's dream, could now proceed unchecked by international agreements; and the keels were laid of the world's two largest battleships, *Yamato* and *Musashi*.

Yet despite these signs of the times – or was it because of them – the man in the street (of the town, not the village) often seemed more interested in sport and pleasure than in official sermons on Japan's matchless spirit and national destiny; for the fever of the early thirties was not fully sustained in the second half of the decade. By 1937 the country – as a Japanese scholar remarked to the writer at the time – was like a bus descending a mountain road, without a driver at the wheel. But unemployment (thanks to the 'semi-wartime economy') had fallen steeply, prices seemed steady, and in 1940 the Olympic Games were due to be held in Tokyo. There was not likely to be war before then. And in June 1937 a youngish, popular Kyoto nobleman, Prince Konoye, took office as Premier, forming a nicely balanced Cabinet of bureaucrats and party politicians, designed to transcend the sectional interests of any group, however powerful. Konoye, protégé of the last surviving *Genro* (the aged Prince Saionji), had sufficient standing, it was believed, to control the army, which would hardly dare to upset a Cabinet welcomed enthusiastically by the press and the public at large. Within eight weeks, however, the Japanese were fighting in North China and Shanghai, and their planes were flying up the Yangtze to bomb Nanking.

IV

There is still obscurity surrounding the hostilities that broke out near Peking early in July 1937. Post-war revelations, which clarified the Mukden conspiracy of September 1931, did little to throw light on the 'Marco Polo Bridge Incident', named after a famous old bridge some miles from Peking, where Japanese troops on night manoeuvres exchanged shots with the Chinese. On what followed from this first clash there is an instructive comment by the Chinese-speaking British scholar, Lord Lindsay of Birker, who had first-hand experience of China in those years:

The Japanese army leaders [writes Lord Lindsay] would have been pleased to settle the fighting of July 1937 as a local incident if they could have got further concessions to strengthen their position in North China, but Chiang Kai-shek could not afford to concede more. Lo Chia-lun, an old and very loyal member of the Kuomintang, once described to me his fears that there would be further concessions at this date and his relief on hearing from a member of Chiang Kai-shek's secretariat that Chiang had decided to send eight divisions into Hopei. Since this was contrary to the terms of an earlier agreement with Japan it showed that the Chinese government had finally decided to fight.[6]

Chiang's determination to fight was the logical consequence of the Sian Affair in the previous year, when under duress (as a temporary prisoner of Chang Hsueh-liang) he agreed to join forces with the

Communists in a united front against Japan. Having failed to crush them while they were on the Long March (November 1934–August 1935) from the Kiangsi–Fukien border to northern Shensi, it was with reluctance that Chiang was obliged to accept the Communists as partners in the struggle with the Japanese.

Meanwhile, there was severe disagreement in Tokyo between the War Ministry, which pressed for strong measures in China, and the Army General Staff, which adhered on the whole to the anti-Russian views of the 'northern school', and therefore urged restraint.

So marked was the split within the army that it was sarcastically said that the 'Nihon-gun' (Japanese army) was in reality the 'nihon-gun' (two-branch army, written with different Chinese characters). Chiang Kai-shek is likewise said to have complained of the difficulty of knowing precisely with whom he should deal in the Japanese army, and one of his aides is reported to have replied that he couldn't go far wrong so long as the other man was only a colonel, a major, or a captain.[7]

That observation by a Japanese writer sums up a situation in which disunity and indiscipline cast a blight on the army and, therefore, on the shaping of national policy, with appalling results for China.

It seems to have been, ironically enough, Prince Konoye, the Premier, who tipped the scales in favour of the War Ministry's tough line; he certainly disappointed 'Old Liberals' who hoped he would bring the army to heel. But on Chinese affairs Konoye appears always to have favoured a strong policy (for which, indeed, he was to admit his blame when the Pacific War was over). All the same, he sent a personal envoy in July on a secret mission to Nanking to negotiate with the Chinese; and it is a telling proof of the army's arrogant power that the military police arrested Konoye's man as he was about to leave the country.

By the end of July 1937 war in North China had started in earnest. The following month a shooting incident in Shanghai supplied a pretext for intervention there in great strength. The ensuing battle was as savage as the fighting in 1932; and this time there was no truce. When Chinese resistance finally collapsed, the Japanese pressed on to Nanking; which fell in December. For several days the invading troops were allowed a free hand, and there were scenes of massacre and rape on a scale rarely known in modern times. These excesses, needless to say, were not reported in the Japanese press; but three generals were recalled home, together with many of the troops involved.

Just before the city was captured, the USS *Panay* was attacked and sunk by Japanese naval aircraft, and HMS *Ladybird* suffered casualties from shellfire by an army artillery unit. The two vessels were on the Yangtze below Nanking, their movements having been notified to the Japanese command. The attacks on these river gunboats, so far from being accidental, were launched by officers on the spot determined to teach the Western powers a sharp lesson: keep clear of the Chinese war zone or suffer the consequences. But the news threw the Japanese government into a state of genuine alarm and created anxiety and regret throughout the country.

This crisis, which caught Tokyo off balance, provided the two leading powers of the West with their last chance of checking Japanese military expansion without resort to war. The Anti-Comintern Pact (which Italy had now signed) had not put an end to Japan's diplomatic isolation, for it did not apply to any dispute Japan might have with the United States and Britain. In fact, the Germans were embarrassed by the scale of Japan's operations in China. Chiang's strategy and tactics were based largely on the advice given him by a team of German military advisers; and German diplomacy was active behind the scenes in trying to get Japan and China to discuss terms of peace.

Given the will, the Roosevelt and Chamberlain governments, acting together, could probably have insisted with success on a Japanese withdrawal from the Yangtze valley. It is true that this would have amounted to a repetition of the humiliation imposed on Japan by the Triple Intervention of 1895. It is undeniable that there would have been some risk of war; and the British government could not have relished the prospect of transferring heavy units of the fleet to the Far East. It can be said, too, that public opinion in Britain and America, although by now deeply stirred by events in the Far East, may not have been prepared for a war that was not obviously one of national self-defence.

Be that as it may, such risks had to be accepted if America and Britain hoped to preserve their interests, not to mention their prestige, in the Far East. There was lacking, however, the necessary Anglo-American unity of purpose that a bold course required. Compensation and apologies, unreservedly offered by Japan, were accepted; Washington and London made no further demands. The sense of relief in Tokyo could be felt on all sides.

Four short years were to elapse before the blows were struck with devastating effect at Hawaii, the Philippines, Hong Kong and Malaya.

The course of developments in the Far East during those years was shaped, to an unusual degree, by the changing situation in Europe. The Munich Agreement of 1938, the fall of France in 1940, the German assault on Russia in 1941 – those three seismic events in the history of twentieth-century diplomacy and war resolved the great debate in Japan between the 'northern' and 'southern' schools. Munich encouraged the army to launch operations from the sea against South China, leading to the capture of Canton, without fear of a significant reaction from Great Britain. The collapse of France ensured that Japan, fearful of 'missing the bus', would hasten to conclude a full-scale alliance with Germany. More than this, French weakness gave the Japanese army and navy an opening in Indio-China for a bridge-head in the shape of airfields and harbours. But it was the outbreak of the German–Russian war that forced an irrevocable choice between a northern and a southern advance.

In July 1941 the Kwantung Army was heavily reinforced; and the Foreign Minister of the day, Matsuoka, uninhibited by the Neutrality Pact he had signed in Moscow a few months earlier, was all for Japan striking hard at the Soviet Far East in support of her German ally. But caution was imposed by the memory of Nomonhan on the Manchurian–Mongolian steppe, where, in 1939 during a prolonged clash with the Russians, the Japanese had suffered a disastrous defeat.

Yet in view of the speed with which the Germans advanced towards Leningrad and Moscow it must be thought surprising that government and high command in Tokyo rejected Matsuoka's pressing advice. In fact, he became an embarrassment to his colleagues. Konoye (Premier for the second time) reshuffled his Cabinet; as reconstituted it did not include Matsuoka.

The preference for the 'southern advance' was indicated as early as July, when France received a Japanese demand for the cession of bases in the south of Indo-China. It does not seem to have occurred to Tokyo that this move further south would attract immediate retaliation from the United States, Britain and the Commonwealth, and Holland. When these countries acting in unison imposed what was in effect an almost total trade embargo it came as a profound shock; the more so because Ambassador Nomura in Washington was having a series of talks with the Secretary of State, Cordell Hull, in the hope of establishing a new understanding between Japan and the United States. The embargo could mean that within about a year and a half Japan's stockpile of oil would be exhausted.

V

So, very late in the day, the United States and Great Britain adopted a policy much more likely to lead to war than would have been the case had they chosen the same course after the *Panay–Ladybird* affair, in the winter of 1937–8. Even so, this likelihood of war with Japan in 1941 was by no means generally accepted in Washington and London – or, if war was seen as probable the prospect was viewed, in some quarters, with unwarranted equanimity, indeed almost insouciance. In the State Department the official in charge of the Far East desk, a China specialist, was confident that Japan would back down. He rated the chance of war as zero. In London the Ministry of Economic Warfare was of much the same mind. The Dutch Foreign Minister was sure the embargo would induce a change of policy in Japan. Churchill's opinion was that if Japan did enter the war certain 'forfeits' – such as Hong Kong – would have to be paid, and Japanese cruisers would be a menace to shipping east of Singapore; but that would be broadly the extent of the damage.

Expert naval and military opinion in America and Britain, however, hoped that any break with Japan would occur in 1942 rather than in the latter half of 1941. Great importance was attached to completing the build-up of the new Boeing 'Flying Fortress' aircraft on the Philippine air bases; a long process that could not be accomplished within 1941. Although the land forces in Malaya had been reinforced by an Australian division, it was certain that the Royal Navy would be able to spare no more than one or two capital ships for Singapore – their function being deterrent. If the deterrent failed to deter, their mission would have failed.

To win time, to delay for as long as possible the breach with Japan; this was the reasoned appreciation of expert opinion. It was shared by the experienced American ambassador in Tokyo, Joseph Grew, and by his British colleague, Sir Robert Craigie. Thus, when Prince Konoye proposed that he should have a meeting with President Roosevelt in Alaska or Hawaii as soon possible, Grew urged Washington to agree. Konoye's plan, it seems, was to muster a powerful delegation, including senior service officers, so that an agreement reached at a 'summit' meeting could be effectively imposed on the armed forces. But the ghost of Munich haunted the West. It appeared only too likely that an American–Japanese settlement would be unattainable save at the expense of China. So the Konoye project came to nothing.

At the beginning of September a conference of Japanese armed service and civilian leaders in the Emperor's presence formally agreed that the country must be prepared for war against the United States and Britain unless, through talks in Washington, the economic blockade was eased by the middle of October.[8] It was a decision reached in a mood approaching desperation.

Plans for the attack on Pearl Harbor had been discussed in the spring, and later there had been secret exercises at Kagoshima where the bay reproduced to some extent the topographical features of the Hawaiian base. The extreme secrecy that surrounded the projected operation was such that the navy, ever jealous of its independence, allowed no detail of its plans to reach the rival service. The War Minister and his colleagues were simply informed that if war should occur, the navy had made plans to meet this emergency. Nevertheless, the lords of the Japanese Admiralty were far from optimistic about the final outcome of a struggle in the Pacific; and they were at least half prepared to accept what Konoye himself recognised as inevitable if war was to be avoided – namely, retreat in face of the pressure of the 'ABCD' (American, British, Chinese, Dutch) powers.

The army's attitude was much less ambivalent. As propounded with vigour by Lieutenant-General Tojo, the Minister of War, it envisaged, as a maximum concession, a withdrawal from the bases in southern Indo-China, while the alliance with Germany and Italy could be left to wilt. There could be no evacuation of occupied China, at least for some time, and certainly not in response to foreign demands: better to risk all than suffer national humiliation. Such was the army's view when mid-October 1941 arrived, with no agreement reached at Washington and with the embargo fully enforced against Japan.

In this crisis, Tojo's stand prevailed. Konoye resigned, Tojo succeeding him, on the understanding that a last effort would be made to cobble together some kind of diplomatic agreement with America; but if this proved impossible, then Japan would resort to war some time after the middle of November.

Japan's final proposal to the United States was a *modus vivendi*, a withdrawal from the southern Indo-China bases in return for a lifting of the embargo – the agreement to be seen as a temporary measure. The Americans hesitated before rejecting this proposal. Throughout 1941 they acted, in effect, as spokesmen for Britain in the Washington talks. Churchill at this juncture encouraged Roosevelt to turn down the *modus vivendi*, although Craigie in Tokyo (concurring with Grew's advice) favoured its acceptance; while the American Chiefs of Staff, since the Japanese proposal had the merit of buying time, also favoured acceptance. Roosevelt and the State Department decided to maintain a firm front. The reply to Tokyo, while not accepting the *modus vivendi*, put forward counter-proposals, reiterating the need for a total reconsideration of her China policy by Japan. In the tense, superheated atmosphere of Tokyo at that time the American reply was interpreted, unjustifiably and in some circles deliberately, as an ultimatum.[9] Nothing now could put the engines of war into reverse.

VI

When the blow was struck at Pearl Harbor on 7 December the reaction in Japan was compounded of astonishment, relief and joy. For it was the general, if irrational, belief that the Empire was encircled by a ring of grimly hostile powers, that Hull's last Note had been a further tightening of the noose.[10] The resort to war, then, seemed fully justified as an act of self-defence. Moreover, the tremendous successes of the first few days – the Pearl Harbor strike, the destruction of the Boeings on the Philippine airfields, the landings in Malaya, the sinking of *Repulse* and *Prince of Wales* – appeared to underline the rectitude no less than the inevitability of Japan's plunge into the Second World War. Heaven, so it seemed, was on her side.

In the chorus of enthusiastic acclaim that greeted the news of these victories, there was a clearly perceptible note of vengeance long postponed but now achieved. There were, of course, private reservations and anxieties; and wise men must have remembered the old adage of the samurai, '*after victory tighten the strings of your helmet*'.

It has often been said that in the past, at any rate, the Japanese had little understanding of equality as a political and social ideal. Nations were ranked, like human beings, in a hierarchy. So in the rhetoric of Japanese nationalism in the thirties a recurring theme was the plea that each nation should find 'its proper place', the implication being that Japan's proper place was at the apex of the pyramid. The undesired intrusion by the West in the nineteenth century had created feelings of inferiority which were largely overcome by Japan's emergence as a world power in the twentieth. Largely overcome; but not entirely. *Sekai Dai Ichi*, 'First in the World'; which country in 1942 could lay claim to this title? Her early victories seemed to place Japan in the running, at last – so it appeared to nationalist true believers. It was a heady prospect, seeing that there were people still living who could have watched in their childhood British soldiers drilling in the foreign settlement at Yokohama. Yet, as we know, 'the violence, fury, skill, and might of Japan' (Churchill as usual found the right words) were to burn up like a falling satellite within four years of Pearl Harbor.

The moral – that nations must know the true potentialities and limitations of their own strength – was grasped with admirable intelligence by Japan after 1945, and for that matter by Great Britain also, and, belatedly, by the United States. Its comprehension in the context of Asia still eludes the Soviet Union; although here perhaps a dearth of facts makes prophecy unwise. But until there is a resolution of the Chinese–Soviet dispute, geographical in its essence, the process initiated by Japan – the redrawing of the map of Asia so as to exclude the West – will remain in a strict sense incomplete.

Chronological Table

1853		Commodore Perry's first visit to Japan
1854		Perry's second visit: first American–Japanese treaty signed
1858		Treaties signed with Russia, Britain, France and other Western powers; the 'unequal treaties', granting extra-territorial rights
1863		British naval bombardment of Kagoshima
1864		British, French, Dutch, and American naval bombardment of forts on the Shimonoseki Straits
1868		Meiji Restoration and the fall of the Tokugawa shogunate
1869– 73		Intergovernmental debate over *Seikan-ron* ('Punish Korea Argument'); final decision is against war
1875		Russo-Japanese agreement on Kuriles and Sakhalin: Japan acquires northern Kuriles in exchange for ceding Sakhalin to Russia
1877		Satsuma Rising under Saigo Takamori
1885		Tientsin Treaty (Li-Ito Convention) between China and Japan: settlement of Sino-Japanese dispute over Korea
1889	February	Constitution promulgated by the Emperor Meiji
1890	November	First session of the imperial diet
1891		Work starts on the Trans-Siberian Railway
1894	July	Revision of the treaty with Great Britain, the 'unequal clauses' to lapse after five years

	July	Outbreak of the Sino-Japanese War
1895	April	Treaty of Shimonoseki, embodying peace terms imposed on China; Japan acquires Formosa and Port Arthur
	April	The Triple Intervention: Russia, Germany, and France 'advise' Japan to return Port Arthur and the Liaotung Peninsula to China
1898	March	Germany obtains the lease of Tsingtao from China
	March	Russia obtains the lease of Port Arthur
	April	France acquires the lease of Kwangchowwan
	April	Outbreak of the Spanish-American War
	June	Britain obtains the lease of the 'New Territories' at Hong Kong
	July	Britain obtains the lease of Weihaiwei 'for as long as Port Arthur shall remain Russian'
	July	The United States' annexation of Hawaii
	December	Peace treaty concluded between the United States and Spain: the United States acquire the Philippines and Guam
1899–1902		The South African War
1899–1902		United States' war against Filipino guerrillas
1900		Boxer Rising
1901	September	The Boxer Protocol
1902	January	Anglo-Japanese Treaty of Alliance signed
1903	August	Japanese–Russian negotiations begin
1904	February	Japanese attack on Port Arthur; Russo-Japanese War begins
1905	January	Surrender of Port Arthur
	March	Battle of Mukden
	May	Battle of Tsushima, Sea of Japan
	July	Taft-Katsura Accord
	August	Russo-Japanese peace conference opens at Portsmouth, New Hampshire

	August	Revised Anglo-Japanese Treaty of Alliance
	September	Portsmouth Peace Treaty signed: riots in Tokyo and other cities against the peace settlement: Japan acquires southern Sakhalin and the lease of Port Arthur and the Liaotung Peninsula
	November	Korea becomes a Japanese protectorate
1906–1907		Anti-Japanese agitation in California; 'war scare' on the West Coast: American fleet transferred to the Pacific
1908	October	American 'Great White Fleet' calls at Yokohama
	November	Root-Takahira Agreement
1910	August	Korea is annexed by Japan
1911–1912		Chinese Revolution; Manchu (Ch'ing) dynasty overthrown
1911	July	Further renewal of the Anglo-Japanese Alliance
1914	4 August	British declaration of war on Germany
	23 August	Japanese declaration of war on Germany
	October	Japanese navy occupies German Pacific islands north of the Equator
	November	Surrender of Tsingtao
1915	January	Twenty-one Demands presented to China
	May	China accepts modified version of the Demands
1916	July	Russo-Japanese Treaty of Alliance signed
1917	February–March	Britain, France, Russia and Italy sign secret agreements with Japan
	March	Russian Revolution; fall of the monarchy
	April	American declaration of war on Germany
	August	Chinese declaration of war on Germany
	November	Bolshevik seizure of power in Petrograd
	November	Lansing–Ishii Exchange of Notes
1918	March	Brest–Litovsk Peace Treaty

	July–August	Rice riots in Japanese cities
	August	Tokyo decision to join Allied expedition to Siberia
	11 November	Armistice on the Western Front
1919	January–June	Paris Peace Conference
	28 June	Peace Treaty signed at Versailles
1920		USA and Allies withdraw from Siberia: Japanese troops remain, and later occupy northern Sakhalin
1921	July	First Congress of Chinese Communist Party, Shanghai
1921	December	Four Power Pact signed at Washington; Anglo-Japanese Alliance to lapse on ratification of the Pact
1922	February	Sino-Japanese agreement at Washington; Japan agrees to evacuate Shantung
	February	Naval Limitation Treaty and Nine Power Pact signed at Washington
1922		Japanese withdrawal from Siberia
1923	September	Kanto (Tokyo/Yokohama area) Earthquake
1926	July	Northern Expedition of Kuomintang under Chiang Kai-shek begins
1928	June	Murder of Chang Tso-lin
1929	Autumn	Wall Street Crash and start of World Depression
1930		London Naval Treaty
1930	November	Attack on Premier Hamaguchi
1931	March	Abortive military conspiracy in Tokyo
	September	*Coup* at Mukden leads to the Japanese occupation of large areas of Manchuria. China appeals to the League
1932	January–March	Sino–Japanese conflict at Shanghai
	March	Establishment of Manchukuo
	May	Murder of Premier Inukai
	October	Publication of the Lytton Report
1933	March	Japan withdraws from the League
1935		Agitation over the Minobe affair

1936	February	Mutiny in Tokyo
	November	German–Japanese Anti-Comintern Pact signed
	December	Chiang Kai-shek agrees, under duress at Sian, to a united front with the Chinese Communists against Japan
1937	July	Outbreak of Sino–Japanese hostilities, Marco Polo Bridge, near Peking
	August	Sino–Japanese hostilities spread to Shanghai
	12 December	USS *Panay* and HMS *Ladybird* sunk by Japanese action on the Yangtze
	13 December	Fall of Nanking
1938	September	The Munich Agreement
	October	Japanese occupation of Wuhan
	October	Japanese campaign in south China and capture of Canton
1939	May– September	Russo–Japanese hostilities in the Nomonhan region of the Outer Mongolia–Manchukuo border
	September	World War II begins in Europe
1940	June	The Fall of France
	September	Franco–Japanese agreement on Japanese use of bases in northern Indo–China
	September	German–Japanese–Italian Tripartite Pact signed
1941	March– April	Foreign Minister Matsuoka visits Berlin and Rome; signs Neutrality Pact with Soviet Union (13 April)
	April	Japanese–American talks open in Washington
	June	Germany attacks the Soviet Union
	July– September	Japanese mobilisation
	July	Japanese occupy bases in southern Indo–China. Economic embargo imposed by United States, British Commonwealth, and Holland

	September	Imperial Conference at Tokyo confirms decision for war in the autumn, if Washington talks fail
	November	Hull's final Note
	7/8 December	Japanese attacks on Pearl Harbor, Hong Kong and Malaya
	December	Sinking of *Prince of Wales* and *Repulse* Capture of Hong Kong
1942	January–	
	May	Japanese occupy Malaya, Philippines, Java, Sumatra, Borneo, Celebes, Burma and the Andamans; Ceylon and Port Darwin, Australia, raided; Japanese naval victories in the Java Strait and Indian Ocean; indecisive Japanese–American Battle of the Coral Sea
	June	Battle of Midway; heavy Japanese losses
	August	Australians repulse the Japanese at Milne Bay, New Guinea
	August	Opening of Guadalcanal, Solomons, campaign
1943	February	Americans complete the recapture of Guadalcanal
1944	April–	
	June	Battle of Kohima–Imphal
	July	Fall of Saipan
	October	American assault on the Philippines; Battle of Leyte Gulf
1945	February	Fall of Manila
	March	Fall of Iwojima
	May	Fall of Rangoon
	May	Surrender of Germany
	June	Capture of Okinawa completed
	26 July	Potsdam Proclamation, calling for the immediate surrender of the Japanese armed forces
	6 August	Atomic Bomb dropped on Hiroshima
	8 August	Soviet Union declares war on Japan
	9 August	Atomic Bomb dropped on Nagasaki
	15 August	Japanese Emperor's broadcast announc-

ing acceptance of the Potsdam Proclamation

2 September   Formal Japanese surrender ceremony on USS *Missouri* in Tokyo Bay

Notes and References

1. DISASTER FOR THE WEST

1. 'Defence of HMS *Peterel* at Shanghai, 1941'; a summary of the official report prepared for the writer by the Historical Section, Admiralty, Whitehall.
2. Ibid.
3. There is, however, a very brief account of the episode in Martin H. Brice, *The Royal Navy and the Sino-Japanese Incident 1937–1941* (London: Ian Allan, 1973) p. 152.
4. Sir William Slim, *Defeat into Victory* (London: Cassell, 1956) pp. 42–3.
5. Ibid., p. 35.
6. S. Woodburn Kirby *et al.*, *The War Against Japan*, vol. II: *India's Most Dangerous Hour* (London: H.M.S.O., 1958) p. 126.
7. Ibid., p. 122.
8. Colin Cross, *The Fall of the British Empire* (London: Hodder & Stoughton, 1968) p. 241.
9. 'Summary of Policy Agreed at Imperial Conference, July 2, 1941', in Nobutaka Ike, *Japan's Decision for War: Records of the 1941 Policy Conferences* (Stanford, California: Stanford University Press, 1967) p. 79.
10. George Alexander Lensen, *The Strange Neutrality: Soviet–Japanese Relations during the Second World War, 1941–1945* (Tallahassee, Florida: The Diplomatic Press, 1972) pp. 37–8.
11. Ian Morrison, *Malayan Postscript* (London: Faber & Faber, 1942) p. 115.
12. Ba Maw, *Breakthrough in Burma* (New Haven and London: Yale University Press, 1968) pp. 311–12.
13. Iyenaga Saburo, cited in Joyce C. Lebra, *Japan's Greater East Asia Co-Prosperity Sphere in World War II, Selected Readings and Documents* (Kuala Lumpur: Oxford University Press, 1975) p. 169.
14. Joyce C. Lebra, *Jungle Alliance: Japan and the Indian National Army* (Singapore: Asia Pacific Press, 1971) p. 88.
15. Mark R. Peattie, *Ishiwara Kanji and Japan's Confrontation with the West* (Princeton, New Jersey: Princeton University Press, 1975) p. 74.
16. Richard Storry, *The Double Patriots: A Study of Japanese Nationalism* (London: Chatto & Windus, 1957) p. 317 (appendix II: 'Land Disposal Plan in the Greater East Asia Co-Prosperity Sphere', December 1941, Ministry of War Research Section, Tokyo).
17. Slim, *Defeat into Victory*, p. 188.
18. Correlli Barnett, *The Collapse of British Power* (London: Eyre Methuen, 1972) p. 592.
19. Ibid.

2. THE YELLOW PERIL AND THE WHITE PERIL

1. Jean-Pierre Lehmann, *The Image of Japan: From Feudal Isolation to World Power 1850–1905* (London: George Allen & Unwin, 1978) p. 49.
2. Cited by Marius Jansen, 'Modernization and Foreign Policy in Meiji Japan', in Robert E. Ward (ed.), *Political Development in Modern Japan* (Princeton, New Jersey: Princeton University Press, 1968) p. 182.

3. One of the best accounts of the *Seikan Ron* dispute, especially in terms of the psychology of those concerned, is in Hilary Conroy, *The Japanese Seizure of Korea 1868–1910* (Philadelphia: University of Pennsylvania Press, 1960) pp. 17–73.

4. Ward, *Political Development in Modern Japan*, p. 175.

5. Akira Iriye, *Across the Pacific: an Inner History of American–East Asian Relations* (New York: Harcourt, Brace, 1967) p. 67.

6. Masao Maruyama, *Thought and Behaviour in Modern Japanese Politics* (London: Oxford University Press [expanded edn] 1969) p. 7.

7. W. G. Beasley, *The Modern History of Japan* (London: Weidenfeld & Nicolson, 1963) p. 158.

8. Kiyosawa Kiyoshi, *Nihon Gaikoshi* (A Diplomatic History of Japan) (Tokyo, 1942) vol. i, pp. 5–7, cited in S. Okamoto, *The Japanese Oligarchy and the Russo-Japanese War* (New York: Columbia University Press, 1970) pp. 41–2.

9. Maruyama, *Thought and Behaviour*, pp. 18–19.

10. George A. Lensen (ed.), *The D'Anethan Dispatches from Japan, 1894–1910* (Tokyo: Sophia University Press, 1967) p. 18.

11. Conroy, *Japanese Seizure of Korea*, p. 196.

12. Basil Hall Chamberlain, *Things Japanese* (London: John Murray, 1905) p. 489.

13. Ibid.

14. Ernst L. Presseisen, *Before Aggression* (Tucson: University of Arizona Press, 1965) p. 141.

15. Ernest P. Young, 'A Study of Personalities in Japan Influencing the Events Leading to the Sino-Japanese War (1894–1895)', in *Papers on Japan* (East Asian Research Center, Harvard University, August 1963), p. 257.

16. Conroy, *Japanese Seizure of Korea*, p. 242, n. 26.

17. Quoted by Young, *Papers on Japan*, p. 251.

18. Ibid., p. 267.

19. Tatsuji Takeuchi, *War and Diplomacy in the Japanese Empire* (London: Allen & Unwin, 1936) p. 116.

20. Ian H. Nish, *The Anglo-Japanese Alliance* (London: The Athlone Press, 1966) p. 28.

21. J. K. Fairbank, E. O. Reischauer and A. M. Craig, *East Asia: The Modern Transformation* (Tokyo: Tuttle, 1965) p. 384.

22. Nish, *Anglo-Japanese Alliance*, p. 31.

23. *Jiji Shimpo* (21 June 1895), cited by Jean Lequiller, *Le Japon* (Paris: Editions Sirey, 1966) pp. 129–30.

24. Ibid.

25. Arthur Diosy, *The New Far East* (London: Cassell, 1904) pp. 332–3.

26. George A. Lensen (ed.), *Korea and Manchuria between Russia and Japan 1895–1904, The Observations of Sir Ernest Satow* (Tallahassee, Florida: The Diplomatic Press, 1966) p. 120.

3. A QUESTION OF ALLIANCES

1. Richard W. Van Alstyne, *The United States and East Asia* (London: Thames & Hudson, 1973) p. 91.

2. The text of the Boxer Protocol may be found in Theodore McNelly (ed.), *Sources in Modern East Asian History and Politics* (New York: Appleton-Century-Crofts, 1967) pp. 13–21.

3. A map illustrating the prospective division of China can be found in David Dallin, *The Rise of Russia in the Far East* (London: World Affairs Book Club, 1950) p. 67.

4. L. K. Young, *British Policy in China 1895–1902* (Oxford: Clarendon Press, 1970) p. 252.

5. Cited (from Witte's *Memoirs*) in Dallin, *Rise of Russia*, p. 35.

6. Andrew Malozemoff, *Russian Far Eastern Policy 1881–1904* (Berkeley and Los Angeles: University of California Press, 1958) p. 40.

7. Malozemoff argues powerfully that Russian policy was muddled rather than aggressive. David Walder, in *The Short Victorious War* (London: Hutchinson, 1973) p. 51, writes: 'At no stage did one man, or group of men, positively advocate war. There was never a war party, as there was eventually to be in Japan.' This is probably true; though it may be worth noting that in 1903 Plehve is alleged to have told Kuropatkin: 'What this country needs is a short victorious war to stem the tide of revolution.' (Ibid., p. 56).

8. Sakamoto Taro, *Nihon-shi Kojiten* (A Short Dictionary of Japanese History) (Tokyo: Kawakami Shuppansha, 1963) p. 318.

9. Ibid., pp. 124–5.

10. Malozemoff, *Russian Far Eastern Policy*, p. 155. Malozemoff's defence of the proposed treaty is ingenious rather than convincing.

11. Ibid., p. 151.

12. Nish, *Anglo-Japanese Alliance*, p. 120.

13. The letter is quoted in full as an appendix to Nish, *Anglo-Japanese Alliance*.

14. Max Beloff, *Imperial Sunset* (New York: Knopf, 1970) vol.i, p. 93.

15. Quoted in Nish, *Anglo-Japanese Alliance*, p. 213.

16. Cited by Foster Rhea Dulles, *America's Rise to World Power* (New York: Harper, 1963) p. 67.

17. The Katsura memorandum and the later memorandum by Komura are given as Appendices at the end of Nish, *Anglo-Japanese Alliance*, pp. 381–5.

18. Ibid.

19. Ibid., p. 151.

20. Roger F. Hackett, *Yamagata Aritomo in the Rise of Modern Japan* (Cambridge, Mass.: Harvard University Press, 1971) p. 218.

21. The treaty text is in Nish, *Anglo-Japanese Alliance*, pp. 216–17.

22. Ibid., p. 212.

4. 'THESE LITTLE PEOPLE WILL FIGHT'

1. Shumpei Okamoto, *The Japanese Oligarchy and the Russo-Japanese War* (New York: Columbia University Press, 1970) pp. 66–7.

2. Hyman Kublin, *Asian Revolutionary, the Life of Sen Katayama* (Princeton, New Jersey: Princeton University Press, 1964) p. 148.

3. Ibid., p. 145.

4. Margaret Blunden, *The Countess of Warwick* (London: Cassell, 1967) p. 171. Katayama's excellent English was the fruit of a college education in the United States.

5. Kublin, *Asian Revolutionary*, p. 181.

6. Cited in Tatsuo Arima, *The Failure of Freedom, a Portrait of Modern Japanese Intellectuals* (Cambridge, Mass.: Harvard University Press, 1969) p. 34.

7. Okamoto, *Japanese Oligarchy*, p. 8.

8. John Albert White, *The Diplomacy of the Russo-Japanese War* (Princeton, New Jersey: Princeton University Press, 1964) p. 352. This work has a useful appendix (pp. 351–8) setting out in parallel columns the Japanese and Russian proposals and counter-proposals from August 1903 to February 1904.

9. William Leonard Schwartz, *The Imaginative Interpretation of the Far East in Modern French Literature 1800–1925* (Paris: Librairie Ancienne Honoré Champion, 1927) p. 131. In Pierre Loti's *Madame Chrysanthème* the Japanese are portrayed as essentially unserious and superficial, almost childish indeed.

10. The experienced Belgian Minister in Tokyo (he had been there for ten years) wrote in a dispatch to Brussels (May 1904): ' "No war of race, no war of religion", says Count

Katsura, and he speaks not only as a private individual, but as Prime Minister in the name of the Emperor. His view is shared by all policy-makers.' Lensen (ed.), *D'Anethan Dispatches*, p. 188.

11. Payson J. Treat, *Diplomatic Relations between the United States and Japan 1895–1905* (Gloucester, Mass.: Peter Smith, 1963) p. 194. (Dispatch from Lloyd Griscom to the Secretary of State, 21 January 1904.)

12. Quoted by White, *Diplomacy of the Russo-Japanese War*, p. 127.

13. 'Long ago I stated that "East was East and West was West and never the twain should meet". It seemed right, for I had checked it by the card, but I was careful to point out circumstances under which cardinal points ceased to exist.' Rudyard Kipling, *Something of Myself* (Leipzig: Bernhard Tauchnitz, 1938) p. 202.

14. Walder, *Short Victorious War*, p. 163.

15. Lo Hui-min (ed.), *The Correspondence of G. E. Morrison 1895–1912* (Cambridge: Cambridge University Press, 1976) p. 287.

16. Kuroha Shigeru, *Sekaishi-jo yoru mitaru Nichiro Sensoshi* ('A History of the Russo-Japanese War from the Viewpoint of World History') (Tokyo: Shibundo, 1966) p. 231.

17. James W. Morley (ed.), *Japan's Foreign Policy 1868–1941, A Research Guide* (New York: Columbia University Press, 1974) pp. 196–7.

18. H. M. Hyndman, *The Awakening of Asia* (London: Cassell, 1919) p. 143.

19. Cited in Chushichi Tsuzuki, *H. M. Hyndman and British Socialism* (London: Oxford University Press, 1961) p. 225. The quotation is from *New Europe*, XI (29 May 1919) 154–8. The war 'now being concluded' refers of course to the First World War.

5. THE NECESSARY AND UNPOPULAR PEACE

1. White, *Diplomacy of the Russo-Japanese War*, pp. 229–30.

2. Raymond A. Esthus, *Theodore Roosevelt and Japan* (Seattle: University of Washington Press, 1966) pp. 38–9.

3. See Nish, *Anglo-Japanese Alliance*, pp. 298–344, for a judicious account of the 1905 treaty, including the debate within and between government departments in Whitehall and Calcutta on whether or not to press for a Japanese military contribution to the defence of India.

4. Roosevelt, letter to Taft (5 October, 1905), quoted in Esthus, *Theodore Roosevelt and Japan* (cited) p. 104.

5. Okamoto, *Japanese Oligarchy*, pp. 154–5.

6. Ibid.

7. Esthus, *Theodore Roosevelt*, p. 92.

8. It is only fair to emphasise that this is a supposition that Professor Esthus would scarcely accept. Indeed, he declares that Roosevelt 'regarded the Japanese claim for the island as so strong that it doubtless never entered his mind that Japan might consider giving back the entire island to Russia'. Ibid., pp. 92–3.

9. John M. Maki (ed.), *Conflict and Tension in the Far East, Key Documents, 1894–1960* (Seattle: University of Washington Press, 1961) pp. 18–21.

10. Lo Hui-min (ed.), *Correspondence of G. E. Morrison*, p. 333. Morrison up to now had been strongly anti-Russian and correspondingly pro-Japanese; but within months of the ending of the war his views changed and he became a resolutely hostile critic of Japan. One suspects that the seeds of disenchantment were sown that summer at Portsmouth, New Hampshire.

11. The literary critic, Eto Jun, in 'The Staff of the Asahi Shimbun', *The Pacific Rivals, A Japanese View of Japanese–American Relations* (New York and Tokyo: Weatherhill/Asahi, 1972) p. 60.

12. Conroy, *Japanese Seizure of Korea*, p. 334.

13. Marius B. Jansen, *The Japanese and Sun Yat-sen* (Cambridge, Mass.: Harvard University Press, 1954) p. 117.
14. Joseph Gallieni, *Neufs ans à Madagascar* (Paris: Hachette, 1908) p. 270.
15. 'Obermann Once More' (1862), cited in Stephen C. Hay, *Asian Ideas of East and West* (Cambridge, Mass.: Harvard University Press, 1970) p. 6.
16. The words are from a poem sent by Katsura to the journalist and political commentator, Tokutomi Soho, owner of the *Kokumin Shimbun*, a paper whose premises were attacked by the Tokyo rioters in 1905 for its support of the Portsmouth peace terms.

6. TROUBLE AT THE GOLDEN GATE

1. Ian H. Nish, *Alliance in Decline, A Study in Anglo-Japanese Relations 1908-1923* (London: Athlone Press, 1972) p. 20.
2. Esthus, *Theodore Roosevelt*, p. 307. In the letter to Taft there is also a reference to a meeting with Kitchener (in England in 1909) at which the latter told Roosevelt that Japan was laying down triple lines of track on the SMR as an answer to Russia's double-tracking of the Trans-Siberian.
3. Hosoya Chihiro, 'Japan's Policies toward Russia', in Morley (ed.), *Japan's Foreign Policy*, p. 376.
4. Akira Iriye, *Pacific Estrangement, Japanese and American Expansion, 1897-1911* (Cambridge, Mass.: Harvard University Press, 1972) p. 133.
5. Ibid., p. 136.
6. 'The American who is flattered at first by the politeness of his Japanese servant will later on, perhaps, cite as a reproach against the race the fact that "we can never tell what a Japanese is thinking about"' (the sociologist, Robert E. Park) quoted by Stanford M. Lyman, 'Generation and Character: The Case of the Japanese–American', in Hilary Conroy and T. Scott Miyakawa, *East Across the Pacific* (Santa Barbara, California and Oxford: Clio Press, 1972) p. 280.
7. Esthus, *Theodore Roosevelt*, p. 191.
8. Ibid.
9. Charles E. Neu, *The Troubled Encounter, the United States and Japan* (New York: John Wiley, 1975) pp. 54–5.
10. Esthus, *Theodore Roosevelt*, p. 213.
11. Ibid., p. 363..
12. Neu, *Troubled Encounter*, p. 64.
13. Iriye, *Pacific Estrangement*, p. 151.

7. JAPAN, CHINA AND THE FIRST WORLD WAR

1. K. Takahashi, *The Rise and Development of Japan's Modern Economy* (Tokyo: Jiji Tsushinsha, 1969) p. 366.
2. One of the best studies of such activities is Jansen, *The Japanese and Sun Yat-sen*.
3. Nish, *Alliance in Decline*, p. 96.
4. Ibid.
5. Cited in Peter Lowe, *Great Britain and Japan, A study of British Far Eastern Policy 1911-1915* (London: Macmillan, 1969) p. 182.
6. Nish, *Alliance in Decline*, p. 137.
7. Lowe, *Great Britain and Japan*, p. 199.
8. Jansen, *The Japanese and Sun Yat-sen*, p. 189.
9. Lowe, *Great Britain and Japan*, p. 221.
10. Maki (ed.), *Conflict and Tension in the Far East*, p. 34. The full text of the 'Twenty-One Demands' is to be found in this work.

11. Ibid., p. 31.
12. Ibid., p. 34.
13. *The Times* (13 February 1915), cited in Lowe, *Great Britain and Japan*, p. 232.
14. Chow Tse-tung, *The May Fourth Movement* (Cambridge, Mass.: Harvard University Press, 1964) p. 87.
15. Burton F. Beers, *Vain Endeavor: Robert Lansing's Attempt to End the American–Japanese Rivalry* (Durham, North Carolina: Duke University Press, 1962) p. 116.
16. Ibid., p. 109.

8. THE NINETEEN-TWENTIES

1. Captain Malcolm D. Kennedy, *The Estrangement of Great Britain and Japan 1917–35* (Manchester: Manchester University Press, 1969) p. 13.
2. David Footman, *Civil War in Russia* (London: Faber & Faber, 1961) p. 303.
3. Shuichi Kato, 'Taisho Democracy as the Pre-Stage for Japanese Militarism', in Bernard S. Silberman and H. D. Harootunian (eds), *Japan in Crisis: Essays on Taisho Democracy* (Princeton, New Jersey: Princeton University Press, 1974) p. 221.
4. Ibid., p. 233.
5. Putnam Weale cited by W. Roger Louis, *British Strategy in the Far East 1919–1939* (Oxford: Clarendon Press, 1971) p. 108.
6. Nish, *Alliance in Decline*, p. 381.
7. Barnett, *Collapse of British Power*, p. 254.
8. Ibid., p. 257.
9. Akira Iriye, 'The Failure of Economic Expansionism: 1918–1931', in Silberman and Harootunian (eds), *Japan in Crisis*, p. 261.
10. Cited in Ian Nish, *Japanese Foreign Policy, 1869–1942: Kasumigaseki to Miyakezaka* (London: Routlege & Kegan Paul, 1977) p. 155.
11. Nobuya Bamba, *Japanese Diplomacy in a Dilemma: New Light on Japan's China Policy, 1924–1929* (Vancouver: University of British Columbia Press, 1972) p. 275.
12. John J. Stephan, 'The Tanaka Memorial (1927): Authentic or Spurious?', *Modern Asian Studies*, vol. VII, part 4 (October 1973), 745. Dr Stephan's article demolishes the case for supposing Tanaka had any connection with the supposed 'Memorial'.
13. Cited in Stephen E. Pelz, *Race to Pearl Harbor: The Failure of the Second London Naval Conference and the Onset of World War II* (Cambridge, Mass.: Harvard University Press, 1974) p. 15.

9. THE END OF THE ROAD

1. Cited by Christopher Thorne, *The Limits of Foreign Policy: The West, the League and the Far Eastern Crisis of 1931–1933* (London: Hamish Hamilton, 1972) p. 4.
2. Ibid., p. 387.
3. Edwin O. Reischauer, 'What Went Wrong?', in James W. Morley (ed.), *Dilemmas of Growth in Prewar Japan* (Princeton, New Jersey: Princeton University Press, 1971) pp. 507–8.
4. The Minobe Affair receives scholarly attention in Frank O. Miller, *Minobe Tatsukichi, Interpreter of Constitutionalism in Japan* (Berkeley and Los Angeles: University of California Press, 1965).
5. The fullest account in English of the Tokyo insurrection is Ben-Ami Shillony, *Revolt in Japan: The Young Officers and The February 26, 1936 Incident* (Princeton, New Jersey: Princeton University Press, 1973).
6. Michael Lindsay, *The Unknown War: North China, 1937–1945* (London: Bergstrom & Boyle Books, 1975) (pages unnumbered).

7. Saburo Shiroyama (trans. John Bester), *War Criminal: The Life and Death of Hirota Koki* (Tokyo: Kodansha International, 1977) p. 176.

8. The main proceedings of this conference (Imperial Conference, 6 September 1941) may be found in Nobutaka Ike (trans. and ed.), *Japan's Decision for War: Records of the 1941 Policy Conferences* (Stanford, California: Stanford University Press, 1967) pp. 133–63.

9. The famous Hull Note of 26 November 1941, containing ten proposals (including the withdrawal by Japan of 'all military, naval, air and police forces from China and from Indo-China'), although described by Grew in his diary at the time as 'a broad-gauge, objective, and statesman-like document', was not helpful; but it contained no kind of warning or implied threat. Furthermore, it was headed '*Tentative and Without Commitment*'. Yoshida Shigeru points this out in his post-war memoirs and tells us that he went to see the Foreign Minister (Togo Shigenori) to draw his attention to that aspect of the Note. 'I suggested to him that if he could not prevent a Japanese declaration of war on the United States he should resign, an act which would hold up Cabinet deliberations and give the Army something to think about; and that if as a result of such a gesture he should be assassinated, such a death would be a happy one' (Shigeru Yoshida, *The Yoshida Memoirs*, London: Heinemann, 1961, p. 18). Yoshida also says that the Japanese government 'embellished the official translation of the Hull Note with certain touches calculated to excite popular feeling' and implies that the words 'tentative and without commitment' were omitted (ibid., p. 20). But perhaps the best comment is Grew's:

It is true that the draft proposal was not presented as an ultimatum, but coming when it did, after the conversations had dragged on futilely for some seven or eight months, permitting the pro-Axis and extremist forces of opposition in Japan to organize and consolidate their strength and allowing them to convey to the Japanese public the impression that the United States was merely playing for time and had no real intention of reaching a settlement, it was definitely regarded in Japan as an ultimatum, and it consequently was followed by the almost immediate outbreak of war. (Joseph C. Grew, *Turbulent Era*, Boston: Houghton Mifflin, 1952, vol. II, p. 1338).

It has to be remembered that when Hull composed the Note, Washington, thanks to having broken the Japanese diplomatic code, knew that Japan's military preparations for an attack were well advanced.

10. 'The formidable cordon of naval and air bases which America has developed round Japan in concert with Britain, the Netherlands, East Indies, Australia, and Chungking constitutes a direct threat against the Japanese Empire' (editorial column, *Japan Times and Adviser*, 18 November 1941), cited in Joseph C. Grew, *Ten Years in Japan*, London: Hammond & Hammond, 1944, p. 415.

Select Bibliography

(Including books not mentioned in the Notes and References.)

LOUIS ALLEN, *The End of the War in Asia* (London, 1976).

TATSUO ARIMA, *The Failure of Freedom, A Portrait of Modern Japanese Intellectuals* (Cambridge, Mass., 1969).

ASAHI SHIMBUN STAFF, *The Pacific Rivals, A Japanese View of Japanese-American Relations* (New York and Tokyo, 1972).

BA MAW, *Breakthrough in Burma* (New Haven, Conn., 1968).

NOBUYA BAMBA, *Japanese Diplomacy in a Dilemma: New Light on Japan's China Policy, 1924–1929* (Vancouver, 1972).

CORRELLI BARNETT, *The Collapse of British Power* (London, 1972).

W. G. BEASLEY, *The Modern History of Japan* (London, 1963).

BURTON F. BEERS, *Vain Endeavour: Robert Lansing's Attempt To End The American–Japanese Rivalry* (Durham, N. C., 1962).

MAX BELOFF, *Imperial Sunset* (New York, 1970).

JOHN BESTER (trans.) SABURO SHIROYAMA, *War Criminal, The Life and Death of Hirota Koki* (Tokyo and New York, 1977).

DOROTHY BORG and SHUMPEI OKAMOTO (eds) *Pearl Harbor as History; Japanese–American Relations, 1931–1941* (New York, 1973).

MARTIN H. BRICE, *The Royal Navy and the Sino-Japanese Incident 1937–1941* (London, 1973).

ROBERT J. C. BUTOW, *Tojo and the Coming of the War* (Princeton, N. J., 1961).

BASIL HALL CHAMBERLAIN, *Things Japanese* (London, 1905).

CHOW TSE-TUNG, *The May Fourth Movement* (Cambridge, Mass., 1964).

HILARY CONROY, *The Japanese Seizure of Korea 1868–1910* (Philadelphia, 1960).

——, T. SCOTT MIYAKAWA, *East Across the Pacific; Historical and Sociological Studies of Japanese Immigration and Assimilation* (Santa Barbara, Calif. and Oxford, 1972).

COLIN CROSS, *The Fall of the British Empire* (London, 1968).

JAMES B. CROWLEY, *Japan's Quest for Autonomy: National Security and Foreign Policy, 1930–1938* (Princeton, N. J., 1966).

DAVID J. DALLIN, *The Rise of Russia in the Far East* (London, 1950).

ARTHUR DIOSY, *The New Far East* (London, 1904).

FOSTER RHEA DULLES, *America's Rise to World Power* (New York, 1963).

PETER DUUS, *The Rise of Modern Japan* (Boston, Mass., 1976).

RAYMOND A. ESTHUS, *Theodore Roosevelt and Japan* (Seattle, 1966).

JOHN K. FAIRBANK; EDWIN O. REISCHAUER; ALBERT M. CRAIG; *East Asia, The Modern Transformation* (Boston, Mass., 1965).

DAVID FOOTMAN, *Civil War in Russia* (London, 1961).

JOSEPH GALLIENI, *Neufs ans à Madagascar* (Paris, 1908).

K. K. GHOSH, *The Indian National Army: Second Front of the Indian Independence Movement* (Meerut, 1969).

JOSEPH C. GREW, *Ten Years in Japan* (London, 1945).

——, *Turbulent Era: A Diplomatic Record of Forty Years, 1904–1945* Vol. II (Boston, Mass., 1952).

ROGER HACKETT, *Yamagata Aritomo in the Rise of Modern Japan 1838–1922* (Cambridge, Mass., 1971).

STEPHEN C. HAY, *Asian Ideas of East and West* (Cambridge, Mass., 1970).

H. M. HYNDMAN, *The Awakening of Asia* (London, 1919).

NOBUTAKE IKE (trans. and ed.), *Japan's Decision for War: Records of the 1941 Policy Conferences* (Stanford, Calif., 1967).

AKIRA IRIYE, *After Imperialism, the Search for a New Order in the Far East 1921–1931* (Cambridge, Mass., 1965).

——, *Across the Pacific: An Inner History of American – East Asian Relations* (New York, 1967).

——, *Pacific Estrangement: Japanese and American Expansion 1897–1911* (Cambridge, Mass., 1972).

MARIUS B. JANSEN, *The Japanese and Sun Yat-sen* (Cambridge, Mass., 1954).

—— (ed.), *Changing Japanese Attitudes Toward Modernization* (Princeton, N. J., 1965).

MALCOLM D. KENNEDY, *The Estrangement of Great Britain and Japan 1917–35* (Manchester, 1969).

S. WOODBURN KIRBY and others, *The War Against Japan*, vol. II, *India's Most Dangerous Hour* (London, 1958).

HYMAN KUBLIN, *Asian Revolutionary, the Life of Sen Katayama* (Princeton, N. J., 1964).

JOYCE C. LEBRA, *Jungle Alliance: Japan and the Indian National Army* (Singapore, 1971).

JOYCE C. LEBRA, (ed.), *Japan's Greater East Asia Co-Prosperity Sphere in World War II: Selected Readings and Documents* (Kuala Lumpur, 1975).

——, *Japanese-Trained Armies in Southeast Asia: Independence and Volunteer Forces in World War II* (Hong Kong, 1977).

LEE CHONG-SIK, *The Politics of Korean Nationalism* (Berkeley and Los Angeles, 1965).

BRADFORD A. LEE, *Britain and the Sino-Japanese War 1937–1939, A Study in the Dilemmas of British Decline* (London, 1973).

JEAN-PIERRE LEHMANN, *The Image of Japan: From Feudal Isolation to World Power 1850–1905* (London, 1978).

GEORGE A. LENSEN (ed.), *Korea and Manchuria Between Russia and Japan 1895–1904, The Observations of Sir Ernest Satow* (Tallahassee, Florida, 1966).

—— (ed.), *The D'Anethan Dispatches from Japan, 1894–1910* (Tokyo, 1967).

——, *Japanese Recognition of the USSR: Soviet–Japanese Relations 1921–1930* (Tokyo, 1970).

GEORGE A. LENSEN, *The Strange Neutrality: Soviet–Japanese Relations during the Second World War, 1941–1945* (Tallahassee, Florida, 1972).

——, *The Damned Inheritance: The Soviet Union and the Manchurian Crisis, 1924–1935* (Tallahassee, Florida, 1974).

JEAN LEQUILLER, *Le Japon* (Paris, 1966).

MICHAEL LINDSAY, *The Unknown War: North China, 1937–1945* (London, 1975).

LO HUI-MIN (ed.), *The Correspondence of G. E. Morrison, 1895–1912* (Cambridge, 1976).

WILLIAM W. LOCKWOOD, *The Economic Development of Japan: Growth and Structural Change, 1868–1938* (Princeton, N. J., 1954).

—— (ed.), *The State and Economic Enterprise in Japan* (Princeton, N. J., 1965).

W. ROGER LOUIS, *British Strategy in the Far East, 1919–1939* (Oxford, 1971); and *Imperialism at Bay, 1941–45* (Oxford, Clarendon Press, 1977).

PETER LOWE, *Great Britain and Japan, 1911–1915: A Study of British Far Eastern Policy* (London, 1969).

PETER LOWE, *Great Britain and the Origins of the Pacific War: A Study of British Policy in East Asia* (Oxford, 1977).

THEODORE MCNELLY (ed.), *Sources in Modern East Asian History and Politics* (New York, 1967).

JOHN M. MAKI (ed.), *Conflict and Tension in the Far East, Key Documents, 1894–1960* (Seattle, 1961).

ANDREW MALOZEMOFF, *Russian Far Eastern Policy 1881–1904* (Berkeley and Los Angeles, 1958).

MASAO MARUYAMA, *Thought and Behaviour in Modern Japanese Politics* (London, 1969).

FRANK O. MILLER, *Minobe Tatsukichi, Interpreter of Constitutionalism in Japan* (Berkeley and Los Angeles, 1965).

JAMES W. MORLEY, *The Japanese Thrust into Siberia* (New York, 1957).

JAMES W. MORLEY (ed.), *Dilemmas of Growth in Pre-war Japan* (Princeton, N. J., 1971).

—— (ed.), *Japan's Foreign Policy 1868–1941, A Research Guide* (New York, 1974).

IAN MORRISON, *Malayan Postscript* (London, 1942).

CHARLES E. NEU, *The Troubled Encounter: The United States and Japan* (New York, 1975).

WILLIAM L. NEUMANN, *America Encounters Japan: From Perry to MacArthur* (Baltimore, 1963).

IAN H. NISH, *The Anglo-Japanese Alliance* (London, 1966).

——, *Alliance in Decline, A Study in Anglo-Japanese Relations, 1908–23* (London, 1972).

——, *Japanese Foreign Policy, 1869–1942: Kasumigaseki to Miyakezaka* (London, 1977).

SADAKO N. OGATA, *Defiance in Manchuria; The Making of Japanese Foreign Policy, 1931–1932* (Berkeley and Los Angeles, 1964).

SHUMPEI OKAMOTO, *The Japanese Oligarchy and the Russo-Japanese War* (New York, 1970).

MARK R. PEATTIE, *Ishiwara Kanji and Japan's Confrontation with the West* (Princeton, N. J., 1975).

STEPHEN E. PELZ, *Race to Pearl Harbor; The Failure of the Second London Naval Conference and the Onset of World War II* (Cambridge, Mass., 1974).

ERNEST L. PRESSEISEN, *Before Aggression: Europeans prepare the Japanese Army* (Tucson, Arizona, 1965).

EDWIN O. REISCHAUER, *The Japanese* (Cambridge, Mass., 1977).

ROBERT A. SCALAPINO, *Democracy and the Party Movement in Pre-War Japan* (Berkeley, Calif., 1952).

WILLIAM LEONARD SCHWARTZ, *The Imaginative Interpretation of the Far East in Modern French Literature 1800–1925* (Paris, 1927).

ARON SHAI, *Origins of the War in the East: Britain, China and Japan 1937–1939* (London, 1976).

BEN-AMI SHILLONY, *Revolt in Japan; The Young Officers and the February 26, 1936 Incident* (Princeton, N. J., 1973).

BERNARD S. SILBERMAN and H. D. HAROOTUNIAN (eds), *Japan in Crisis; Essays on Taisho Democracy* (Princeton, N. J., 1974).

SIR WILLIAM SLIM, *Defeat into Victory* (London, 1956).

JOHN J. STEPHAN, 'The Tanaka Memorial (1927): Authentic or Spurious?', *Modern Asian Studies* (Cambridge, 1973).

RICHARD STORRY, *The Double Patriots: A Study of Japanese Nationalism* (London, 1957).

——, *A History of Modern Japan* (Harmondsworth, Middlesex, 1976).

ROGER SWEARINGEN and PAUL LANGER, *Red Flag in Japan* (Cambridge, Mass., 1952).

K. TAKAHASHI, *The Rise and Development of Japan's Modern Economy* (Tokyo, 1969).

TATSUJI TAKEUCHI, *War and Diplomacy in the Japanese Empire* (London, 1936).

CHRISTOPHER THORNE, *The Limits of Foreign Policy; The West, the League and the Far Eastern Crisis of 1931–1933* (London, 1972).

——, *Allies of a Kind: The United States, Britain and the war against Japan, 1941–1945* (London, 1978).

GEORGE OAKLEY TOTTEN III, *The Social Democratic Movement in Pre-War Japan* (New Haven, Conn., 1966).

PAYSON J. TREAT, *Diplomatic Relations between the United States and Japan 1895–1905* (Gloucester, Mass., 1963).

RYUSAKU TSUNODA; WM THEODORE DE BARY; DONALD KEENE, *Sources of the Japanese Tradition* (New York, 1958).

RICHARD W. VAN ALSTYNE, *The United States and East Asia* (London, 1973).

DAVID WALDER, *The Short Victorious War* (London, 1973).

ROBERT E. WARD (ed.), *Political Development in Modern Japan* (Princeton, N. J., 1968).

JOHN ALBERT WHITE, *The Diplomacy of the Russo-Japanese War* (Princeton, N. J., 1964).

GEORGE M. WILSON (ed.), *Crisis Politics in Pre-War Japan: Institutional and Ideological Problems of the 1930s* (Tokyo, 1970).

SHIGERU YOSHIDA, *The Yoshida Memirs* (London, 1961).

ERNEST P. YOUNG, 'A Study of Personalities in Japan Influencing the Events Leading to the Sino-Japanese War (1894–1895)' in *Papers on Japan*, Vol 2, Aug. 1963 (Harvard East Asia Research Center).

L. K. YOUNG, *British Policy in China 1895–1902* (Oxford, 1970).

Index